Fictions of Globalization

CONTINUUM LITERARY STUDIES SERIES

Also available in the series:
Character and Satire in Postwar Fiction by Ian Gregson
Joyce and Company by David Pierce
Masculinity in Fiction and Film by Brian Baker
Women's Fiction 1945–2000 by Deborah Philips

Forthcoming titles:
Beckett's Books by Matthew Feldman
English Fiction in the 1930s by Chris Hopkins
Novels of the Contemporary Extreme edited by Alain-Phillipe Durand and Naomi Mandel
Re-writing London by Lawrence Phillips

Fictions of Globalization

JAMES ANNESLEY

LONDON • NEW YORK

Continuum
The Tower Building   80 Maiden Lane
11 York Road   Suite 704
London SE1 7NX   New York
                                 NY 10038

© James Annesley 2006

All rights reserved. No part of this publication may be reproduced or transmitted in any form or by any means, electronic or mechanical, including photocopying, recording, or any information storage or retrieval system, without prior permission in writing from the publishers.

James Annesley has asserted his right under the Copyright, Designs and Patents Act, 1988, to be identified as Author of this work.

British Library Cataloguing-in-Publication Data
A catalogue record for this book is available from the British Library.

ISBN: 0–8264–8937–0 (hardback)

Library of Congress Cataloging-in-Publication Data
A catalog record for this book is available from the Library of Congress.

Typeset by RefineCatch Limited, Bungay, Suffolk
Printed and bound in Great Britain by MPG Books Ltd, Bodmin, Cornwall

Contents

	Acknowledgements	vi
1	Introduction: Culture Incorporated	1
2	Cash Rules Everything Around Me	13
3	Branding, Consumption and Identity	27
4	The Fictions of Globalization	60
5	Pure Shores	102
6	Migrating Globalization	128
	Notes	164
	Bibliography	183
	Filmography	196
	Discography	197
	Index	199

Acknowledgements

I would like to thank Tim Armstrong, Tom Betteridge, Humphrey Couchmann, Mick Gidley, Richard Godden (for the title), Avril Horner, Anna Kiernan, Judith Newman, Pete Nicholls, Eithne Quinn, David Rogers and Ellen Rose for their help and advice. I am also very grateful for the support of the staff at Continuum, particularly Anna Sandeman, Rebecca Simmonds and Joanne Allcock, and the financial assistance I have received from the Faculty of Arts and Social Sciences at Kingston University, the British Academy and the Arts and Humanities Research Council. Finally, I am indebted to Karen and Conrad – nothing would have been possible without their contributions.

1
Introduction: Culture Incorporated

The successes of Eric Schlosser's *Fast Food Nation* (2002) and Morgan Spurlock's *Super Size Me* (2004) offer striking illustrations of the extent to which a whole range of contemporary fears and anxieties have coalesced into a broad critique of consumption, corporate power and the complex and often loosely interpreted network of socioeconomic forces that have come to be known as globalization.[1] Employing the image of the unhealthy body to dramatize anxieties about consumer society, both *Fast Food Nation* and *Super Size Me* use the consumption of fast food as an emblem for a world bloated by greed and weighed down by materialism. Stuffed full of junk, these accounts suggest, the body politic is making itself terminally ill.

The symbolism of the healthy body offers a ready comparison with the images of mental illness that inform Joel Bakan's *The Corporation* (2004). Drawing on the discourses of psychology, he argues that the corporation is a psychopathic institution, explaining that:

> As a psychopathic creature, the corporation can neither recognize nor act upon moral reasons to refrain from harming others. Nothing in its legal make-up limits what it can do to others in pursuit of its selfish ends, and it is compelled to cause harm when the benefits of doing so outweigh the costs. Only pragmatic concern for its own interests and the laws of the land constrain the corporation's predatory instincts, and often that is not enough to stop it from destroying lives, damaging communities, and endangering the planet as a whole.[2]

Selfish, unfeeling and focused solely on its own interests, the corporation is thus demonized in an argument that conjures up a host of dark and apocalyptic fears. A position rehearsed in the work of Naomi Klein, George Monbiot and Michael Moore, *The Corporation*, in terms that extend the insights offered by Spurlock and Schlosser, thus reinforces the increasingly commonly held belief that the interrelated forces of globalization and consumer society are having an ever more malign influence on daily life.

Prevalent in popular accounts of contemporary experience, these perspectives have their origins in longstanding academic debates about consumption. Published with a cover depicting riot police protecting the front of a Niketown store, Basic Books' decision to produce a 25th Anniversary edition of *Captains of Consciousness* is grounded in the belief that Stuart Ewen's famous account of the advertising industry's ability to control, manipulate and persuade is even more relevant today than it was when it was first published in 1976. Ewen's preface reinforces this point.

> Since the mid-1970s, when *Captains of Consciousness* was published, the global reach of American commercial culture has only accelerated. In the 1980s commercialism mushroomed into a vehement global religion. Where advertising once inhabited circumscribed arenas – television, radio, newspapers, magazines, billboards – today nearly every moment of human attention is being converted into an occasion for a sales pitch, while notions of the public interest and non-commercial arenas of expression are under assault.[3]

Alluding to a world characterized by branding, idents, ambient advertising, viral communication, guerrilla marketing, spam and the penetration of sponsorship into sport and the arts, Ewen seems to be stating the obvious when he suggests that the contemporary period is characterized by ever greater levels of commercial influence and control.

Ewen is not, of course, the only commentator to adopt this kind of position. In, for example, *The Threat of Globalism* (1998), a special issue of the British journal *Race and Class*, Ambalavaner Savanandan describes 'the havoc being wreaked . . . by capital in its latest avatar', a process that John Berger, writing in the same edition, argues is linked to a 'reductionism' in which 'human intelligence is reduced to greed'.[4] Josef Stiglitz's *Globalization and its Discontents* (2002) and Dani Rodrik's *Has Globalization Gone too Far?* (1997) share this vision, as does Fredric Jameson, who, commenting upon what he calls 'omnipresent consumerism', argues that it is both the consequence of and the foundation for 'the popularity of the rhetoric of market abnegation and the surrender of human freedom to a now lavish invisible hand.'[5] What Ewen calls the 'vehement global religion' of commercialism is thus not only defining contemporary experience, but also, all of these commentators agree, damaging and denuding it in innumerable ways.

Appealing to intuitions shaped by everyday experience of a world in which branding, commodities and advertising seem to be becoming ubiquitous, the apocalyptic vision of a culture in which the influence of commerce has, to use Ewen's word, 'mushroomed' is grounded in truths that appear both self-evident and unquestionable. The problem with this argument, however, is that its gloomily prophetic tone and its appeal to common sense conceal the fact that it is based on a set of unexamined assumptions. The first assumption is that the apparent increase in the volume and visibility of advertising messages, company names and commodities in the contemporary period is incontrovertible evidence of a world that is ever more commercial and ever more subject to the persuasive power of the corporation.[6] Overlooking the possibility that greater advertising volumes could be the sign of a waning of marketing's influence, it presupposes that greater levels of promotional activity necessarily increase the pressure to consume.

The second questionable assumption made by these accounts is the claim that *if* it is true that the contemporary period is subject to increased levels of commercialization, heightened exposure to commercial messages and a proliferation of commodities, that this change should then *necessarily* have a negative impact on social experience. Rooted in a traditional sense of commodification as a form of deathly reification, and flavoured by romantic beliefs that distinguish the apparently pure realms of nature and the arts from the corrupt worlds of industry and the market, this argument equates the commercial with the inferior.[7] Linked to the Frankfurt School's view that a commercial culture is one that has been fully incorporated by the interests of capital in terms that standardize it, homogenize it and strip it of critical potential, these arguments portray the market as a wholly negative entity.⁸ The problem is, however, as countless critiques of the Frankfurt School's thinking make clear, there is no real reason why a culture linked to commerce should necessarily be inferior to one that looks to resist commercial encroachments. Marked by the pejorative associations that accompany the fear of the sell-out, grounded in an implicit contempt for mass society and hinged upon an instinctive and emotional rejection of commercialized culture, these positions seem not only idealistic, but also unable to engage with the relationships that, for good or ill, bind culture, social experience and the market together.⁹

Behind these specific concerns lies a more general anxiety about the ways in which globalization is known and understood. By its very nature, the idea of globalization seems to defy easy definitions. Providing explanatory contexts for phenomena as diverse as global tourism, climate change, Jihadi terrorism, the power of transnational brands, mass migrations, the spread of the English language and the growth of global media, and understood as the product of complex, interrelated changes in the organization of social, political and economic life that are in turn read in relation to technological developments, the danger is that globalization offers both a theory of everything and an explanation of nothing.¹⁰ Used in some contexts as part of complex readings of the contemporary meaning of modernity (Anthony Giddens and Arjun Appadurai) and/or imperialism (Nestor Garcia Canclini, Leslie Sklair, Michael Hardt and Antonio Negri) and in others as a simple shorthand for a culture that can be characterized by clichéd images of a child wearing a Chicago Bulls T-Shirt in a remote corner of the Amazon, there is little doubt that globalization is a concept that is porous, unstable and increasingly overstretched.

Despite these concerns, it is still possible to identify a consensus. Though many have contested his conclusions, few would argue with the way Giddens frames the debate by suggesting that

> Globalization can ... be defined as the intensification of worldwide social relations which link distant localities in such a way that local happenings are shaped by events occurring many miles away and vice versa. This is a dialectical process because most local happenings may move in an obverse direction from the very distanciated relations that shape them.¹¹

Introduction

In Gary Teeple's terms, globalization can thus be conceived as:

> The unfolding resolution of the contradiction between ever expanding capital and its national and public formations. Up to the 1970s, the expansion of capital was always national, capital with particular territorial roots and character. Afterwards, capital began to expand more than ever as ... ownership began to correspond less and less with national geographies.[12]

Growth in patterns of investment that cross national boundaries and a related reduction in the power and influence of the nation state produces, according to these accounts, a globalized market that in turn provides the fuel for the creation of increasingly internationalized forms of culture. It is these forms of culture that have become central to understandings of globalization's processes; processes that, as commentators like Appadurai and Roland Robertson have emphasized, are grounded not just in economic and infrastructural changes, but in transformations that have affected the cultural representation and social perception of that world. In simple terms, the globalization thesis argues that a combination of 'engines' or 'drivers' linked to technology, economics and politics are creating a world that either is, or appears to be, ever smaller and more homogeneous.[13]

Beyond this point, however, the debate becomes much more fractured. Arguments about, for example, the relative importance of different causal factors compete with discussions of the effects of particular changes and the work of commentators that question the extent to which these changes can be said to have taken place at all. These are all important areas for discussion, but it is not the intention of this book to offer yet another intervention into this debate. Focused on cultural representations of globalization and the patterns of contemporary consumerism, particularly those offered in recent American writing, *Fictions of Globalization* is not concerned with clarifying or resolving these difficulties, but interested instead in an analysis of the discourses that surround contemporary understandings of globalization and consumer society. It is not the historical realities of globalization that are at stake here, but the ways in which the debate raised by those realities is structured, known and understood. Though, as later chapters demonstrate, *Fictions of Globalization* does problematize some of the interpretations that inform certain versions of the globalization thesis, the significance of these questions lies not in the illumination they shed on the realities (or otherwise) of the conditions in a globalized world, but the ways in which they help clarify a response to the understanding of, following Appadurai, 'something critical and new in global cultural process: *the imagination as a social process.*'[14]

Such a claim is, of course, central to this discussion and forms a key part of the analysis of the relationships that connect contemporary American fiction with the processes of globalization and consumer society. The aim is not, however, to read these novels in terms that evidence the reality of globalization, or to present them as homological expressions of the specifics of these material conditions, but to use the analysis of different texts to refine ways of knowing globalization's discourses. Though there are questions about the shape and character of globalization, there can be little doubt that the concept has a powerful grip on the contemporary imagination. The suggestion is that the examination of recent American fiction and a consideration of the ways in which globalization's processes are represented offers an insight into the shape and character of concerns that have a key bearing on the interpretation of contemporary cultural, social and political life. In these terms, the aim is neither to celebrate nor condemn globalization, but to find ways in which it might be possible to read contemporary fiction in terms that add to knowledge about, and understanding of, its discourses.

Fiction and globalization

Fictions of Globalization's analysis of recent American fiction is prompted not simply because these concerns are central to any understanding of contemporary experience, but because, in more straightforward terms, so many recent novels seem to be energized by a focus on issues of this kind. As the following discussions of fiction by writers like William Gibson, Jhumpa Lahiri, Bharati Mukherjee, Paul Beatty, Don DeLillo, Chuck Palahniuk, Sandra Cisneros, Dave Eggers and Bret Easton Ellis set out to demonstrate, not only do these debates provide both the context and the subject matter for a significant number of recent narratives, they also inform the metaphors and styles employed in these texts. Alongside discussions of this kind are readings that identify the continuities that tie contemporary fiction's concern for globalizing consumer culture with American literature's enduring preoccupation with business, economics and the market. In brief discussions of Herman Melville and Ernest Hemingway, *Fictions of Globalization* argues that the recognition of these relationships not only helps provide a context for the understanding of contemporary narratives but also raises important questions about the ways in which the globalization debate is understood.

At this stage it is also important to emphasize that the contemporary novels discussed here are not isolated examples, but in fact fairly typical of the currents and trajectories that characterize recent American writing. Many modern winners of the Pulitzer Prize, for example, raise issues that have a real bearing on understandings of globalization and consumer society. Steven Millhauser's *Martin Dressler* (1996) is a novel focused on business and its relationship to emergent forms of American popular culture and leisure. In similar terms, Philip Roth's *American Pastoral* (1997) uses the internationalization of capital and its effect on the glove-making business as a key part of its portrait of the Swede's life, a theme echoed in Richard Russo's *Empire Falls* (2001).

It is not, of course, just winners of the Pulitzer who set out to develop concerns of this kind. Equally relevant to the kinds of debates raised in *Fictions of Globalization* is the exploration of consumer society and the emergence of the post-Soviet states offered in Jonathan Franzen's *The Corrections* (2001), and the large number of recent fictions like Amy Tan's *The Joy Luck Club* (1990) and Junot Diaz's *Drown* (1996) that are centred on questions linked to national and postnational identity. Even novels focused on slavery like Toni Morrison's *Beloved* (1987) and Edward Jones's *The Known World* (2004) (both themselves winners of the Pulitzer), or fictions that explore the impact of Manifest Destiny on Native Americans, like David Treuer's *Little* (1995) and Louise Erdrich's *Tracks* (1988) make an important contribution to readings of the history (or prehistory) of globalization, a realization that provides further evidence of the centrality of these concerns to contemporary American fiction.

There is, of course, neither time nor space to consider all of these text or ideas in detail, or to make this thumbnail sketch of recent American fiction more comprehensive. The important point, however, is that the examples discussed here are chosen not because they are exceptional, but because they are exemplary. The analysis of these particular texts thus promises not just an insight into the wider patterns of contemporary American fiction, but, more importantly, ways of knowing and interpreting contemporary culture's relationships with, and responses to, globalization and consumer culture.

Recognizing that these narratives offer rich evidentiary sources, *Fictions of Globalization* suggests that the process of interpreting the representation of these patterns in contemporary literature provides a way of developing significant critical insight into relationships that connect the dynamics of contemporary culture with the wider contexts of globalization and consumption. The result is a study that uses the analysis of literature as the cue for discussions that include: the connections that tie ethnicity, identity and consumption together; the representation of globalization and the globalization debate; dreams of escape from, and rebellion against, consumer society and the forces of globalization; and the impact and consequences of tourism and migration. The suggestion is that the analysis of recent fiction generates a unique way of knowing and understanding the dynamics that define the relationship between contemporary culture and the market.

With these motivations to the fore, it is also worth noting that it is the attempt to read recent American fiction in terms that engage with the contextual and conceptual debates generated around consumption and globalization that provides a key distinction between its ambitions and other accounts of contemporary literature. Despite the prevalence of concerns linked to consumption and the world market in recent American fiction and the ferocity of the wider debate around globalization in many areas of both the humanities and the social sciences, it is surprising that there has not been a systematic attempt to develop a critical discussion of these debates in relation to American literature. Recent criticism of contemporary American fiction has instead tended to follow different approaches.

Some studies, for example, use arguments linked to ethnicity, identity and gender to bring together their overviews of recent American literature. Books like Julian Murphet's *Literature and Race in Los Angeles* (2001) and the later sections of Maria Balshaw's *Looking for Harlem* (2000), for example, develop their reading of contemporary fiction around the intersection of text, place, gender and ethnicity.[15] Of more relevance to this discussion are the positions raised in special issues of *PMLA* (Proceedings of the Modern Language Association of America) and *Modern Fiction Studies* that concentrate on the relationships between globalization and readings of colonialism and post-colonialism and connect these approaches with interpretations of writers like Salman Rushdie and Jamaica Kincaid. Though focused more on theoretical arguments about the links between globalization and established critical perspectives rooted in the debate around post-colonialism and on readings of English writing from across the globe than on American fiction, the essays in these collections do have an important bearing on certain parts of this discussion and, in particular, as later chapters demonstrate, on the analysis of representation of migration and identity.

Also relevant to *Fictions of Globalization* are books like Nick Heffernan's *Capital, Class and Technology in Contemporary American Culture* (2000), Philip Simmons's *Deep Surfaces* (1997) and Stephen Baker's *The Fiction of Postmodernity* (2000) that use frameworks derived from the analysis of postmodernism as the central focus for their readings of contemporary American literature.[16] The problem is, however, that though all of these discussions pursue arguments linked to technology, the media, mass culture and consumerism, arguments that shadow the kinds of issues explored in *Fictions of Globalization*, their reliance on postmodernism as a frame of reference problematizes their approach. The point is not that these accounts fail to produce effective commentaries upon the texts in hand, but that the very foundations upon which their arguments depend seem to have become exhausted. Using postmodernism, a framework developed initially in relation to the analysis of literature and culture from the 1960s and 1970s, to interpret texts from the end of the twentieth century, these approaches are forced to broaden and extend this perspective to the point that it loses its specificity.[17] More a problem with postmodernism than the fault of these studies, the tired, contradictory and diffuse nature of these familiar terminologies seems to diminish the effectiveness of the insights they generate.

Having said that, there are clear connections between the concerns raised in the postmodernism debate and the issues generated around the discourses of globalization. Indeed for some, like Susie O'Brien and Imre Szeman, postmodernism can be read as an early attempt to shape arguments that are now more properly understood in relation to concepts linked to globalization.[18] The very fact that some of the most well-known commentators on postmodernism and postmodernity seem to have used the globalization debate as part of an attempt to rebrand and refresh these old ideas seems to add weight to this suggestion.[19] Globalization cannot, however, be read in simple terms as a refurbished version of the debates around postmodernism and postmodernity. Stepping beyond postmodernism's preoccupation with representation and simulation and avoiding its Eurocentric bias, arguments linked to globalization promise more productive ways of interpreting the relationships that link culture with socio-economic conditions. As Paul Jay argues, 'literature's relation to the processes of globalization as they manifest themselves in a variety of historical periods – indeed literature's facilitation of economic and cultural globalization – is becoming a potentially important field of study that might get short-circuited if we think of globalization only as a postmodern eruption.'[20] In short, though it is possible to think about globalizing some of the debates linked to postmodernism in constructive terms, recasting concerns tied to globalization in relation to postmodernism seems both less meaningful and less productive. This is the point that Michel Bérubé makes when he writes, 'postmodernism aligns with postcolonialism not because they're both post-something or because they're both sceptical of legitimating narratives, but because they are epiphenomena of globalization itself'.[21]

Fictions of Globalization thus sets out to read the debates around globalization and consumption in terms that open up the analysis of recent American fiction and, at the same time, to use the interpretation of contemporary literature and culture to develop critical perspectives upon the understandings and positions that inform those same debates. Recognizing that many of these novels are sceptical of readings of consumption that work in terms linked to social control and wary of arguments that see globalization as an 'unstoppable' process, the suggestion is that recent American fiction offers an alternative to pessimistic visions of a contemporary culture characterized by ever greater levels of coordination.[22] A broader reflection on the problem of critique is, in consequence, a central part of this discussion.

Questions about the extent to which it is possible for a product of a market society (in this case the novel) to develop a critical perspective upon that same society in terms that are neither hopelessly co-opted nor dangerously complicit are enduring parts of the debate around the relationship between culture and society. As the histories of romanticism and realism in the nineteenth century, modernism and the avant-garde at the start of the twentieth and the movements linked to situationism and punk in the post-war period all suggest, processes of rebellion and co-option seem doomed to couple and re-couple. In one version of events, this process has a tragic cast as artists and artworks battle to escape commodification only to find their chosen strategies twisted back upon themselves. The result is that the seemingly endless ability to assimilate antagonistic gestures and to convert rebellious dreams into seductive commercial fantasies becomes yet another demonstration of the market's flexibility, resilience and strength.

Pessimism is not, however, *Fictions of Globalization* argues, the only possible response to these conditions. Apocryphal stories of anti-globalization protesters hurling scaffolding poles at McDonald's restaurants while wearing Nike shoes may prompt an ironic view of the impossibility an uncompromised critique, but the contradictions illustrated by this anecdote are perhaps more productive than they first appear. Instead of oscillating between pure moments of utopian opposition and grimly ironic accounts of complicity and co-option, the process of interrogating the oppositions that inform accounts rooted in either utopianism or pessimism furthers the understanding of contemporary culture's critical potential. Through the process of analysing the binaries that divide the commodified from the uncommodified, the commercial from the uncommercial, the free from the co-opted, *Fictions of Globalization* recognizes that such oppositions are largely unsustainable and limit and narrow understandings of the possibility that culture can be both commercial and at the same time critical of commerce. The suggestion is that the play between the commercial and the uncommercial merits not further exploration of these tensions in the hope of finding a resolution, but as part of a critical interrogation of the binaries upon which these positions depend.

Foregrounding an understanding of globalization as a complex and multi-layered phenomenon, *Fictions of Globalization* thus rejects polarized accounts of consumption and the market. Recognizing the ways commerce and culture engage in fluid and multi-dimensional negotiations, the discussion of recent American fiction that follows suggests that this back-and-forth is not just characteristic of contemporary culture, but a central part of its creative process, a process that offers a privileged insight into the ways in which it might be possible to find expression in the changing geography of a globalizing world. The central argument explored in the following discussion is that this culture does not simply reflect the incorporating power of consumer capitalism and globalization, but offers instead a sense of the ways in which critical and creative possibilities can be sustained within a globalizing consumer society and through relationships with consumption.

2
Cash Rules Everything Around Me

An illustration of the prevalence of commodities in contemporary culture more vivid than that manifested in hip-hop would be hard to find. With its visual and linguistic codes steeped in a commercial iconography of Benzes, Hilfiger and Hennessy, and its personalities keen to portray themselves as conspicuous consumers, hip-hop seems wedded to the currents of contemporary capitalism. The feeling is that hip-hop culture has been bought and sold in a fast-moving commercial frenzy. Tupac Shakur's observation on his first (non-fatal) brush with gunplay dramatizes this process. Shot when entering a New York recording studio and robbed of $50,000 dollars worth of jewellery, he recalled the experience in the following way: 'I could see the gunpowder and the hole ripped in my Karl Kani drawers.'[1] In this context it is not hard to understand why so many commentators are willing to see these processes of commercialization in destructive terms. bell hooks, for example, argues that 'to a grave extent, the commodification of blackness has created the source for an intensification of opportunistic materialism and longing-for privileged class status among black folks'.[2] Her regretful tone is echoed by Nelson George, who argues that the pursuit of individual gain and material success is having a negative impact on broader patterns of social and communal action, Cornel West, who links the rise of 'corporate market institutions' with what he calls 'nihilism in black America', and Ellis Cashmore, who sees these processes as a co-option of political agency, part of a sequence in which something that 'started as ... radically different and, in many ways, dangerous ... was appropriated and ultimately rendered harmless.'[3] Echoes of these sentiments can also be heard from inside hip-hop culture itself. DJ Shadow's *Endtroducing*, for example, includes a track entitled 'Why Hip Hop Sucks in '96', a question that he answers with the rolling refrain 'it's the money'.[4] Commerce and avarice have, it seems, consumed hip-hop's radical potential and bonded it to the corporate aspirations of the entertainment industry. These general perspectives find a precise focus not only in the ghetto-fabulous styles popular with so many contemporary hip-hop, R'n'B and crossover artists, but also in the language and rhetoric of innumerable hip-hop tracks.

The relationships that exist between the priorities of commerce and those of hip-hop artists are not, however, unique. In many respects hip-hop simply exemplifies the broader characteristics of culture's relationship with the market in the contemporary period. Paul Gilroy makes these points explicit when, writing about Spike Lee's advertisements for Nike, he states that 'Lee set the power of street style and speech to work not just in the service of an imagined racial community but an imaginary blackness which exists exclusively to further the interests of corporate America.'[5] Robert Goldman and Stephen Papson echo this position when they suggest that 'the appropriation of ghetto speech and hip-hop signifiers has become rampant in consumer-goods advertising.'[6] The consensus is that these patterns of appropriation have wholly negative consequences, ones that do not simply enforce the subjugation of African Americans, but have wider implications for an understanding of Western society's general relationship with the market. Fuelled by a straightforwardly critical account of consumer society, these perspectives thus seem to offer a pessimistic vision of a globalizing society in which 'the scope of commodification is now so wide that everything, including difference, can be reshaped into a package.'[7]

Leaving aside, for the time being, general concerns about the ways in which these arguments conceive and interpret consumption, the key problem with such positions is that they fail to engage with the specific elements underpinning African-American consumerism. Preferring the rhetoric of the sell-out to an understanding of the issues at hand, there is no historicity to this reading of hip-hop's relationship with the market. In describing the corporate bondage of contemporary culture, for example, it fails to recognize the specific resonance that ideas linked to enslavement might have for African Americans. The implication is that any interpretation of the commodity-heavy styles of hip-hop needs to be connected with a broader historical interpretation of the African American's relationship with consumer society. Reflecting upon Zora Neale Hurston's thoughts on the ways in which advertising images are assimilated into the patterns of 'negro expression' provides a way of introducing such a perspective.

Hurston's 'Characteristics of negro expression' (1934) includes the following observations on the meaning of advertising for the African American:

> On the walls of the homes of the average Negro one always finds a glut of gaudy calendars, wall pockets and advertising lithographs. The sophisticated white man or Negro would tolerate none of these, even if they bore a likeness to the *Mona Lisa*. No commercial art for decoration. Nor the calendar nor the advertisement spoils the picture for this lowly man. He sees the beauty in spite of the Portland Cement Works or the butcher's announcement.[8]

Reading these characteristics in relation to a wider analysis of what she calls the 'will to adorn', Hurston identifies a process that involves remaking and renegotiating the relationship between the African American and the conditions of dominant culture, particularly with regard to language. As Hurston explains, 'the American Negro has done wonders to the English language . . ., has made over a great part of the tongue to his liking and has had his revision accepted by the ruling class.'[9] Developing this point into a wider framework of ideas rooted in an analysis of the relationships between marginalization and identity, Hurston rejects essentialist accounts of this love of 'adornment' and interprets it instead in relation to the specific social history of the African American. The advertising message is not one-dimensional in Hurston's mind, but is seen to generate meanings that step beyond commercial purposes. In this context the 'will to adorn' allows the 'American Negro' to recognize the 'beauty in spite of the Portland Cement works'. An individual with a long history of accepting the imposition of master-codes and at the same time well-used to finding ways of adapting and recycling those codes, does so here with advertising, one of the twentieth century's most visible expressions of corporate power. This promotional material is thus given a private meaning that has nothing to do with marketing or sales.

The suggestion is that this reading of the 'will to adorn' could be used to interpret the yearning for consumer durables articulated in hip-hop tracks. Far from being a simple reflection of co-option or sign of a childishly gullible response to the claims of marketing and the lure of conspicuous consumption, the desire to make repeated references to commodities can be seen instead as a representation both of an ability to find private meaning in public symbols and as part of a broader challenge to power and authority. Revising, in Hurston's terms, the established codes of consumerism and encouraging the 'ruling class' to adopt that revision, the African American both adorns and remakes those discourses in terms that have important implications for the understanding of the relationship between ethnicity and consumption. In the same way that seeing or reading the words of an articulate ex-slave like Frederick Douglass jolted nineteenth-century Americans out of complacent prejudice, the sight of the African-American male in possession of the tools and trappings of the boardroom does not signal corporate colonization, but marks a challenge to control and co-option. As Paul Mullins's book *Race and Affluence* (1999) explains, 'brand consumption had a . . . symbolic appeal to African Americans: brands harbored the prospect of consumer and civil citizenship . . . to possess garments bearing the trademarks of well-known advertisers, sold for the most part in the better stores . . . [was an] important indicator of status.'[10]

In this regard it has to be recognized that there is something aspirational and even democratizing about the enthusiasm for consumption. Hip-hop's version of the Horatio Alger story, describing the move from poverty to wealth through the opportunities created by music, drug dealing and sport is, of course, a subject explored in countless rap tracks. The Wu-Tang Clan's 'C.R.E.A.M.' typifies this trend. The grim naturalism of a chorus that states 'Cash rules everything around me' is matched to rhymes like those in which Raekwon explains how he joined a gang and started dealing drugs in the expectation of making 'forty Gs' a week, in a song that offers a definitive statement on the relationship between wealth and social opportunity.[11] The point is that the Wu-Tang Clan are not simply selling the myth of the ghetto, they are rewriting popular American narratives and articulating long-standing historical concerns about marginalization and exclusion. This is an argument developed in William Shaw's book *Westsiders* (2000) through his discussion of what he calls hip-hop's 'fecund vocabulary of desire'.[12] 'It says a lot', writes Shaw, 'that the topic of wealth is such a rich source of hip-hop slang. There are dozens of words all meaning basically the same thing.'[13] The fact that hip-hop artists themselves are intensely professionalized and determined to represent themselves as workers only adds to this impression. Rejecting creative mystification, 'they understand better than their audiences that music is a business and rapping . . . a job.'[14]

Hip-hop's dedicated pursuit of money and its celebration of consumer goods thus needs to be interpreted not as a sign of its complicity or the mark of a general passivity in the face of dominant commercial and political forces, but as part of a longstanding search for equality and social status. E. Franklin Frazier's essay in Alain Locke's *The New Negro* (1927) makes exactly these points when he writes, 'two hundred and fifty years of enforced labor, with no incentive and just rewards, more than any inherent traits, explain why the Negro has for so long been concerned chiefly with consumption rather than production.'[15] Frazier goes on to suggest that though the African American's 'desire for color and form has been the cause of mockery . . . his desire to work for only enough to supply his wants is . . . the ideal that has motivated economic activities in former ages. Moreover, the love of leisure and interest in consumption are aristocratic virtues.'[16] In terms that force a re-evaluation of straightforwardly condemnatory accounts of African-American culture's enthusiasm for conspicuous consumption, Franklin recognizes that the specific history of Africans in America creates very particular relationships with and responses to consumer goods. As Paul Mullins' book *Race and Affluence* explains, 'rich with symbolic possibilities . . . and carrying tacit promises of citizenship, material goods provided a seemingly innocuous, yet meaningful mechanism to reposition African Americans in opposition to racialized inequalities.'[17]

Positions of this kind are not, however, without their critics. bell hooks, for example, insists that 'black capitalism is not black self-determination.'[18] In her terms these processes simply mimic the patterns of domination and reinforce the marginalization of African Americans. Her argument is that 'hedonistic materialism ... [is] a central aspect of an imperialist colonialism that perpetuates and maintains white supremacist capitalist patriarchy.'[19] A more specific expression of these anxieties can be found in the work of Michael Dyson (1993).

Examining the rise of fashions for sportswear and sneakers, Dyson writes:

> The sneaker ... epitomizes the worst features of the social production of desire and represents the ways in which the moral energies of social conscience about material values are drained by the messages of undisciplined acquisitiveness promoted by corporate dimensions of the culture of consumption. These messages of rapacious consumerism supported by cultural and personal narcissism, are articulated on Wall Street and are related to the expanding inner-city juvenocracy, where young black men rule over black urban space in the culture of crack and illicit criminal activity, fed by desires to 'live large' and to reproduce capitalism's excesses on their own terrain ... Moreover, while sneaker companies exploited black cultural expressions of cool, hip, chic and style, they rarely benefit the people who both consume the largest quantity of products and whose culture redefined the sneaker companies *raison d'etre*.[20]

Flavoured by apocryphal tales of sneaker rage and touched by a puritan concern for those who try to live too 'large', Dyson's position is intensely problematic. In his terms, consumerism produces a 'lethal' exploitation, a suggestion that seems to offer an implicit endorsement of Washingtonian humility. Sneakers are not only a form of mass deception but also, it seems, uppity and connected to criminality. The fundamental problem with such arguments is, however, that they are unable to engage with the kind of contradictory processes that Robin Kelley identifies when he writes 'in the struggles of urban youths for survival and pleasure inside of capitalism, capitalism has become their greatest friend and greatest foe.'[21] A return to consider Hurston's reading of the 'will to adorn' provides a way of refining the interpretation of these issues.

Reading the 'will to adorn' as part of a desire to reshape dominant codes and languages, Hurston identifies the system of borrowings and appropriations that characterize this process.

One particular example of the folkloric borrowings that attract Hurston's attention is the mythification of well known industrialists. Hurston writes:

> Negro folklore is not a thing of the past. It is still in the making. Its great variety shows the adaptability of the black man: nothing is too old or too new, domestic or foreign, high or low, for his use. God and the Devil are paired and are treated no more reverently than Rockerfeller and Ford. Both of these men are prominent in folklore, Ford being particularly strong, and they talk and act like good-natured stevedores or mill-hands.[22]

In Hurston's terms, the inclusion of Ford and Rockerfeller alongside more familiar figures in a folk tale does not signal the co-option of that form of expression, but stands instead as sign of the ways in which these stories are looking to equalize social relations by appropriating distant figures of power and influence. These ideas have important implications for the interpretation of the use of brands and commodities in hip-hop. Suggesting that the processes of appropriation used in rap are not signs of some new and unique commercial threat to the authenticity and integrity of hip-hop, but part of well-established patterns of negotiation between the forces of industry and the dynamics of African-American culture, Hurston's work opens up a way of historicizing the hyper-commodification that characterizes so much of contemporary hip-hop and thus provides a response to arguments that see its reliance on brands as a simple image of its complicity with the forces of capitalism and the market. Characteristic of 'negro expression', hip-hop's blizzard of labels and logos is thus read as part of the long history of the African American's struggle to reshape and renegotiate a place in American society.

Such arguments can be developed by reflecting upon the specifics of the historical relationships that link African Americans with brands and advertising. Adding the pun on the word brand, the burnt marker or emblem of ownership, to a sense that the advertising poster might always in some respects echo either the announcement of a sale or the reward for the capture of a fugitive, gives a quick sketch of the peculiar relationship that exists between the African American and the processes of advertising. A number of studies have developed these thoughts by exploring the historical origins of the African American's relationship to branded goods. Paul Edward's book *The Southern Negro as Consumer* (1932), for example, considers the history of food purchases and discusses the existence of a preference for expensive branded food staples like coffee, flour and baking powder.[23] Two reasons are offered for this. The first is that 'brand goods provided product "security" by tacitly evading the deceits of local marketers who sold goods in bulk . . . African Americans were not the sole target of such fraud, but they certainly were systematically subjected to it.'[24] This point is linked to a second argument that suggests 'African-American consumers most valued the power brands gave them in the act of shopping itself [by providing] . . . consumers [with] sway over local merchants by investing decision-making power in the consumer, rather than the merchant.'[25] Such arguments do not, of course, mean that these consumers were immune to the traditional influences of advertising or free from the patterns of desire. They do, however, suggest that African-American consumption needs to be understood in relation to a broader reading of the specifics of their historical situation.

Clearly these ideas are moving this discussion beyond a simple reflection on the music, styles and cultures of hip-hop and towards an engagement with *Fictions of Globalization*'s wider focus on the connections that link culture to the patterns of a globalizing consumer culture. The significance of this focus on hip-hop is that it illustrates the importance of conceiving culture not in opposition to commerce, but through a series of multi-dimensional relations that include, as the discussion of contemporary African-American music suggests, an understanding of the historical experiences of particular social groups. The fact that hip-hop culture is itself increasingly influential in so many areas of contemporary American life only adds fuel to this sense of the broader relevance of these ideas. Evidence of this crossover can be found, not only in hip-hop's impact on a whole range of popular styles of music (rock, metal, dance and R'n'B all show evidence of its influence) but also in ways in which hip-hop stars are penetrating the film business. Sean Combs, Nas, DMX, Tupac, Beyonce and Mos Def are some of the many hip-hop artists who have, in recent years, crossed from music into film. Rap's influence can also be detected in fine art, fashion, sport, graphic design and advertising, with the implication being that contemporary culture can be characterized by increasing patterns of hip-hopization. This process of extension can also be traced in the currents of recent African-American fiction. Writers like Sapphire in *Push* (1997) and *American Dreams* (1996), and Ray Shell in *Iced* (1995) have looked to trace the contours of marginality in the ghetto experience in terms that reflect some of the more mournful chronicles of hip-hop. Both Jess Mowry, in *Way Past Cool* (1993), and Sister Souljah in *The Coldest Winter Ever* (1999) have offered fictional versions of familiar gangsta narratives. These tales have their own particular resonance, but it is discussion of the work of Paul Beatty that seems to offer some of the most suggestive insights into the relationships that connect contemporary fiction with both hip-hop and the dynamics of consumer society.

Paul Beatty

Originally a poet, Beatty has written two novels, *White Boy Shuffle* (1996) and *Tuff* (2000) and been lauded as the 'laureate of hip-hop.'[26] Characterized by a linguistic exuberance and a propensity for riffing, Beatty's fiction reverberates to the sound of hip-hop. These qualities are most readily detectable in his novel *Tuff*. Describing the life of Winston Foshay, Tuffy for short, a young man caught in a cycle of violence and limited opportunities in Spanish Harlem, the novel follows him as he is given an opportunity to run for local elections. In a journey that sees Beatty explore a whole range of characters and situations from African-American urban culture, it is the richness of Beatty's writing that is most immediately striking, a richness that emerges in forcible terms through representations of consumerism and consumer goods.

> Whenever Winston was in Midtown, doing the things he couldn't do in Harlem, such as seeing a movie or shopping for logo-free clothes, and got a craving for a Thirstbuster, his favourite drink was impossible to find. Stocked with colas and nectars, the shelves in the clean East Side delicatessens had natural waters from every lake in Europe ... Winston would ask the shopkeeper for a grape or a pineapple Thirstbuster and get a blank stare in return [he would be] forced to exit the store examining [a] two-dollar bottle of melted glacier water.[27]

Leaving Harlem behind, Tuffy steps outside the branded spaces that are familiar to him and enters the 'logo-free' terrains of Midtown. Representative of a shift that operates in terms of both ethnicity and class, for Tuffy the absence of recognizable brands becomes a sign of his status as an outsider in this part of Manhattan. Familiar commodities, this passage suggests, are thus tied to Tuffy's sense of identity and make him sceptical about the purity of products that present themselves as both logo free and natural. In this respect, Tuffy's loyalty to a particular brand of soft drink is not a sign that he is the dupe of marketing and product promotion (he is clearly resistant to the charms of 'melted glacier water'), but a preference that is connected to his sense of self.

These relationships are developed further in a scene that depicts the meeting between Tuffy and his future wife Yolanda, an episode that takes place inside a Burger King restaurant. Beatty writes:

> She looked into Winston's cupcake-brown face and repeated his order. Remembering her customer protocol, Yolanda pushed the fries and beverages. 'Would you like to try our new cheddar cheese curly fries or something to drink?'
> 'I'll take an orange soda.'
> 'What size?'
> 'Bout your size.'
> Yolanda blushed but didn't waver a second. 'That be about a medium.'[28]

Though restrained by business protocols and uniformed in Burger King fatigues, Yolanda is able to remake the sales formulas into her own flirtatious language. This is not a dialogue that simply survives its exposure to the controlled and commodified spaces of the fast-food restaurant, but one that is actually made possible by the very limits of that terrain. Yolanda and Tuffy use the corporate language to forge a personal connection and thus, like so many of the commodities depoloyed in hip-hop, this interaction illustrates the ways in which it is possible to speak a commercialized language with an accent that does not simply reflect, sustain or reproduce the forces of commerce.

The importance of a scene of this kind to a novel in which the central protagonist weighs 320 pounds can be extended by thinking about the ways in which his intake of food represents broader consumerist desires. When Beatty writes: 'The butt end of a flauta de pollo disappeared down Winston's gullet. His napkin already saturated with grease stains, he licked his finger tips and wiped his mouth with the corner of the linen tablecloth' he emphasizes the fact that Winston is trying to live large in both senses of the word.[29] Like Hype Williams's celebrated music video for Missy Elliot's track 'The Rain' in which he inflates her already robust frame with a black vinyl jump-suit ('supersizing' her in the language of the take-out restaurant), here Beatty performs a similar function with his XXL protagonist. Tuffy is thus shown to articulate himself through acts of consumption and uses them to find not just satisfaction, but also self definition, a sense of place and a way of interacting with those around him. In these terms, the novel suggests that, like many hip-hop tracks, the emphasis on consumption does more than simply reflect the market's hegemony.

Concerns of this kind are also apparent in Beatty's first novel *White Boy Shuffle* (1996), a coming-of-age story focused on the life of Gunnar Kaufman. In one sequence Gunnar, having moved with his parents from a white suburban world in Santa Monica to the black terrains of West Los Angeles, finds himself ostracized for his speech, style and education. His response is to escape from the world of the street and find refuge in a display tent pitched in the camping goods section of a local department store. Beatty writes:

> I started playing Thoreau in the Montgomery Ward department store over in the La Cienega Mall, turning its desolate sporting goods department into a makeshift Walden. I moved the pond, a flimsy dark blue plastic wading pool decaled with big-eyed, absurdly happy black and yellow ducks, next to the eight-man tent tucked away in the wilds of the camping section.[30]

Once again it is Beatty's sensitivity to his protagonist's place within the commercialized spaces of contemporary society that underpins this description. Seeking release inside the mall, not in an escape from it, Gunnar, like Tuffy, finds that commerce does not always constrain him. It is not simply an attempt to suggest, as Mark Neal does in his reading of *White Boy Shuffle*, that this incident 'implies that these artists can never escape the impositions of mass culture', but an image which demonstrates that the market even, while it imposes itself on individuals and intrudes into their lives, cannot be regarded as the architect of commercial slavery.[31] The implication is that like hip-hop, Beatty's novels demonstrate that the individual retains agency and holds on to particular creative and expressive freedoms. These texts can thus be read in terms that interrogate Cornel West's fear that 'the saturation of market forces' creates the conditions for a 'jungle ruled by cutthroat market morality.'[32]

Triple Crown

Though these arguments seem sustainable when applied to Beatty, a self-consciously literary writer (as the reference to Thoreau in *White Boy Shuffle* suggests) who seems determined to explore complex social and aesthetic issues, questions remain about the applicability of these ideas to other strands of contemporary African-American literature, particularly the large number of popular novels that in recent years have set out to document and celebrate African-American street life. Championed by Triple Crown Publications, an Ohio-based company founded on the success of editor-in-chief Vickie Stringer's first novel *Let that be the Reason* (2001), the last few years have seen the publication of a large number of widely read tales of ghetto life and gangsterdom, including K'Wan's *Gangsta* (2003) and *Road Dawgz* (2003), Nikki Turner's *A Hustler's Wife* (2003) and *A Project Chick* (2004) and T. N. Baker's *Sheisty* (2004). As the titles suggest, these novels offer familiar stories of gang banging and hustling and tend to focus upon characters drawn or coerced into criminal acts in the pursuit of economic stability and/or social status. At the heart of all of these tales is an implicit appeal to authenticity, an appeal sustained by Vickie Stringer's own life story.

Writing *Let That be the Reason* while on a seven-year prison sentence for drug-trafficking offences, Stringer set up Triple Crown on her release, determined both to publish her own novel and to establish herself in a legitimate business. Like many hip-hop stars, the desire to tell her story is thus intimately linked with a need to secure economic success. To see the books published by Triple Crown as evidence of a desire to commodify and exploit the supposedly authentic experiences of African Americans would, however, be a mistake. Just as the rap narratives of Dre, Scarface and 50-Cent provide key commentaries on the African American's place within and responses to consumer society at the same time as they offer marketable products to that society, Triple Crown novels work in terms that are equally multidimensional.[33] Such a view is sustained not simply through a broad cultural reading of the general significance of the popularity of these texts that considers their location in the publishing industry and the ways in which they articulate legitimate desires for a place within mainstream society, but also through an analysis of the dynamics of the texts themselves. Populated by characters like Tressa, the protagonist in Nikki Turner's *A Project Chick*, a woman who carries diapers and a switchblade in her Gucci pocketbook, and the narrator of *Shiesty* who introduces himself with the statement 'I'm 22 years old, pushing a 325 BMW, living in a $700 a month apartment', the novels tend to be characterized by straightforward desires to use commodities in terms linked to conspicuous consumption.[34] Such perspectives need to be tempered, however, by the recognition that they also include episodes that articulate a more complex view of the significance of consumerism. One such moment comes in the opening to Kwan's *Road Dawgz*.

Returning from prison at the start of a criminal odyssey, K-Dwag makes a classic journey from his arrival at Port Authority in Midtown up to Harlem and observes the changed world around him. Kwan describes these transformations in the following terms:

> There were no more rope chains or African medallions, and the guys were flossing big jewels and bracelets. Everyone was wearing oversized jeans with T-shirts sporting some kind of logo or statement. Even the color scheme was different. Everything was bright and festive. It seemed that the black love fad had given way to the age of the baller. If this was the case, then K-Dawg wanted in.[35]

Though Triple Crown novels often share their subject matter with Paul Beatty, they tend not to match the self-consciousness of his style. In this section, however, there are clear echoes of the ways in which Tuffy conceives himself and his relationships to place and ethnicity in terms linked to consumption. Like Tuffy, K-Dawg is making a journey not just up Manhattan to Harlem, but also through time as he crosses from the old world before he went into prison, into the present and like Tuffy, it is branding that promises to give him a sense of his location. The logos on the clothes worn by the people around him are not, in these terms, the badges of the co-opted but markers of their place in this new world. K-Dawg, naturally wants 'in'. Looking to find an identity in this changed environment, he does not want to reject this branded world, but seeks a position within it. Acknowledging the symbolic possibilities of consumer goods and recognizing the ways in which consumption offers a route towards self-definition to an individual well-used to inhabiting roles prescribed by society's racialized discourses, this episode, like moments in Beatty's fiction and the images of conspicuous consumption in so many hip-hop tracks, thus uses commodities as part of an attempt to forge a distinct sense of African American identity.

If, as Russell Potter has it, hip-hop is a 'spectacular vernacular', then it is appropriate that it should turn to the signs and symbols of the society of the spectacle for its reference points.[36] This pattern, echoed not just in the lyrics, the clothes, the music videos and the films associated with hip-hop, but also in Beatty's fiction and novels published by Triple Crown, is thus read not as a mute emblem of incorporation but the sign of a more complex relationship with consumerism. Registering the underlying concern that the tendency to see African Americans as consumers who are more willing than most to consume conspicuously and, by implication more gullible and passive in the face of commercial pressures, runs the risk of aligning itself with discourses that infantilize the African, this chapter has insisted upon a historicized analysis of the relationships that connect consumer behaviour with the specific experiences of different ethnic groups. Fostering a wider critique of approaches that see the consumer as a dupe, the analysis of the representation of consumption in hip-hop and contemporary African-American fiction thus opens up a perspective on the significance of brands and consumption in contemporary culture, a perspective that is sharpened in the following chapter's analysis of novels by Bret Easton Ellis, Candace Bushnell and Chuck Palahniuk.

3
Branding, Consumption and Identity

With his prose patterned with a profusion of brand names and logos that might seem excessive even by the standards set in the world of hip-hop, Bret Easton Ellis assaults his readers with novels that read more like catalogues than works of fiction. Characteristic of all Ellis's writing, this tendency is taken to extremes in his novel *Glamorama* (1998). Depicting a world in which commodities have replaced relationships and identities become subsumed by branding, aspirations towards celebrity and the ideals of advertising, *Glamorama* offers a critique of consumption and constructs a portrait of a world lost in a commercial frenzy. Building a disturbing mood through the combination of elements of realism with moments of fantasy, *Glamorama* develops an apocalyptic feel in a narrative that features exploding skyscrapers, violent terrorists and consumer-fuelled insanity. In terms that are most obviously comparable to the work of J. G. Ballard and the recent stories of George Saunders, the text creates an overblown vision that retains an unsettlingly realistic texture. Central to the novel is a powerful sense that consumerism has reached a destructive intensity, and it is around the representation of consumption in *Glamorama* that this discussion turns. This emphasis does not simply raise questions about the representation of consumption in literary texts, but prompts a wider reflection on the ways in which consumerism is known and understood. The suggestion is that the analysis of a novel like *Glamorama* can be used to develop further questions about the relationship between the aesthetics of a literary text and the patterns of consumer culture and globalization.

Bret Easton Ellis

Centred on the life of Victor Ward, a 27-year-old 'model-slash-actor', *Glamorama* begins with the countdown to the opening of Victor's new club in Manhattan.[1] These sections introduce Victor, his supermodel girlfriend Chloe and various characters including Damien, the club's backer and Damien's fiance Alison Poole, a character who steps into the novel from the pages of Jay McInerney's *The Story of my Life* (1988).[2] The description of the launch of this club allows Ellis the opportunity to explore his signature concerns with wealth, consumption, popular culture, fashion and celebrity. The result is a comedy of manners focused on the dim-witted narrator and his banal world that includes reflections on Victor's desire to secure a part in *Flatliners II*, his obsession with the minutiae of interior design and the constant repetition of his mantra that 'the better you look ... the more you see'.[3]

At the start of the novel, Victor seems on the verge of stardom and the launch of this club is meant to propel him higher into the firmament. Instead of adding to his celebrity, however, the opening night proves a personal and professional disaster and leads to the exposure of his various infidelities, the demise of his relationship with Chloe and the end of his business partnership with Damien. While experiencing this collapse, Victor becomes involved with the sinister Palakon, an individual who offers him money to go to Europe in search of a missing actress. With his life in disarray, Victor accepts this offer and begins a journey that brings him into contact with an international terrorist cell that draws its recruits from the worlds of fashion and celebrity. A series of atrocities follow, with Victor implicated in various ways, before the cell implodes in violence. As the disintegration of the organization accelerates Victor is briefly reunited with a now-pregnant Chloe, who then dies in suspicious circumstances. Following Chloe's death, Victor returns to New York, where he attempts to live a more normal life. His enrolment in law school is, however, short lived as Victor finds himself drifting towards the life he knew before. Drawn back not only into the world of fame and fashion, but also into violence, the novel ends with Victor travelling to Europe and becoming involved in another murder.

As this outline of the plot suggests, *Glamorama* re-ploughs familiar fields. This tale of violence, terrorism, media intrusion and excess seems almost like the last possible permutation of the themes explored in Ellis's *Less Than Zero* (1985) and *American Psycho* (1991). This repetitive quality signals a narrative dissipation and creates the feeling that Ellis is constructing a decadent, degenerate novel, fashioned from the glittering scraps left over from his first four books. Returning to the original meaning of the word 'glamour' Ellis casts a glittering spell that makes clarity and fixed meanings seem distant and remote. This impression is strengthened by the novel's use of plot devices that force the reader to question the reality and plausibility of almost everything on the page. Most obvious of these is the fact that Victor's life is being documented by a variety of film crews, a situation that means the reader sees him having his words and gestures scripted and directed as part of some unnamed film or TV production. That Victor is also forced to contemplate the possibility that while he is in Europe a series of doppelgangers seem to be living his life for him in New York adds to this impression. Layering fantasy and reality together in these terms, Ellis thus creates a text that is intensely self-conscious and possessed with an exaggerated sense of its own artificiality. Developing along these parallel planes (reality and the film set, Victor and his alter-ego), many of the events in the novel thus appear to cancel each other out. Everything that follows the end of Victor's relationship with Chloe and his fall from fashionable standing seems to involve a kind of breakdown in which a whole series of violent fantasies merge together. The film crews that follow Victor everywhere, his conversations with various directors and the violent and/or sexually explicit episodes that punctuate the text (sequences that seem heavily inflected with the imagery of a high-concept action movie) all add to this feeling. The implication is that the novel can be read as the product of a nightmarish fantasy brought on by Victor's obsession with fashion, brands and media celebrity. This hyperbolic text, with its extreme emphasis on consumption and its relentless determination to mix reality with unreality, thus seems intended to function as a lengthy satire on both the banality of Victor's life and the shallow concerns that dominate the worlds of fashion, media and celebrity.

The problem is, however, that many of *Glamorama*'s reflections on the superficiality of contemporary life, the derealizing effect of the contemporary media and the impact of contemporary culture's relentless preoccupation with commodities on personal identity and relationships seem to add little to the concerns explored in Ellis's earlier fiction. In this respect Ellis's portrait of Victor falls short of the kind of vicious insights that fuelled *American Psycho* or the complex moral and cultural realities explored in *Less Than Zero*. The result is one of Ellis's least interesting novels. It is, however, in the nexus of ideas that link branding and identity together that it offers its most suggestive insights and it is upon these moments that this discussion is focused.

Ellis has always used brands and commercial languages in his writing, but *Glamorama* takes this tendency to extremes. Almost everything in the novel bears the mark of one kind of brand or another. On a simple level, the use of these labels functions as further evidence of Victor's blank reflection of the tastes and mores of contemporary capitalism. Ellis complicates this impression, however, by linking brands to the violent terrorist acts he describes in his text.

> The second bomb in the Prada backpack is now activated.
>
> Dean and Eric, both splattered with Brad's flesh and bleeding profusely from their own wounds, manage to stumble over to where Brad has been thrown, screaming blindly for help, and then, seconds later, the other blast occurs.
>
> This second bomb is much stronger than the first and the damage it causes is more widespread, creating a crater thirty feet wide in front of Café Flore.
>
> Two passing taxis are knocked over, simultaneously bursting into flame.
>
> What's left of Brad's corpse is hurled through a giant Calvin Klein poster on a scaffolding across the street, splattering it with blood, viscera, bone.[4]

The purpose of this scene, one typical of many of the violent episodes that punctuate the novel, seems to be to suggest that, like a time bomb in contemporary culture, these labelled items (in this case part of the highly successful diffusion of the Prada brand in the late 1990s) reduce the world to a rubble of things.[5] 'Creating a crater' a hole in the heart of modern life, the brand explodes in the faces of the consumer, shattering experience, reducing human life to its basic physical constituents: 'blood, viscera, bone'. Bloodying the Calvin Klein poster with Brad's splintered corpse, the bomb literalizes consumption's reification of the human body.[6]

This critical view of the brand, one that harks back to the descriptions of Patrick Bateman's violent acquisitiveness in *American Psycho*, raises a number of questions, the most pressing of which is a concern about the ways in which the text attacks branding and consumer society, while revelling in a language drawn from the very culture it is looking to condemn. The result is that Ellis finds himself caught in a paradox, crowding his pages with commercial details while seeming to criticize the confetti of logos and images that swirl through everyday life. In one typical section, Ellis describes Victor's return to New York in the following terms: 'I'm walking through Washington Square Park, carrying a Kenneth Cole leather portfolio that holds my lawbooks and a bottle of Evian water. I'm dressed casually, in Tommy Hilfiger jeans, a camel-hair sweater, a wool overcoat from Burberry's.'[7] Everything about this scene seems as carefully art-directed and styled as a magazine advertisement.

The point is that though in some respects Ellis's tactics articulate a sense of Victor's enslavement to the world of commodities, he struggles to establish any critical distance between the text and consumer society. Ellis's images are offered in a manner that appears entirely unmediated, with the result being that it becomes hard to distinguish between Ellis's fiction and the advertising images it is intending to satirize. The reader may, it is true, react against the lifestyles and values Ellis portrays, but such a critical response could equally well have been prompted by reading a fashion magazine. The implication is that Ellis is struggling to differentiate his detailed portrait of hyper-consumption from the forces of hyper-consumption themselves with the consequence being that the text seems consumed by the very brands, labels and logos it is seeking to interrogate. The result is a weakening of the satirical impact of the novel. As a statement on the extent to which brands and celebrity have penetrated the identity and imagination of the novel's vacuous protagonist, Ellis's approach seems effective enough, and as an insight into the wide-ranging influence of commercial forces it works well, but as films like Woody Allen's *Celebrity* (1998), Robert Altman's *Prêt-à-Porter* (1994) and Ben Stiller's *Zoolander* (2001) demonstrate, the worlds of fame and fashion are easy targets for satire.[8] It is, in these terms, difficult to see what *Glamorama* actually adds to these satires beyond simply reinforcing the straightforwardly critical points they all make. This is Ellis's longest novel, but the precise purpose of its repetitive focus on commercial details is hard to fathom. The question is why would Ellis have gone to such extreme lengths to attack such vulnerable targets?

The answer lies in a focus on the novel's extremity. Ellis's writing is wilfully repetitive and hyperbolic. The impact is numbing as he offers an endless series of commercial images and brands. Like Andy Warhol's absorption in the emblems and logos of popular culture, an aesthetic that draws its power from the patterns of similarity and the serial nature of the images, Ellis seems to be making a statement about language and contemporary culture.[9] Collapsing the boundaries that divide his fiction from these terrains, Ellis offers not simply an overblown satire, but a text that engages with the fabric of contemporary consumerism. This is more than just a critique of fashion and celebrity, it is an attempt to create an aesthetic from those worlds. Not only does the presence of commercial language generate an 'instant verisimilitude' in his work, it does so in ways that overshadow more traditional senses of realism.[10] Just as Warhol's images of Coca-Cola and Elvis offer defining visual portraits of mid-to-late-twentieth-century American life, the storm of names and brands that blow through Ellis's text signals his sense of the extent to which these commercial priorities are informing not just creative cultures (as evidenced in his own aesthetic), but the languages and psychological realities of contemporary societies.

Glamorama, a novel that sees consumerism not just as a potential subject matter, but as a raw material, thus rejects any sense that the artwork should have a distance from these terrains. More self-consciously artistic and experimental than Ellis's other work, the novel does not simply *talk about* the world of brands and commodities but actually *speaks* its language. The implication is, as far as *Glamorama* is concerned, that this approach offers the most appropriate response to the incorporated cultures of contemporary capitalism. The novel thus strives towards a panoramic vision of a world preoccupied with the glamour of commodities in terms that do more than simply satirize contemporary culture. Questions remain, however, about the extent to which the novel achieves this ambition. With plot a secondary consideration and repetition a fundamental part of Ellis's design, the stylistic experiment is pursued relentlessly. The resulting effects are alienating, a legitimate artistic ambition in itself, but one problematized by the sense that while Ellis is effective in creating a novel that *speaks* the language of brands, he is less clear about what such a novel *says* about consumption.

Ellis is not, of course, the only contemporary writer to use the milieu inhabited by affluent urbanites as the settings for his novels. In recent years a whole range of popular novelists have explored these terrains in different ways. Indebted in part not only to Ellis' early work, but also to New York novels from the 1980s and early 1990 like McNerney's *Bright Lights, Big City* (1986) and Tama Janowitz's *Slaves of New York* (1987), a large number of writers, particularly women, have, in recent years, set out to explore this world. Helen Fielding's *Bridget Jones's Diary* (1996), novels by Jennifer Belle and titles like Plum Sykes's *Bergdorf Blondes* (2004) and Lauren Weisberger's *The Devil Wears Prada* (2003) all owe a debt to the themes and styles popularized by Ellis and his contemporaries. Though these 'chick lit' novels have swapped his satire for bright comedy and plots based around romance, clear continuities can be traced both in terms of setting and with regard to the ways in which they deploy brands and logos in their prose.[11] The most famous exemplar of this trend is Candace Bushnell's *Sex and the City* (1996).

Candace Bushnell

Assembled from columns written for the *New York Observer*, *Sex and the City* was a relatively minor novel until it was taken up by HBO and transformed into one of the most acclaimed TV shows of recent years. Though differing substantially from the original, the show popularized the adventures of Carrie Bradshaw and established Bushnell as a successful writer of contemporary fiction. *Sex and the City* has been followed by *Four Blondes* (2001) and *Trading Up* (2003), with all three novels sharing a focus on the social, sexual, romantic and professional experiences of ambitious metropolitan women. What makes Bushnell's fiction more interesting than some of her contemporaries is that she is willing to offer a darker portrait of the women who inhabit the urban

Fictions of Globalization

elite. These insights can be traced by looking in greater detail at *Sex and the City*.

In some ways, Bushnell's fiction uses brands in fairly straightforward ways. Offering a ready indicator of wealth and taste, the logo functions as the perfect way of delineating characters and defining their status. A typical scene begins:

> At just that moment Amalita walked in . . . and her coat and packages were whisked away. She was wearing a tweedy Jil Sander (the skirt alone cost over a thousand dollars) and a green cashmere shell. 'Is it hot in here?' she said, fanning herself with her gloves. She removed her jacket. The entire restaurant gauped.[12]

Operating in terms that seem to affirm the success of the Jil Sander brand, Amalita's outfit gives the entire restaurant something to admire and in using this product to identify her as wealthy, beautiful and fashionable, the text focuses the reader on what is, in effect, a promotional spectacle. In this respect, *Sex and the City* simply nurtures and reinforces patterns of conspicuous consumption. One only has to look at the ways in which the constant allusions to Monolo Blahnik shoes in the *Sex and the City* TV series have increased both the profile and the sales of that particular brand to find evidence of the relationships that bind this type of fiction to the worlds of fashion and commerce.[13]

Such a view is compromised, however, by the fact that Bushnell's novel includes moments that generate a much more critical account of the relationships between the women she describes and the consumer society they inhabit. Though in the main the tone of the novel is light, there are a number of darker insights. The scene with Amalita, for example, develops in the following way when she starts to describe the life another woman, Ray. In response to Carrie's question 'how does she [Ray] survive?' Amalita replies,

> She takes gifts. A Bulgari watch. A Harry Winston necklace. Clothing cars, a bungalow on someone's property, someone who wants to help her. And cash. She has a child. There are lots of rich men out there who take pity. These actors with their millions. They'll write a check for fifty thousand dollars. Sometimes just to go away . . . well is there any future? And you've got to keep up. With the clothes and the body. The exercise classes. The massages, facials. Plastic surgery. It's

expensive. Look at Ray. She's had her breasts done, lips, buttocks; she's not young, darling, over forty. What you see is all she's got.[14]

Conjuring a grim vision of a woman forced to commoditize her life, her relationships and her body, this passage makes it clear that Bushnell recognizes the costs and consequences of the glamorous world she portrays. The aspirational mood that characterizes so much of the writing is thus shaded with bleaker moments that see women weighed down by the need to consume, and trapped in the reflective surfaces of consumer culture.

This is not, of course, an insight that Bushnell can claim as her own. Concerns of this kind can be found in novels as familiar as Theodore Dreiser's *Sister Carrie* (1900), Jane Austin's *Pride and Prejudice* (1813) and Edith Wharton's *The House of Mirth* (1905). Indeed, at various moments in *Sex and the City* Bushnell draws self-consciously on elements from Wharton's New York novels and it is possible to see parallels between Carrie Bradshaw and both Lily Bart and Ellen Olenska. What differentiates Bushnell from these traditional accounts of the relationships between women, consumption and society, however, is the tendency to colour the world she describes with a more apocalyptic vision of consumerism. This view is most forcefully articulated in a scene that sees Carrie walking home alone through a hot New York night and allowing herself to become absorbed in cannibalistic fantasies. Bushnell writes:

> The city is hot. She feels powerful, like a predator. A woman is walking down the sidewalk a few feet in front of her. She's wearing a loose white shirt, it's like a white flag and it's driving Carrie crazy. Suddenly Carrie feels like a shark smelling blood. She fantasizes about killing the woman and eating her. It's terrifying how much she's enjoying the fantasy . . . Carrie envisions tearing into the woman's soft, white flesh with her teeth.[15]

In terms that echo the violence of *Glamorama*, *American Psycho* and, most obviously, the vampiric fantasies that dominate Ellis's *The Informers* (1994), Carrie responds to the spectacular world of consumption around her by imagining brutally violent acts. Suggesting that consumerism not only dehumanizes, but also reifies in ways that turn every living thing, even the human body, into an object to be greedily consumed, Carrie's fantasy stands as what is Bushnell's most potent critique of consumption. Modern New

York, this image suggests, is a cruel and destructive place in which people seem to feed off each other. Clearly apparent in Ellis's fiction and readily detectable in the apparently superficial surfaces of Bushnell's romance, these ideas are even more strongly articulated in Chuck Palahniuk's writing, particularly in *Fight Club* (1996), a novel that will be discussed later in this chapter. Before moving to the analysis of Palahniuk's text, however, it is worth pausing to reflect upon the history of the use of brand names in literature and considering the extent to which the analysis of this tradition can add to the understanding of writers like Ellis and Bushnell.

Hemingway's brands

Though the use of brand names in literature is a feature that seems to characterize contemporary writing, there is no sense that either Ellis or Bushnell are doing anything new or unique. It may be true that Ellis's novels use an unprecedented number of logos, but he is certainly not the first writer to employ commercial language. Though it would be impossible (and indeed, perhaps, pointless) to identify the earliest example of the inclusion of a logo in a work of literature, even the most casual survey would demonstrate that branded language is present in a great many literary texts (with works by Alexander Pope, Samuel Pepys and Tobias Smollett prominent amongst them) written since, at the very latest, the start of the eighteenth century. These patterns are even more obvious in novels from the early part of the twentieth century. James Joyce, for example, makes a rigorous attempt to engage with the meanings of advertising and consumption in *Ulysses* (1922) through his portrait of Bloom the 'canvasser' and the significances attached to references to products and companies (both real and imaginary) like Plumtree's Potted Meat, The House of Keyes, Bass and J. C. Kino.[16] Like Joyce, John Dos Passos also saw the need to incorporate brands and advertising into his writing. In a typical scene from the opening of *Manhattan Transfer* (1925), Dos Passos describes a Jewish man staring 'abstractedly at a face on a green advertising card ... under it in copybook writing was the signature King C. Gillette.'[17] Having seen this poster the man then buys the razor and shaves off his beard, a sequence of events that dramatizes both the power of branding

Branding, Consumption and Identity

and Dos Passos's sense of the ways in which commerce plays an essential role in processes of cultural assimilation and mechanisms of self-fashioning.

Patterns evident in the fiction of this period can also be discerned in the visual arts. As paintings by Charles Demuth, Stuart Davis and Edward Hopper demonstrate, American artists were starting to incorporate brands into their compositions throughout the 1920s and 1930s.[18] In terms that prefigure the artistic apotheosis of the logo affected by Warhol, all three of these painters reveal an awareness of the brand's presence in the vernacular and iconography of everyday life. These tendencies are also apparent in earlier works by European artists, particularly in the cubist experiments of Pablo Picasso and Georges Braques. As the collages of paint and packaging used to create pieces like Braques' *Packet of Tobacco* (1914) and Picasso's *Packet of Cigarettes and Newspaper* (1911–12) and *Glass of Pernod and Cup* (1911) make clear, brands and packaging were not just seen as suitable subjects for art, but also as appropriate raw materials for the making of artworks.

There are, however, exceptions. Though Gertrude Stein's list of 'Objects' in *Tender Buttons* (1914) includes portraits of items of clothing and various umbrellas, few of these things are known in relation to brands or trademarks.[19] The same applies to an earlier text like Kate Chopin's *The Awakening* (1899). Concerned with conspicuous consumption and the status of Edna as a commodity it is, perhaps, surprising that Chopin's text contains no references to brands. Revealing as the lack of logos in *The Awakening* is, more striking is the absence of almost all trademarks from F. Scott Fitzgerald's *The Great Gatsby* (1926). Though offering extensive descriptions of Gatsby's many possessions, the novel almost wilfully omits details of their manufacturers. This is most apparent in the play between Tom Buchanan's 'coupé' and Gatsby's 'yellow' car. With identification of the vehicles crucial to the plot, it is significant that Fitzgerald should choose to leave them both so pointedly unbranded.[20] William Faulkner, unlike Fitzgerald, does include brands in his work. Jason Compson chases a 'ford' and drinks a 'cocacola' in *The Sound and the Fury* (1931), but Faulkner's decision not to capitalize either trademark indicates an unwillingness to accept them without a degree of qualification.[21] It thus appears that for Stein, Fitzgerald and, to some extent,

Faulkner, there is a reluctance to embrace the language of brands, a reluctance that suggests an attitude towards modernity and consumption that contrasts with the responses offered in texts by Joyce and Dos Passos.

A similar hesitation can be identified in Ralph Ellison's *Invisible Man* (1952). Though the car that plays such an important role in the opening section of the book is known to be 'powerful' and filled with the smell of 'mints and cigar smoke', the manufacturer remains unidentified.[22] In contrast, Richard Wright's *Native Son* (1940) seems much more attuned to the social and cultural significance of brands. Hired to drive for the Daltons, Bigger wonders, 'What make of car was he to drive? . . . He hoped it would be a Packard, or a Lincoln, or a Rolls Royce . . . he would make those tires smoke.'[23] In this regard, Wright shadows Zora Neale Hurston's awareness of the significance of brands and logos in African-American culture and articulates ideas that offer ready connections with the discussion of the commodity-heavy styles of contemporary African-American culture raised in the preceding chapter. Alive to the precise significances property, commodities and brands have for the descendents of slaves and intensely aware of the rich range of social, cultural and political meanings generated by consumption, Wright's use of the names of particular companies serves a necessary and specific function in his text.

The tendencies apparent in this brief survey of twentieth-century literature and visual culture are interesting in part because they offer insights into the relationships these different texts have with modernity and consumer society. They are also significant in terms of the light they shed on the prevalence of logos in contemporary culture and on the ways in which recent film, fiction and the visual arts deploy brands. Where Joyce, Wright and Dos Passos saw fit to include references to the occasional product in their work, many contemporary writers, as the discussion of Ellis and Bushnell demonstrates, seem content to fill the pages of their fiction with a host of such allusions. The obvious interpretation is that this tendency offers a direct reflection of what seems to be the increasingly branded nature of everyday experience. The brand, according to commentators like Naomi Klein, is expanding into all areas of contemporary experience, and as a result it seems unsurprising that logos should colonize all areas of culture and take their place on the pages of contemporary novels.[24] Leaving aside, for the time being at least, questions about the extent to which Klein is right to insist that early twenty-first century life is the victim of uniquely invasive forms of commercial penetration, these arguments raise the problematic suggestion that the inclusion of brands in fiction signals a straightforward commercialization of culture, a process that co-opts and diminishes creativity.

This position is mirrored in one of the few academic studies to make an extended attempt to address the presence of brands and labels in fiction, Monroe Friedman's *A 'Brand' New Language* (1991). Offering a statistical analysis of the increasing frequency of the use of brands in fiction written in the postwar period, Friedman argues that, 'If authors of best-selling novels and hit plays in the 1940s and 1950s referred in their works to motor vehicles as "cars" and "autos", while their 1970s and 1980s counterparts referred to them as "Fords", "Cadillacs", or "Toyotas", this would suggest increasing commercial influence over the course of the postwar period.'[25] The problem is, however, that because he is only able to see the use of trademarks as the sign of 'commercial influence', Friedman neglects the kinds of social and cultural significances generated by the use of brands in the work of Joyce, Dos Passos and Wright. He also fails to appreciate that brands bring verisimilitude to a text. Film-makers and television producers have known for years that the failure to include recognizable brands in their work often prompts vigorous complaints about unreality. Part of the fabric of everyday life, logos provide an efficient way of rooting a text to a particular milieu and connecting it to specific contexts and social experiences. To condemn the presence of labels in film and fiction out of hand as the sign of an unhealthy 'commercial influence' or a suspect form of product placement is, in these terms, to run the risk of ignoring the complex social dimensions of consumption, the sophistication of the consumer's relationship with branded products and the aesthetic and symbolic effects created by the use of a familiar logo. A brief discussion of the use of brands in Ernest Hemingway's 'Hills like white elephants' (1927) can make this range of forces, meanings and effects more readily understood.

Like his contemporaries Joyce, Dos Passos and Picasso, Hemingway makes a deliberate effort to explore the status of branded products in his fiction. In terms that prefigure the kinds of commodity-heavy prose used by more contemporary novelists, Hemingway is not only very aware of the social status of branded goods, but also determined to demonstrate a wider sense of the logo's communicative function. Reflecting Hemingway's personal desire to present himself as a knowledgeable and experienced consumer, his fiction is littered with revealing lifestyle details and references calculated to offer precise insights into the tastes of his protagonists. Hemingway's characters drive Buggatis, carry Louis Vuitton luggage, read *Le Monde* and drink in the cocktail bars of exclusive European hotels.[26] This brief discussion of his fiction thus promises both a more detailed understanding of these forces and a wider insight into the traditions that inform the characteristics of more recent writing. Hemingway is not the originator of this aesthetic tendency, but he is a writer who, as the discussion that follows will suggest, employs commercial languages in terms that pre-empt contemporary approaches. The analysis of his fiction thus provides an important perspective on the use of brands in recent fiction and combines that with a wider historical understanding of the development of these traits. Prioritising the recognition that the use of brands is not a unique feature of contemporary fiction and linking that position with an interpretation of the social meaning of logos, the suggestion is that Hemingway's text can be read in terms that suggest branded languages do more than simply reflect the interests of commerce and the market.

Richard Godden's *Fictions of Capital* (1990) offers a powerful account of the relationship between Ernest Hemingway's fiction and consumerism. Identifying a contradiction at the heart of Hemingway's project, Godden argues that his search for experiences distanced from modernity and consumer society and his pursuit of a simple, direct literary style, makes his fiction complicit with processes of commodification. Godden's argument is that Hemingway 'experiences the contradiction that to revel in the surface of things within nature is to revel in their reproduction with exchange. In its extreme form that contradiction becomes a confused revulsion for what is celebrated.'[27] Recognizing that Hemingway's 'shop windows sell the escape from shop windows', Godden identifies Hemingway as the 'laureate' of capitalist realism.[28] Hemingway's desire for an uncommodified reality is thus set against a sense of the indissociability of that reality from the processes of capital in terms that illustrate the increasing influence and ubiquity of the market and the force of its 'assault on perception'.[29] In this respect, the images of consumption in Hemingway foster a critical reading of the history of the commodity and initiate historicizing processes that are at odds with capitalism's desire to make all that is solid melt into air.[30] Though these observations are elegant and authoritative, there is still a sense that there is more to say on the function of commodities in Hemingway's fiction, a suggestion that can be developed by shifting away from Godden's emphasis on consumption's relationship with the market and towards an approach that focuses on its role in processes of social communication. Discussion of the meanings generated by the references to the aniseed spirit Anis del Toro in 'Hills like white elephants' can be used to introduce these ideas and to establish a broader sense of the function of brands and commodities in fiction.

When the male protagonist in 'Hills like white elephants' steps out from the interior of the bar and on to the station platform he passes through a beaded curtain that stands as an obvious metaphor for the growing separation between himself and his partner. That Hemingway should develop this image by describing the logo for Anis del Toro painted onto the curtain brings an additional level of complexity to the scene. With the couple engaged in the process of translating their feud over her pregnancy into an argument about their itinerant lifestyle and their constant search for new experiences, the drink finds itself turned into a repository for a whole range of values and meanings. The dispute builds from her reference to the white elephants, an allusion that hints at realms of knowledge that lie beyond his ken. Revealing both an exotic past and (perhaps) her affluence, the simile unsettles him, an irritation that arises, it seems, because these markers of wealth and independence imply that both she and her unborn child could survive without him.

The power she accrues from this observation is, however, wrested from her the moment she asks for 'Anis del Toro'. Her experience of Africa is suddenly eclipsed by his cultural and linguistic familiarity with Spain. Not only does he speak the language, he knows the country's products too. In ordering the drink he is thus able to satisfy her appetites for knowledge and commodities and as a result finds himself restored, momentarily at least, to the role of guide and mentor. This authority is reinforced by the fact that her curiosity seems both impulsive and childish. In terms that reflect familiar portrayals of the female consumer as emotional and spontaneous, she responds instinctively to the advertiser's stimuli and is, in consequence, infantilized by her request.[31] This is, of course, exactly the way he wants her to behave. He wants a childlike woman, a girl who can be manipulated into agreeing to a termination.

His power, however, is short lived. On sampling the drink and discovering that it tastes like 'liquorice', she puts the glass down on the table.[32] Recognizing that this apparently exotic experience is just another version of Pastis, she unmasks the Spanish branding of the product and erodes his status as a result. She, a woman who has seen real elephants, seems unimpressed that he can only offer her ersatz anisette. The sense of division generated in the responses to Anis del Toro is developed further at the end of the story when the man steps away from the table, walks around the station and slips surreptitiously into the bar through the door on the other side of the platform. Once inside he orders another Anis del Toro and drinks it, before stepping back through the beaded curtain to rejoin his companion. Obviously a sign of his anger and anxiety, this secret drink is also an attempt to re-establish the values she has stripped away. Determined to re-instate the cultural status of the drink, he purchases and consumes it alone. His actions suggests that Anis del Toro isn't simply 'liquorice', but an emblem of his familiarity with Europe and a symbol for the kind of independent lifestyle he fears will be lost if the child is born. The fact that the brand name articulates a range of meanings linked to masculinity and sexual potency only adds to the importance of this particular scene and develops the general sense of the significance of the Anis del Toro brand in the text. There can be little doubt that allusions to Anis del Toro (literally 'the bull's aniseed spirit') have a particular resonance in a story about pregnancy and sexual power.

The beaded curtain and the drink could, of course, have remained unbranded without substantially altering the meaning of the story. The fact that Hemingway chooses to use the Anis del Toro marque does, however, add to the narrative both with regard to the precision of the description and in terms of the ways in which it generates a very specific focus on the couple's relationship.

The commodity embodies a whole range of social meanings and forms part of the communicative codes used by the two individuals. Its 'cultural capital' is traded between them in ways that have little to do with commerce.[33] As Pierre Bourdieu explains, 'consumption is . . . a stage in a process of communication . . . an act of deciphering, decoding, which presupposes practical or explicit mastery of a cipher or code.'[34] Not just another sign of the commodification of Hemingway's style or a straightforward mark of his preoccupation with things, the references to the Anis del Toro brand thus play a key role in the text and demonstrates the ways in which responses to logos and the ability, in Bourdieu's terms, to master and decipher their codes are central elements in the ongoing transactions between the man and the woman. Hemingway's references to commodities and the descriptions of consumption are thus not purely and simply emblems of commercial incorporation, but moments that communicate a wide range of meanings about the relationships that connect individuals. The implication is that the logo is not always the sign of deathly reification, but forms part of the living fabric of everyday life.

Such positions stand apart from traditional accounts of consumption that draw on problematic distinctions between legitimate needs and false desires in terms that can be linked to a wider reading of consumer society as a form of mass deception. The implication is that branding and marketing form part of what Raymond Williams calls advertising's 'magic system', an industry aimed at resolving and displacing the contradictions of capitalist society. In Williams's terms:

> If the consumption of individual goods leaves the whole area of human needs unsatisfied, the attempt is made, by magic, to associate this consumption with human desires to which it has no real reference . . . The magic obscures the real sources of general satisfaction because their discovery would involve radical change in the whole common way of life.[35]

The problem with such a position, however, is that it sees consumption only in relation to capitalism. The result is a perspective that is unable to recognize the ways in which consumer activities can be read, not only as forms of communication (in terms that shadow the work of commentators like Bourdieu) but also as central components in the anthropological formation of social groups. The common concern that links works as diverse as Dick Hebdige's *Subcultures* (1979), Mary Douglas and Baron Isherwood's *The World of Goods* (1978) and Mihaly Csikszentmihalyi and Eugene Rochberg-Halton's *The Meaning of Things* (1984) is a sense that consumption can operate as a social indicator. The implication is that commodities need to be understood, in Douglas and Isherwood's terms, as a 'nonverbal medium for the human creative faculty.'[36] It is the failure to recognize these dimensions of consumer behaviour that problematizes the accounts of consumption offered by Williams and the Frankfurt School.[37]

As the analysis of 'Hills like white elephants' shows, the trademark provides one more element in the array of aesthetic effects available to Hemingway. Reading this story in these terms thus sheds a revealing light on the broader social meaning of logos, brands and advertising. More than simply the badges of capitalism, these insights privilege the understanding of brands as forms of social communication. In terms that dramatize the complex social symbolism that surround logos and trademarks, 'Hills like white elephants' thus reveals a strong sense of the ways in which both particular products and commodities in general can been seen as the carriers of values that are more than simply commercial. Linked to gender identity, functioning as the signs of social status and operating as shorthand devices for communicating details of place and culture, the use of brands thus works to generate a rich range of significances not just in this piece, but in many of his novels and stories. The implication is that, like his contemporaries Joyce, Picasso, Dos Passos and Braques, Hemingway demonstrates a sensitivity to the emerging significance of branded goods in twentieth-century society and seems concerned to explore the meanings generated by these products in his fiction.

Though for some the incorporation of brands into his prose, and the ways in which his texts appear to emulate processes and patterns of commodification reveal an affirmative relationship with consumer capitalism, the suggestion is that the presence of these commercial elements in his texts work in terms that do much more than simply mimic the interests of commerce. This argument, developed through readings of Hemingway's 'Hills like white elephants', and relevant, as this discussion has suggested, to the works of a significant number of his contemporaries, has a particular importance for contemporary culture. Living in an age in which brands and commodities are not only a common presence on the pages of recent novels, but also, it seems, all areas of social and cultural experience, the debate around the status and significance of brands and commodities has a specific urgency and currency. The general importance of this discussion is that it makes a contribution to this debate and provides a sense of the ways in which processes of branding and commodification can be seen not simply as the sign of commercial co-option, but as part of ongoing processes of negotiation between capitalism's interests and the concerns of individuals and social groups. Turning to consider Chuck Palahniuk's *Fight Club*, a novel in which men of the Hemingwayan type battle corporate power and the influence of consumption, provides an even clearer focus on the forces that shape and define these relationships.

Chuck Palahniuk

A host of similarities unite Ellis's *Glamorama* with Palahniuk's *Fight Club*. Terrorism, violence, consumption and the banality of advertising are themes that dominate both books and it is interesting in itself that these two novels should turn independently towards subjects of this kind when constructing their portraits of late twentieth-century life. Though similar in terms of general conception, there are, however, significant differences between the texts, the most obvious of which is that *Fight Club* seems to address consumer society in a much more direct and confrontational way. Like Ellis's, Palahniuk's novel is patterned with explosions and hyperbolic acts, but unlike *Glamorama*, *Fight Club* seems to offer an unambiguous vision of both the problems at hand and the remedies needed to cure them. Where Ellis's text is preoccupied with aesthetic experiments and the comedy of fashionable manners, *Fight Club* is driven by the clearly articulated critical agenda framed through the thoughts and gestures of the narrator's alter ego, Tyler Durden.

Vigorously opposed to consumption in all its forms, Durden is the catalyst for the development of the network of 'fight clubs' and the founding of 'project mayhem', an anti-capitalist, terrorist organization bent on taking America back to year zero. Durden dreams of 'stalking elk past department store windows and stinking racks of beautiful rotting dresses and tuxedos on hangers; you'll wear leather clothes that will last you the rest of your life, and you'll climb the wrist-thick kudzo vines that wrap the Sears Tower.'[38] Privileging the durability and authenticity of leather clothes over the superficiality of fashion, Durden is not a futurist yearning for a radical (or indeed reactionary) kind of modernity, but an individual looking to take a step back in time.[39] Dreaming of leather-stockinged heroes from the American past, he seeks to bring down the Sears Tower and leave only wilderness in its place. Central to these ambitions is a very specific image of masculinity that is defined as antithetical to consumption. Where the shop windows of contemporary culture are filled with flimsy dresses and tuxedos, Durden looks to reject these commodities in favour of durable items of clothing that are, one assumes, crafted by manly, unalienated labour. The implication is that real men aspire to things not commodities.

These ideas are supported by moments in the text that privilege what Durden regards as images of authentic masculinity over displays of a more synthetic kind. One section reads: 'the gyms you go to are crowded with guys trying to look like men, as if being a man means looking the way a sculptor or art director says.'[40] The relationship between identity and consumption described here is one that echoes familiar accounts of the relationship between contemporary masculinity and consumption. Susan Faludi's *Stiffed* (2000), for example, explores what she calls 'ornamental masculinity' and sees this need to ornament as one of the causes of the 'betrayal of modern man'.[41] Faludi's argument is that after the Second World War the 'more productive aspects of manhood, such as building or cultivating or contributing to a society, couldn't establish a foothold on the shiny flat surface of a commercial culture, a looking glass before which men could only act out a crude semblance of masculinity.'[42] In her mind there is an unproblematic distinction between 'productive' and unproductive 'aspects of manhood' and an adherence to traditional senses of the ways in which masculinity is tied to action, cultivation and work. Consumption is thus explicitly identified with the feminine. As Faludi explains, 'the dictates of a consumer and media culture had trapped men and women in a world in which top billing mattered more than building, in which representation trumped production, in which appearances were what counted. This was good for no one of either sex, but at least "femininity" fit[ted] more easily into the new ethic.'[43]

Seeing men as diminished by consumption, a position linked with a sense that consumerism is implicitly feminine, is an argument that has an obvious relationship with the ways in which Durden conceives and constructs his fight clubs. Exclusively male, the fight clubs promise an escape from 'ornamental' masculinity. Fighting, the raw punching of fist on skin, thus becomes both a release from the mundane currents of consumer society and a visceral critique of that society. These fights, in contrast to the seemingly false images peddled by advertising and the media, are presented as moments of truth, authenticity and reality. Durden's claim is that 'You aren't alive anywhere like you're alive at fight club.'[44] In his mind, 'Fight club is not football on television. A bunch of men you don't know halfway around the world beating on each other live by satellite with a two-minute delay, commercials pitching beer every ten minutes, and a pause now for station identification. After you've been to fight club, watching football on television is like watching pornography when you could be having great sex.'[45] Fight club, it seems, provides reality and authenticity and offers an antidote to the synthetic spectacles and the banality of everyday life.

Advertising, interrupting football games and promoting apparently false desires is at the heart of his sense of contemporary culture's vacuity. As one of Durden's acolytes explains, 'You have a class of young strong men and women, and they want to give their lives to something. Advertising has these people chasing cars and clothes they don't need. Generations have been working in jobs they hate, just so they can buy what they don't really need.'[46] The solution appears to be simple: reject consumption (and it seems femininity) and return to a more primal, unornamented sense of masculine selfhood. Promised first by the fight clubs and then developed into a more direct assault on the structures of capitalism itself by project mayhem, the answers seem to lie in these straightforwardly adversarial acts, gestures that punch through the superficial facades of modern life and expose the rawer, more authentic experiences lying beneath.

It is this idealism that informs one of the key moments in the text, the destruction of the narrator's perfectly maintained condo in an explosion. Having met (or imagined) Durden for the first time on a business flight, the narrator returns home to find his home ablaze, an event that bears all the hallmarks of project mayhem. When questioned by the police about the suspicious circumstances, the narrator responds

> I told the detective, no, I did not leave the gas on and then leave town. I loved my life. I loved that condo. I loved every stick of furniture. That was my whole life. Everything, the lamps, the chairs, the rugs were me. The dishes in the cabinets were me. The plants were me. The television was me. It was me that blew up. Couldn't he see that?[47]

Both a moment of loss for the narrator and a release, the destruction of property ties the narrator more firmly to both Durden and the fight clubs. Palahniuk makes this point explicit by having their first fight take place immediately after this explosion and following that with a scene that shows the narrator moving into Durden's temporary abode, the decrepit and blighted house on Paper Street. Losing his home and property he is thus able to shed the weight of consumer society and find, it seems, freedom. Crucially this freedom is also a moment in which he rejects the domestic. The implication is that the destruction of his comfortable home and his neatly arranged domestic objects does not simply liberate him, but destroys the feminine dimensions of his existence and makes him both more real and more of a man.

Fighting and the rejection of consumption are thus tied together as the novel constructs an image of masculinity that is both aggressive and immune to the pleasures of consumer society. Consumerism, the text suggests, diminishes not just selfhood, but masculinity. These ideas are, however, extremely problematic. The relentless typing of consumption in terms of femininity, for example, hinges upon, as many commentators have suggested, an essentialist account of women as natural consumers.[48] In similar terms, the bald ways in which Palahniuk's characters seem able to make categorical distinctions between authentic and inauthentic experiences are equally awkward and bring to mind a whole range of familiar Baudriallardian critiques linked to debates around simulation. Though these dynamics are interesting in themselves, the focus of this discussion is on the ways in which these two assumptions are linked to the novel's general vision of consumer society. It is through an examination of the text's contradictory representation of consumption and its apparent anti-capitalism that many of these tensions around gender, identity and authenticity can be interpreted.

On one level Palahniuk seems to construct an unproblematic opposition between commodified and uncommodified experiences. The fight clubs and the terrorism of project mayhem that emerges from those clubs stand as clear attempts to oppose consumption. In this respect there is a strongly reactionary quality to Durden's ideology. Like a Pol Pot for the world of consumer goods, he dreams of destroying everything and starting again, creating a new world freed from inauthentic displays. In the novel's terms: 'It's project mayhem that's going to save the world. A cultural ice age. A prematurely induced dark age. Project mayhem will force humanity to go dormant or into remission long enough for the Earth to recover.'[49]

This reactionary position is, however, founded on a fundamental complicity with the systems and structures it is reacting against. In simple terms, the brutal battles fought out on the floor of the fight clubs echo the *laissez faire* patterns that characterize contemporary capitalism.[50] This sense of complicity is strengthened by the understanding that members of fight club seem to have exchanged idealized commercial images of grooming and dress for a kind of narcissism of pain, one that celebrates the injuries and disfigurements picked up through fighting in ways that become an alternative form of ornamental masculinity.[51] The implication is that the ideal of the fighting male does not shatter inauthentic displays of self, but simply replaces one stylized construction of masculinity with another. These entanglements are also apparent in the organization of project mayhem. With its rigorous selection policy and bureaucratized structures, the movement develops in a fashion that starts to mimic the ordinary business cultures it is seeking to oppose. Like the narrator's work in recall coordination, project mayhem takes on an increasingly institutionalized quality. The industrial nature of the production of explosives and the strict employment criteria make it clear that the alternatives offered by Durden are simply mirror images of the world he is trying to destroy.

These complications suggest the presence of a powerful contradiction at the heart of the novel. Rejecting capitalism and consumption, while continuing to be tied to its meanings and structures, Durden, the fight clubs and project mayhem remain complicit with the world they are looking to oppose. What makes this complicity interesting, however, is that the text seems to explore these contradictions in terms that generate a broader perspective on the conflicts and complexities that characterize the relationship between individuals and consumerism. The suggestion is that the text frames Durden's naive opposition to consumption within a wider consciousness of the paradoxes that characterize his endeavours. The most telling insight into this consciousness comes through the patterns of ideas generated by the nature of the production of first soap and then nitro-glycerine.

Durden's 'Paper Street Soap Company' renders fat from liposuction to make glycerine. Breaking into medical waste incineration plants, the 'goal is the big red bags of liposuctioned fat we'll haul back to Paper Street and render and mix with lye and rosemary and sell it back to the very people who paid to have it sucked out. At twenty bucks a bar, these are the only people who can afford it.'[52] Extracted from the bodies of the wealthy, processed and sold at a premium to those same individuals, there is a tight ironic symbolism in these images. That the same fat should then be used, the reader is led to believe, to make the explosives that will be deployed in assaults on commercial institutions only adds to the significance of these images. Cleansing and destruction, favoured images in project mayhem's rhetoric, thus come together in the text's focus on the manufacture of soap and nitroglycerine. The point is, however, that both of these products are manufactured in ways that reveal an intimate connection between project mayhem and the world it is looking to purge with the implication being that it is tied to the systems it is opposing in a parasitical relationship that problematizes its antagonism. Bonded to the circuits of wealth, it can only challenge consumerism with products of its own, commodities that depend upon affluence and luxury for their manufacture and the wealth of consumers for their dissemination. The metaphor of the soap and the liposuctioned fat thus becomes an image of the circuits and interrelationships that characterize contemporary experience. Tyler Durden may see himself as an outsider, challenging the structures and patterns of consumerism, with his fight clubs, rigorously organized terrorist cells, soap and nitro-glycerine, but all of these gestures and products remain wedded to the society he is looking to oppose. The dream of landing a clean and successful knock-out punch on consumerism is thus undermined by a novel that questions the possibility of such a straightforward attack.

This conflict is equally apparent in the film version of Palahniuk's novel. Made by David Fincher, a film-maker who emerged in the 1980s as a director of high-profile music videos for Madonna, Sting and Paula Abdul and commercials for Nike, Pepsi and Coca-Cola, the critique of consumption in the film version of *Fight Club* (1999) could be seen as Fincher's attempt to bite the commercial hand that once fed him. Such an argument would be sustainable were it not, however, for the complicated sense of the relationship between the individual and consumer culture constructed in his version of the novel. Not only does the film borrow many of the strategies of television advertising, techniques learned, one presumes, while on agency-funded shoots, but at times it seems to incorporate the very aesthetics of advertising itself into the substance of its creative fabric. One of the most obvious of these moments comes when Durden (Brad Pitt) and the narrator (Edward Norton) get onto a bus and stand by a poster of the sculpted physique of a male model advertising Gucci underwear. The narrator asks Tyler 'is that what a man is supposed to look like?' and receives the dismissive reply 'self improvement is masturbation'.[53] That this scene should then give way to shots of a semi-naked Pitt rising bloodied but triumphant from the floor of the fight club and standing illuminated in a shaft of light that catches perfectly on his famously toned body while his fellow fight-clubbers look on adoringly only adds to the audience's contradictory response to the movie.

Mocking the idealized body in one scene and then celebrating its seductive beauty in another, Fincher's film thus reveals a powerful consciousness of the contradictions that characterize both consumerism in general and the particular dynamics of male consumption. Durden's contempt for consumerism is a classic image of cool. It becomes the emblem of his own position as the ideal man and as such prompts the envious commodifying gaze of the men who surround him. Leaving the viewer in no doubt, Fincher offers the audience a shot of the semi-naked Pitt as if to reconfirm his status as an idealized image of masculinity, a man who is both contemptuous of consumption and free from the constraints of advertising. The irony is that articulating these ideas only makes the character more attractive and heightens his status as an object of desire. Casting Brad Pitt in the role of Durden adds an additional layer of meanings to these images. Knowing that Durden is the product of the narrator's imagination, a seemingly ideal image of free, libidinous and unfettered masculinity, Fincher's decision to cast Pitt in the part stands as an acknowledgement of his status as a contemporary icon.[54] Recognizing that Pitt would function well as many men's favourite alter ego, Fincher plays on the seductive appeal of Pitt's image and his status as a star and uses him to portray the perfectly packaged embodiment of freedom and uncircumscribed masculinity.

The play between the film's celebration of anti-capitalist ideals and its deployment of these commodified images is typical of the kinds of complexities that characterize Fincher's movie. Much of the film seems to work around the tension between these two poles, a process articulated in particularly clear terms in the scene that sees Edward Norton drawn into the world of IKEA. Opening on a shot of him in his bathroom flicking through the Ikea catalogue and ordering 'dust ruffles' through the mail order service, the sequence develops as the narrator steps out into his flat.[55] In the scene that follows, a number of film techniques combine to create the effect of the apartment being magically furnished around Norton as he moves through its spaces until it resembles the images we have already seen on the pages of the catalogue. His desires become real, falling into their allotted places, as he steps through his condominium. This mirroring effect is completed by the appearance of prices, specifications and descriptions in superimposed type over the images. Fincher adds to this scene by partnering the visuals with a voiceover that has the narrator observe, 'like so many others I had become a slave to the IKEA nesting instinct . . . we used to read pornography, now it was the Horchow collection'.[56] The implication seems clear: the narrator has become chained to possessions, enclosed and absorbed by them in ways that stunt his emotional and sexual potential.

Such a reading is, however, complicated by the fact that in order to develop this point, Fincher has borrowed heavily from the medium of advertising itself. To explode these consumerist myths, Norton has to step onto the pages of the catalogue and come to inhabit them. The sequence itself looks like an advertisement, and even though the tone is ironic, this does not completely cancel out the lingeringly affirmative sense of the desirability of IKEA products. The apartment looks seductive, even as that image is being interrogated. So strong, in fact, are the images used in *Fight Club* that IKEA have themselves, it seems, borrowed heavily from this scene for a recent commercial. Using the strapline 'Live Unlimited', the campaign depicts a man sitting alone in an empty apartment. As the music begins, sofas, rugs, lamps and shelving units all appear around him as, like Norton in Fincher's film, he finds his home being magically furnished by IKEA in ways that give him unlimited lifestyle opportunities. The connections that link culture with commerce could not, it appears, be more circular. Fincher, a director who first established himself in advertising, uses techniques he learnt directing commercials to make a film that interrogates consumption and then finds that his aesthetic approach has itself been appropriated by advertising agency creatives. The point is that the film seems so knowing about these cyclical processes of appropriation and re-appropriation that it seems unlikely that Fincher would be troubled by this circulation of references. Reliant on an aesthetic that draws on a constant slippage between the realms of commercial art and creative culture, it seems right that IKEA should now borrow from *Fight Club* as it once borrowed from them.[57]

The suggestion is that Fincher, in terms that echo Ellis's techniques in *Glamorama*, marries his critical vision of contemporary consumerism to images of its pleasures in ways that complicate the possibilities of any straightforwardly oppositional response to consumption. Just as Norton's character in early parts of the narrative seems to derive his identity from the objects he buys from the IKEA catalogue, Fincher both derives his aesthetic inspiration from this commercial medium and relies upon its visual techniques to communicate his message. In what is one of the most visually complex scenes in the film (it combines voice-over, dialogue, image, layered editing effects and superimposed text), Fincher creates a sequence that owes its aesthetic complexity to the devices and techniques of advertising. The suggestion is that Fincher is offering the audience an understanding that the commercial codes and commodities that surround us are not simply the signs of the deadening encroachment of commerce into culture, but elements that retain a rich range of expressive possibilities. To see advertising as a source of cinematic experiment rather than its antithesis is particularly interesting, as it forces an appreciation of the ways in which commercial imperatives feed into and revitalize creative cultures, even as they seem to be reified and deadened by them. Fincher's film thus offers a critique of consumerism, while raising a range of questions about the contradictory relationship the modern consumer has with consumption. Perhaps because of his experience of working in both commercial and creative worlds, Fincher seems able to explore the mutually informing relationships that connect these two terrains and combine them in the structure, content, aesthetic and meaning of his version of *Fight Club*. Though there are elements within the film that seemed determined to reject consumption outright, the film itself frames these straightforwardly condemnatory attitudes within a more subtle articulation of the nature of the individuals' relationships with consumerism.

The fact that Fincher generates these different layers of meaning is not simply interesting in itself and revealing in terms of the perspective it offers on Palahniuk's original text, but significant because it raises broader questions about the nature of contemporary culture's relationship with consumption. It is the figure of Durden, the narrator's seductive, anti-capitalist alter ego, that represents these contradictions most vividly and it is through him that the novel develops its most potent expression of the contradictory status of consumerism in contemporary life.

From the beginning of the novel onwards it becomes increasingly clear that Durden is a product of the narrator's imagination, part *doppelganger*, part alter ego. The world Durden constructs must, as a result, be interpreted as an insane fantasy, a 'hallucination'.[58] With the narrator finding himself in an asylum at the end of the text, Palahniuk offers two possible interpretations. The first is that the effort to escape the ordinary currents of life has driven the narrator insane, the second is that the desire to reject or transcend these currents leads to insanity. Added to these concerns is the role of Marla Singer. As the narrator says at the start of the text, 'I know all of this, the gun, the anarchy, the explosion is really about Marla Singer . . . This isn't about *love* as in *caring*. This is about *property* as in *ownership*.'[59] This romantic dimension, Marla's role as the only woman in the text, a woman who seems to represent a world apart from the rigorous masculinity of the fight clubs, adds an additional level of complexity to the understanding of the nexus of ideas that connect gender, identity and consumption.

Linking the narrator's *amour fou* with Marla Singer to the divided sense of self expressed in his creation of the Tyler Durden alter ego thus creates an understanding of the ways in which the text explores an image of romantic desire that seems to lead inevitably toward madness and dislocation. Palahniuk's point appears to be that it is the romantic yearning for Marla, coupled to the desire for some kind of absolute release from the dictates of consumerism that creates his insanity. It is important to note that Tyler first appears to the narrator on a business flight, springing to life in exactly the kind of numb, empty spaces of 'supermodernity' that characterize, in the narrator's mind, the dead world of the business traveller.[60] The point once again is that Durden stands as an expression of consumer desire, a commodity that appeals because he seems to be outside the ordinary currents of consumerism. Seeing him in these terms and connecting him with the narrator's desire for Marla, suggests that Palahniuk understands that the problem with contemporary life is not consumerism in itself, but the kind of divided attitude towards consumption offered by the narrator. His yearning to be both inside and outside the market seems to create the schizophrenia which destroys him in the end. His desire for idealized experiences free from the taint of commerce both bind him more fully to consumerism, while making him less able to understand and engage with it.[61]

These dynamics can be developed further by reflecting more precisely on the ways in which Palahniuk writes. Like the subtleties of Fincher's film version that links the narrator's critique of consumption to an aesthetic that draws its language and techniques from contemporary advertising, Palahniuk's style offers a way of resolving the kind of schizophrenic response to consumerism articulated through the characterization of the narrator. Littered with 'how to' instructions (like, for example, advice on the construction of a silencer, the production of napalm and the manufacture of soap) and loaded with details gleaned from the bureaucratic protocols that govern everyday life (like, for example, the principles that guide airline searches of luggage and the code used to alert cinema projectionists that a reel of a film is coming to an end), *Fight Club* has an intense, immediate feel that develops from the text's grip on these banal, technical details. This texture is enhanced by a preference for short sentences and paragraphs. One typical passage reads:

> You wake up at O'Hare.
> You wake up at LaGuardia.
> You wake up at Logan.[62]

This aesthetic is rooted in the empty experiences it describes and contributes to the creation of a style that seems deeply enmeshed in the blank, flat terrains of contemporary capitalism.

The sense of familiarity and enclosure created by these effects is strengthened by Palahniuk's structure. Starting at the end, the events that follow simply count down to the apocalypse described in the opening chapter with the result being a sense of inevitability. There is a rigorous plan at work and no possibility for deviation. Like the foreshortened narratives beloved of the television advertiser, the reader is rarely allowed to stray away from the clearly defined plot. Instead of revelation *Fight Club*, like many television commercials, simply offers reinforcement of the message it has established in its opening scene. Palahniuk's tendency to stud his prose with exhortations and nugatory moments of philosophical insight only adds to this impression and gives the writing an immediacy that makes it both compelling and seductive.

True of *Fight Club*, these tendencies are equally apparent in the rest of Palahniuk's fiction. Indeed, so similar are many of his novels that they seem almost mass produced. All centred on ingenious conceits and written in an identikit prose, the branding of Palahniuk's work is always clear and identifiable. Distinct continuities also exist in terms of plot between his work in *Fight Club* and his other novels: *Invisible Monsters* (1999) deals with cosmetic surgery and celebrity; the protagonist in *Choke* (2001) makes his living by extorting money from customers by feigning choking fits in restaurants; *Lullaby* (2002) and *Dairy* (2003) differ slightly from these others but still retain many of his signature concerns. Of all Palahniuk's novels, *Survivor* (1999) offers the clearest parallels with *Fight Club*.

Telling the story of Tender Branson's life in the 'Creedish Death Cult' as he flies a doomed plane out over the Pacific, the novel describes his time as a member of this extreme religious sect and explains his work as a domestic servant. Branson is characterized by his incredible memory for the rituals of bourgeois behaviour, codes learned in the Creedish Death Cult. The result is a novel patterned with long litanies of domestic advice that work as an obsessive expression of the regulations of contemporary society. Tender can be certain, for example, that:

> Thanks to my lessons, these people know all three acceptable ways to place your desert silver. It's my doing that they can drink iced tea the right way with the long spoon still in the glass. This is tricky, but you have to hold the spoon handle between your index and middle fingers, against the edge of the glass opposite your mouth.[63]

Though critical of the rituals, vanity and objectifications that are produced by consumer culture, the novel's aesthetic remains entangled in these codes in terms that compromise and complicate the force of its critique.

The suggestion is that both in his plots and in the shaping of his aesthetic, Palahniuk appears to work with, rather than against, these processes of complicity and co-option. This ambiguous, shifting approach is ideally suited to the exploration of the complexities and contradictions that characterize life in contemporary consumer society. Never content to establish a simple adversarial position, Palahniuk's prose recognizes that consumption is a way of life, a network of ideas and meanings that both constitute a mechanism for the extension and reinforcement of globalization's power and hegemony, and at the same time a structure that provides individuals and cultures with meanings and values. As his writing shows (and as Fincher's film version demonstrates), meaning and creativity can be fashioned from and within the cultures of consumption. In many ways he can be seen to share these aesthetic ambitions with Bret Easton Ellis. The difference between Palahniuk and the work of Ellis and many of his contemporaries (including Candace Bushnell), however, is that *Fight Club* marries its form to a content that adds to the sense of the connections that tie consumption with identity. The alter ego device, the metaphorical associations linked to glycerine and the stylistics of the novel thus combine to create his portrait of the lived experiences of consumerism. The key difference is that where these understandings are generated in implicit terms through the hyperbolic qualities of Ellis's prose, Palahniuk's novel makes them explicit.

Palahniuk thus offers a vision of a consuming self that is able to do more than simply reflect the power of the market. Exploring the contradictory nature of the desires of his protagonists allows him to recognize the life that exists within the seemingly dead and deadening objects peddled by globalizing consumer society. As a final thought, however, it is worth noting that though all of these novels generate critiques of consumerism, they seem to accept the existence of a fundamental link between consuming and selfhood and, as a result, imply that consumerism is one of the defining realities of contemporary life. The problem with such a point of view, however, is that while it provides insights into the nature of the culture of those living within consumer society, it offers nothing for the multitude outside it. Though critical of consumerism, none of these texts pay any attention to those for whom the opportunity to be oppressed by consumption and consumer goods is a distant dream. The consuming selves portrayed by Ellis, Palahniuk and Bushnell have choices that are rooted in their affluence. Durden's dream of year zero, for example, demonstrates his ability to choose, and thus stands as a further expression of the luxurious rights gifted to the affluent consumer. The novel is silent, however, on the options open to those who lack Durden's opportunities and implicitly fails to appreciate that the risk attached to the process of linking identity to consumption is that it places those without the money needed to consume in danger of being turned into nonentities.[64]

The absence of any attempt to address such questions in these novels is, in conclusion, as revealing as anything they have to say about consumption. Reflecting on this omission prompts a range of questions about the ways in which the rights and habits of affluent consuming selves have become naturalized in Western cultures. It is interesting to note that the patterns of African-American culture discussed in the preceding chapter have, in contrast, little time for any thoughts of a crisis linked to overconsumption and affluence. The implication is that the kinds of anxieties explored by Palahniuk, Ellis and Bushnell are, in themselves, expressions of a luxury that few can afford. These issues, concerns that will be explored in more detail through the discussions of travel, migration and ethnicity later in this book, provide a necessary accompaniment to the analyses of commodities and consumerism offered in *Glamorama, Fight Club* and *Sex and the City*. Before developing these debates, however, there is a need to establish a broader reading of the relationships that link the patterns of branding and consumption with the wider contexts of the global market and the contours of the globalization debate.

4
The Fictions of Globalization

Don DeLillo's *Cosmopolis* (2003) has globalization and the intricacies of the world market at its heart. Describing a day in the life of Eric Packer, an American billionaire, as he is driven through New York's gridlocked traffic on the way to the barbershop, DeLillo shows him tracking the collapse of his investments on monitors inside his limousine, holding meetings with members of staff, and encountering a range of characters that include both his wife and his mistress. As the text moves towards a violent (and improbable) confrontation with a former employee, DeLillo uses Packer's journey to anatomize the contemporary city and to locate that analysis within a wider view of the power of the global market. Packer is what Tom Wolfe would call a 'master of the universe', part Bill Gates, part Warren Buffett.[1] His life is thus intended to offer key insights into contemporary experience by providing readers with a vision of an exceptional individual who stands at the centre of systems that shape and influence the lives of millions of others. DeLillo's central point is that Packer's responses to the world around him have a defining impact on the character of that world. The novel, by taking Packer away from distant boardrooms and remote offices and positioning him on the street, literalizes his centrality. He is, as he drives across New York, not just at the centre of the market (and by implication history), but in the heart of everyday life.

DeLillo reinforces this suggestion in a series of moments that see Packer come into contact with various events of public significance: the funeral of a rap star; the President's motorcade; an anti-globalization riot. It is Packer's interaction with this riot that allows DeLillo to sharpen the novel's focus on the nature of the market. In response to Packer's suggestion that the rioters are, in Marx's terms, capitalism's 'grave-diggers', Kinski, one of his employees, responds:

> These are not the grave-diggers. This is the free market itself. These people are a fantasy generated by the market. They don't exist outside the market. There is nowhere they can go to be outside. There is no outside... The market culture is total. It breeds these men and women. They are necessary to the system they despise. They give it energy and definition. They are market-driven. They are traded on the markets of the world. This is why they exist, to invigorate and perpetuate the system.[2]

Articulating a sense of the power of the market and its endless capacity to contain and re-contain dissenting energies, this passage describes a world in which capitalism seems capable of integrating almost everything. Implicit in the ironies that surround *Fight Club*'s descriptions of project mayhem's anti-capitalism and *Glamorama*'s commodity-heavy prose, *Cosmopolis* makes these ideas explicit by describing capitalism's seemingly unending ability to co-opt and assimilate dissent and goes on to portray the market as the defining horizon of contemporary experience.

This position reflects the view of modern society articulated in many of DeLillo's recent novels, texts that seem to be reaching for an authoritative statement on globalization. Where Ellis, Palahniuk, Bushnell, Beatty and others (including those from the early twentieth century like Hemingway) focus on the individual consumer's relationship with the market, DeLillo takes a broader view and sets out to contextualize these relationship within a reading of the global marketplace. Self-consciously analytical and organized around dense and often theoretical interludes, DeLillo's novels interpret local experiences in relation to wider structures and practices. The analysis of his work thus leads this discussion away from reflections on representations of consumption, and into a more detailed engagement with the globalization debate. The commercial cultures examined in the discussions of *Fight Club*, *Glamorama* and *Tuff* (Beatty 2000) can thus be interpreted by locating them within a broader reflection on the market forces that provide the context for these patterns. It is in *Underworld* (1997) that DeLillo offers his most detailed analysis of these concerns.

Ideas linked to system and order lie at the heart of *Underworld*. A dense network of patterns and connections pulls its shifting cast of characters, expansive historical reach and variations in setting and location together. The novel's title foregrounds this concern for hidden systems and gestures towards the existence of a complex of different underworlds within the text. There are the lives of poverty and misery seen by Sister Edgar in her South Bronx ministry. There are the underworlds of cold war connections investigated by J. Edgar Hoover and the subterranean realm inhabited by Moonman 157, the Basquiat-like graffiti artist whose artwork adorns the sides of New York subway trains. There are landfill pits, underground bunkers, mafias and secret histories. There are constant references to cultural images of the underworld and there is the web of connections that brings the baseball hit by Thompson off Branca in the 1951 Pennant Match into Nick Shay's hands.

This emphasis on covert linkages builds upon the preoccupation with conspiracy that characterizes much of DeLillo's earlier work. The lingering focus on images of secret systems in novels like *Ratner's Star* (1976), *The Names* (1982), *White Noise* (1985) and *Libra* (1988) is not only typical of DeLillo's fiction, but, as both Tom LeClair's *In the Loop* (1987) and Steffen Huntke's *Conspiracy and Paranoia* (1994) suggest, forms a crucial part of his wider examination of the structures of history and knowledge.[3] The impression is that *Underworld*'s portrait of tangled interrelationships constitutes an attempt to extend this exploration of representations of power and paranoia. What disrupts this continuity, however, is the novel's apprehension of the ways in which 'everything is connected in the end.'[4] This Forsterian mantra surfaces in a variety of different forms throughout the novel and gestures towards an underlying sense of the significance of order. Unlike narratives concerned with paranoia and conspiracy, systems that nurture, as Thomas Pynchon has it in *The Crying of Lot 49* (1965), a 'languid, sinister blooming' of anxiety and uncertainty, *Underworld* uses its descriptions of connections and coincidences as an attempt to represent something more integrated and cohesive.[5] This ambition finds expression in the patterns that characterize the narrative's organization, a structure that moves through a series of lengthy, coordinated lines of connection.

Starting with the baseball match in 1951, the novel develops thick networks of relationships. The introductory description of the ballgame functions as a structural axis around which much of the rest of the text revolves. Book-ended off from the rest of the work, these images anchor the narrative as it crosses back and forth through time, and create a powerful sense of the relationships that tie different events to the 'match of the century'. One typical network leads from a description of the advertising executive Charles Wainwright to his son, Chuckie, an individual who is glimpsed navigating a B-52 over Vietnam. It is this plane, 'Long Tall Sally', that ends up forming a central part of Klara Sax's monumental artwork, the same Klara Sax who once took Nick Shay as her lover. These interlocking connections are strengthened by the understanding that Chuckie Wainwright forms one of the many links in the chain that brings the coveted Pennant Match baseball into Shay's possession. Below these patterns are a series of symbolic relationships that tie the baseball that divided the crowd in 1951 to the electron that split the atom in the Russian nuclear test. Connecting the baseball to the bomb and the B-52 brings depth to this system and strengthens the impression of order and structure. When DeLillo interrupts his description of Chuckie's bombing mission with the song fragment 'thigh bone connected to the hip bone', he uses this detail to reiterate the significance of integration in the text.[6]

The construction of this dense web of linkages not only draws the novel's events together, but also forces the reader into a wider reflection on the meaning of these patterns. As William Boyd's review of *Underworld* suggests, the network of 'hidden connections . . . buried meanings' is the novel's 'overriding metaphor'.[7] The problem is, however, that Boyd remains unclear about the precise meaning of this metaphor. He argues that the text is concerned with the 'business of classifying connection', but neither extends nor refines his insight.[8] What is clear, however, is that the process of delineating connections and its attendant sense of stability and structure functions as an emblem for order and integration. The novel begins with an image of a public spectacle (the crowd at the Polo Grounds) and then moves out through a series of what, at first, seem to be unconnected narratives. As *Underworld* progresses, the links that tie the fragments both to each other and to the Dodgers/Giants ballgame begin to come into focus. Unlike the explorations of connections that characterize DeLillo's writing in a work like *Libra*, a novel that sees a world 'linked in a vast rhythmic coincidence, a daisy chain of rumour, suspicion and secret wish', and uses that understanding to produce a vision of a decentered and half-imagined history, a 'mind-spatter, a poetry of lives muddied and dripping in language', *Underworld* imagines a more coordinated and systematised realm.[9] *Libra*'s emphasis on expressionist 'spatter' gives way to *Underworld*'s vision of coordination.

This movement towards integration is discernible not only in *Underworld*'s complex network of plot and character relations, but also in key passages of authorial commentary. In the novel's epilogue, for example, a section entitled 'Das Kapital', DeLillo writes:

> Capital burns off the nuance in a culture. Foreign investment, global markets, corporate acquisition, the flow of information through transnational media, the attenuating influence of money that's electronic and sex that's cyberspaced, untouched money and computer-safe sex, the convergence of consumer desire – not that people want the same things necessarily, but that they want the same range of choices.[10]

Coming at the beginning of the novel's final movement and beneath the unequivocal 'Das Kapital' heading, this sequence identifies itself as a central element in the narrative's design. In this passage, in terms that prefigure the ideas developed in *Cosmopolis*, *Underworld* describes the ways in which contemporary experiences are colonized and coordinated by 'Das Kapital'. 'Nuance' is lost, choice narrowed and diversity contained. Reflecting the patterns of organization that characterize the novel's narrative, the passage identifies capitalism as an integrating force. Unlike the bifurcating networks uncovered by Nicholas Branch in *Libra*, *Underworld* offers an image of 'convergence'. The implication is that the reader need 'only connect' *Underworld*'s structured patterns with this view of contemporary economic conditions to establish an interpretative perspective on the text. The focus on the media, cyberspace and corporate policy combined with the emphasis on ideas linked to 'convergence' and integration discloses a desire to engage with 'Das Kapital' not simply on a general level, but in relation to the specific context of globalization. Global markets, this passage suggests, are eroding nuance and promoting greater conformity and integration. With these patterns to the fore, the novel identifies a relationship between its own integrated narrative trajectories and the coordinating processes of globalization. The underworld DeLillo describes is thus the network of connections that characterize globalization.

This sense of the ways in which the novel's integrated structure connects with globalization can be extended by looking at elements in *Underworld* that offer representations of the impact of contemporary economic forces. Central to certain theories of globalization is an understanding of the relationship between these processes and the transformation of space. In Giddens's terms, for example, one of the key forces is 'distanciation' (the shrinking of times and distances).[11] Propelled by new technologies and the expansion of existing markets, Giddens, in The Consequences of Modernity (1990), suggests that globalization works to restructure and redefine the organization and awareness of contemporary environments. Spatial transformation is not a secondary consequence of globalization, he argues, but a mechanism that is essential to its effective operation. This emphasis on the transformation of space is significant because it provides an opportunity to refine the understanding of *Underworld*'s engagement with the forces of globalization. Not only does the novel use narrative connections to integrate its structure (its textual space), it supports that approach with moments that represent the organization of specific terrains.

Underworld's descriptions of New York in the summer of 1974 offer a number of images of the city as a place integrated and coordinated by commercial priorities. Central to this design are a series of poignant descriptions of the building of the World Trade Center. An image that features both on the pages of the novel and on the cover of early editions, this building becomes not just an iconic symbol of the global covenant of contemporary capitalism (fatally so as it would turn out), but a structure that offers a powerful sense of globalization's impact on urban environments. Towards the beginning of this section, DeLillo has Klara Sax stand and observe the construction of the twin towers.

The World Trade Center was under construction, already towering, twin-towering, with cranes tilted at the summits and work elevators sliding up the flanks. She saw it almost everywhere she went. She ate a meal and drank a glass of wine and walked to the rail or ledge and there it usually was, bulked up at the funnelled end of the island, and a man stood next to her one evening, early, drinks on the roof of a gallery building – about sixty, she thought, portly and jowelled but also sleek in a way, assured and contained and hard-polished, a substantial sort, European.

'I think of it as one, not two,' she said. 'Even though there are clearly two towers. It's a single entity, isn't it?'

'Very terrible thing but you have to look at it, I think.'

'Yes, you have to look.'[12]

The World Trade Center and, by implication world trade, is at the heart of this transformed environment. There might be two towers, but in Klara Sax's mind they have melded into a 'single entity' that exerts a kind of relentless authority over the scene. Sax sees the towers 'everywhere' and the passage identifies them as a 'terrible thing', an object of awe and fearful veneration. Such is the visual power of this building that when Sax reflects on the identity of her companion, she imagines him as 'assured and contained and hard-polished ... substantial', a language which seems to spill off from descriptions of the building in ways that reify his body.

Not only does the World Trade Center represent changes to the physical geography of New York and, by extension, the identity and psychology of the people who live there, the building also functions as an image of the integrating and coordinating forces of globalization. The structure organizes space. It dominates the skyline, shrinking everything else and diminishing the rest of the island's skyscrapers. The process of 'distanciation' is thus given a concrete form by DeLillo who represents the World Trade Center as a public spectacle, a mass experience that absorbs and integrates its spectators. All perspectives converge around this single point.

Set alongside these descriptions of the construction of the World Trade Center are a number of other moments that link the invisible networks explored in his narrative to much more concrete manifestations of integration. Klara Sax becomes, once again, one of DeLillo's primary mouthpieces for these concerns.

The Fictions of Globalization

She sees, 'from the tall windows of her loft . . . fire escapes angled and stepped, this was her principal view, dark metal structures intersecting in depth over the back alleys, and she wondered if these lines might tell her something.'[13] There is, as before, a sense of order here, a feeling that these geometric structures provide clues to deeper patterns and meanings.

These scenes are typical of *Underworld*'s representation of the ways in which a wide variety of contemporary environments reveal the importance of processes of integration. Nick Shay's work as a landfill engineer and Klara Sax's monumental art emphasize this point, an impression that is strengthened in DeLillo's portrait of Shay's home in suburban Arizona. Though at first glance this description of a semi-urban space seems more open and fluid than the strict, integrated grid of New York, the scene is still marked by a powerful sense of coordination.

> From the shimmering bronze tower where I worked I used to gaze at the umber hills and ridges that defined the northeast view . . . I looked out past the miscellaneous miles of squat box structures where you took your hearing aid to be fixed or shopped for pool supplies, the self-replicating stretch I travelled everyday, and I told myself how much I liked this place with its downtown hush and its office towers separated by open space and its parks with jogging trails and its fairy ring of hills and its residential streets of oleanders and palms and tree trunks limed white – white against the sun.[14]

It is, once again, a tower that provides the focus for the image. This is the point of convergence around which the rest of the space is orientated. This organization stretches from a store for the repair of hearing aids to the jogging trails marked out across the land. Even the tree trunks have been incorporated into this structure, their bark painted to protect them (and the real estate investment they represent) from the sun. Once more, through the use of spatial images, *Underworld* reinforces the feeling of integration, a process tied to business and the coordinating forces of the global market. This is a 'self-replicating' world, a space enclosed by the tightening 'ring' of coordination.

These thematic representations of the significance of coordinated environments work alongside the dense narrative networks that characterize the organization of the text. The exploration of the ways in which contemporary experience is increasingly trammelled down 'jogging trails' and dominated by the quickening forces of world trade is thus supported by a narrative organization that encourages the reader to follow long paths of interrelated information and to contemplate the meaning of vast public events. The emphasis on convergence, both in terms of the organization of the plot and in relation to the representation of space in the novel, can thus be identified with the concerns for integration and conformity articulated in the opening paragraph of DeLillo's 'Das Kapital' section. The suggestion is that these elements hold a metaphorical relationship with ideas linked to 'global markets' and, by implication, the context and conditions of globalization. *Underworld* thus appears to be a novel that asks to be read in relation to its understanding of globalization. Contemporary economic conditions provide the novel's context, its metaphorical and imagistic schemes, a focus for its moments of authorial comment and a template for the organization of its narrative. These are the elements that underpin Peter Knight's suggestion that *Underworld* attempts 'to map the impossible complex of interactions in the age of globalization between individuals and larger social and economic forms.'[15]

The problem with DeLillo's position, however, is that it represents globalization as an irreducible reality. There is no room for an interrogation of this vision, nor any sense that the novel can do more than offer a homological reflection of these material conditions. Globalization is, it seems, a reality that the novel is powerless either to interrogate or to resist. The result is a work in which characters like Nick Shay and Klara Sax find themselves 'stuck in whatever national mood is prevailing at that moment, like lost souls to flypaper.'[16] What is interesting about this representation is not just the questions it raises about DeLillo's own perspective, but the extent to which his seeming quiescence echoes the views held by a broad range of commentators on globalization.

Popular accounts as contrasting as the celebratory version of global opportunity outlined in Thomas Friedman's *The Lexus on the Olive Tree* (1999) and the critical vision offered in Klein's *No Logo* (1999) offer a surprisingly uniform vision of the processes at work. Not only are they both published by part of the same global conglomerate (Rupert Murdoch's HarperCollins), their portraits of the underlying forces are remarkably similar. The

Lexus and the Olive Tree sees globalization as a system with 'one overarching feature – integration. The world has become an increasingly interwoven place, and today, whether you are a company or a country, your threats and opportunities increasingly derive from who you are and who you are connected to.'[17] Like Friedman, Klein's *No Logo* builds from the basic premise that 'logos, by the force of ubiquity, have become the closest thing we have to an international language . . . [a] select group of corporate Goliaths . . . have gathered to form our de facto global government.'[18] The patterns of convergence, connection and co-option outlined in *Underworld* echo these versions of the globalization thesis. The loss of 'nuance' and the processes of corporate control described by Klein and the integration and emphasis on consolidation identified by Friedman are patterns that shadow both the novel's general organization and the specific version of the globalization thesis conceptualized by DeLillo in 'Das Kapital'. All three share a common view of the context and conditions of globalization and appear reluctant to question the central premises of this thesis. Globalization is a reality and all DeLillo, Klein and Friedman seem able to do is reflect it.

This understanding raises a number of immediate concerns. The first is that these approaches not only limit criticism but also work to strengthen the ideological and conceptual foundations of globalization itself. Roland Robertson's suggestion that 'globalization as a concept refers both to the compression of the world and the intensification of consciousness of the world as a whole' identifies a relationship between discourses *on* globalization and the mechanisms *of* globalization.[19] The willingness to identify globalization as an unquestionable condition of contemporary life must, in these terms, be regarded as a process that participates in the reproduction and expansion of globalization's coordinating processes. This is a point echoed by Nestor Garcia Canclini when he writes 'globalizing politics arrive at consent, in part, because they excite the imagination of millions of persons promising that two plus two which until now made four can be extended to five or six.'[20]

The second concern is that this kind of approach closes off alternative readings of the contemporary context. When, for example, Andrew Sayer suggests that the globalization thesis is often 'confused in its arguments, long in speculation and hype and based on selected examples', he raises basic questions about the economic realities upon which many accounts of globalization are based.[21] Instead of accepting globalization as a reality and reflecting on possible responses to it, Sayer steps behind the prevailing logic and explores the material conditions upon which the globalization thesis rests. In these terms, the kind of narrow reading of contemporary economic realities offered in DeLillo's introduction to 'Das Kapital', and the positions outlined in the works of Klein and Friedman seem at best unsophisticated and at worst misleading.

Sayer's willingness to probe these basic premises is echoed in John Micklethwait and Adrian Wooldridge's, *A Future Perfect* (2000). They begin with the argument that, 'from an economist's point of view, there is no single, integrated capital market. Even during the 1990s, only 10 percent of investment in emerging countries was financed from abroad.'[22] This position is supported by a discussion of the detail of the globalization thesis and the identification of what they identify as five myths: that 'size trumps all'; that 'universal products' will thrive; that 'economics needs to be rewritten'; that 'globalization is a zero-sum game'; and that the contemporary period will see a 'disappearance of geography'.[23] Like Sayer, instead of reading globalization as an unquestionable reality, they see a network of contradictory and unstable forces and discourses.

Leaving aside any attempt to adjudicate between these two positions, recognizing the existence of this conflict is significant because it problematizes the sense that globalization involves straightforward processes of global coordination. Questioning the foundations of the globalization thesis thus opens up a point of critique, one that instead of simply condemning its impact (or celebrating it as Freidman does), encourages a broader contemplation of the conditions that provide the context for those (alleged) effects. The result is an interrogation of *Underworld*'s claim that 'everything is connected in the end'. In describing a view of a universe increasingly integrated by the forces of the global economy, DeLillo seems to be working as much with fictions of globalization as he does with realities. The result is a tension between, on the one hand, a desire to produce an integrated fictional portrait of contemporary conditions and, on the other, a sense that those conditions refuse to conform to his integrating pattern. This tension emerges most obviously in the novel's conclusion.

The Fictions of Globalization

As many commentators have observed, despite its grand 'Das Kapital' title and the panoramic paragraph of commentary that introduces the chapter, *Underworld*'s concluding vision of Sister Edgar's death and the Internet epiphany that follows offers neither the promised clarity nor an adequate resolution to its version of the globalization thesis. In Tony Tanner's eyes, *Underworld*'s conclusion is nothing less than a betrayal of the work's ambitions, a moment in which 'the novel deliquesces into something close to sentimental piety.'[24] Derek Wolcott echoes this suggestion and observes that 'DeLillo's novels have flubbed to mystification before'.[25]

There is no question that *Underworld*'s conclusion is troubling. Echoing T. S. Eliot's ending to *The Waste Land* (1922), DeLillo seems to gesture toward a kind of transcendence. The closing passage reads:

> The tone of agreement or treaty, the tone of repose, the sense of mollifying silence, the tone of hail and farewell, a word that carries the sunlit ardour of an object deep in drenching noon, the argument of binding touch, but it's only a sequence of pulses on a dullish screen and all it can do is make you pensive – a word that spreads a longing through . . . the city and out across the dreaming bourns and orchards to the solitary hills.
> Peace.[26]

The writing here has a fluid, celebratory quality to it. Emerging from the 'dullish screen' are a series of pastoral havens, 'the dreaming bourns . . . orchards . . . the solitary hills.' The word 'peace' appears, DeLillo writes, 'in the lunar milk of the data stream.'[27] DeLillo thus concludes his novel with a vision of a harmonious, cultivated landscape, a place where sequestration is possible. Sister Edgar is swept away into an internet nirvana, a world where science, economics and mysticism intersect. Identity, religion and technology combine to produce this curious technological apotheosis. Quite why this should be the case, however, is never explained, nor is there any sense that the complex and troubling trajectories of the novel can be resolved into this feeling of 'peace'. The author may feel a fusion of mysticism and technology washing through these final pages, but, as the comments of Tanner and Wolcott suggest, others remain unconvinced. The emphasis on ideas of order, integration and convergence, so important in other areas of the work, thus seems to falter in these final pages. Unable to show that 'everything is connected in the end', DeLillo produces a mystical and mystifying ending that promises integration, but provides none.

The fact that this kind of inconsistency is not limited to the novel's conclusion adds to this impression. The figure of the Texas Highway Killer, for example, an individual who appears early in the narrative and seems to incarnate a dark, serial purpose before dropping out of the text without ever having his role either fully developed or successfully explained, offers a clue to the kind of disintegrations that characterize *Underworld*'s conclusion. These inconsistencies reveal the existence of elements in the text that work against its integrated design. The result is an uneven texture that destabilizes the novel and undermines *Underworld*'s image of an increasingly coordinated society.

These inconsistencies are particularly significant in terms of the ways in which they influence the reading of *Underworld*'s relationship with the discourses of globalization. DeLillo is trying to produce a fictional image of an integrated world. Exploring opportunities for representing these conditions in terms of spatial integration and positioning its insights alongside a broader sense of the connections that tie those processes to the patterns and continuities of social, economic and technological change, he sets out to produce an all-encompassing vision. Klara Sax stares in wonder at the World Trade Center while Sister Edgar drifts off into the harmonized tranquillity of cyberspace. The irony is, however, that in its attempts to offer images of integration and order, DeLillo only really manages to prompt far-reaching questions about the nature of his schematized vision. Instead of embodying the coordination it conceives as the defining feature of globalization, *Underworld* finds itself portraying a world of partial connections, a realm marked by discontinuities that signal the limits of both its ordered design and, by implication, its broader alignment with positions that equate globalization with homogenization.

This disjunction can be tied to a wider conflict between narratives that represent globalization (for good or ill) as a system that produces increasing levels of cohesion and homogeneity, and those that question this sense of unification and coordination. Rather than reading globalization as an incontestable reality in

The Fictions of Globalization

which we are all stuck 'like lost souls on flypaper', the novel's attempt to produce an integrated account actually ends up exposing the problems with such totalizing readings. Just as commentators like Klein and Friedman find their arguments stymied by a reliance on readings that see globalization as a total system, DeLillo's attempt to construct a vision of an integrated world falters. *Underworld*, an epic attempt to map these forces of integration, thus fails to bring the connections together and as a result ends up dramatising the problems with arguments that read globalization in terms of total coordination. The consequence of *Underworld*'s failed attempt to produce a closed, integrated account of life in the contemporary period, is the invigoration of critical responses to readings of globalization in terms of homogenization and coordination. If DeLillo is unable to produce the required coordination in his fiction, then the idea of a world increasingly integrated along economic, social and geographical lines needs to be regarded with equal scepticism. What is interesting is that this more fluid sense of the contexts of globalization is in fact articulated within *Underworld* itself. Not simply implied by the inconsistencies, the mystification of the ending and incompleteness of its integrated scheme, this concern is raised through the presence of trajectories that gesture towards a more dialectical relationship between culture and socio-economic conditions. These trajectories are outlined in Mark Osteen's *American Magic and Dread* (2000), a work that explores 'DeLillo's dialogue with culture'.[28]

Osteen's suggestion is that 'only an art that critically examines ... 'massive' systems from the inside can escape recontainment.'[29] The ideas of coordination that seem to dominate the novel are balanced by moments, according to Osteen, in which a dialogue develops between these forces of integration and more pliable, porous terrains that resist 'recontainment'. Osteen exemplifies his point by considering the status of commodities in *Underworld* and by reflecting, in particular, on the function of an advertisement for Minute Maid. The passage from *Underworld* reads:

> The billboard is unevenly lighted, dim in spots, several bulbs blown and unreplaced, but the central elements are clear, a vast cascade of orange juice pouring diagonally from top right into a goblet that is handheld at lower left ... And the six-ounce cans of Minute Maid

73

arrayed across the bottom of the board, a hundred identical cans so familiar in design and color and typeface that they have personality.[30]

Osteen's argument is that 'if the billboard ... can be read as another example of ... inauthenticity ..., it also suggests that the same forces and conditions that create bad faith ... may also germinate effective counterfaiths.'[31] It is through this process, Osteen suggests, that DeLillo demonstrates how it is possible to 'find transcendence in unlikely places, as the very emblems of capital are transmuted into an economy of grace.'[32] This 'economy of grace' operates within the context of globalization, a world in which nuance and diversity has not, it seems, been lost. Though on one level the billboard is an emblem of global incorporation (and represents once again the ways in these processes can be linked with forces of spatial reorganization), the argument is that this image escapes 'recontainment'. The novel, echoing the use of brands in Ellis, Beatty, Bushnell and others, thus dramatizes this constant process of slippage between the forces of global coordination (signified in this instance by advertising) and creates a sense that those forces work against their own purposes in terms that provide one of the most vivid images of this 'dialogue'.

Instead of producing a fiction of total incorporation, DeLillo thus appears to create a work in which forces of coordination play off against processes that resist such easy closure. Though in some respects the presence of a litter of brand names, commercial images and copy from advertising might signal a further level of integration, Osteen shows that these elements pull in two different directions. The 'dread' of total coordination is weighed against the 'magic' of the communicative possibilities articulated in this image. The result is a work that can be read in terms that not only expose some of the fictions of globalization but also link that exposure to an aesthetic that offers 'an economy of grace', an image of a world characterized by patterns that resist recontainment. *Underworld* is thus not a straightforward fiction *of* globalization, but a fiction *in and about* globalization. It is only when *Underworld* begins to embrace incorporation that it manages to engage with the patterns of contemporary economics and society in successful ways. As a result, the novel ends up interrogating its own representations of an integrated world. This suggestion raises important implications for the understanding of contemporary social and economic conditions and provides the foundation for a broader questioning of all narrow versions of the globalization thesis. Not only are they quiescent, but they also hinge upon an exaggerated sense of the power of coordination with the result being a tendency to neglect the myths and inconsistencies that surround contemporary accounts of globalization. Everything is not connected in the end. Globalization does not simply produce processes of integration. It is, as *Underworld* begins to suggest, something much more complex and contradictory.

DeLillo's *Underworld* can thus be read in terms that open up a wider view of the globalization debate. Introducing a sense of the ways in which globalization provides a context for consumption and aligning itself with arguments that represent globalization as contemporary experience's defining horizon, the novel echoes with many of the globalization debate's most familiar orthodoxies. Unprecedented, all-colonizing and irresistible, the prevailing view is that there is nothing that can be done to oppose these systems. Such a view can, however, be tempered, by recognizing that DeLillo's novel also generates moments of critical friction that suggest not only that there are possibilities for resistance, but also that this resistance can be empowered by the recognition that the systems and structures of globalization are neither as stable nor as all-embracing as they first appeared to be. Setting *Underworld*'s vision of integration against a reflection on the more subtle and suggestive elements in the text thus exposes some of the fictions of globalization.

Further insight into the apocalyptic quality of so many of these accounts can be developed by extending this discussion to include the analysis of a novel that shares DeLillo's global perspective. Though written over 150 years ago, Herman Melville's *Moby-Dick* (1851) prefigures the focus on the global expansion of capital that informs so many areas of *Underworld*. Crucially, as far as this argument is concerned, reading Melville in these terms adds to the critique of the apocalyptic tones that characterize so many of the discourses of globalization by demonstrating that these systems are not only much less absolute and incontestable than these accounts suggest, but also neither as new or as unique as they imply. Interpreting Melville's novel from this perspective

Melville's 'no logo'

When Charles Olson describes *Moby-Dick* as a novel that explains the processes behind the production of the light needed to read it by, he identifies the ways in which Melville's fiction traces the circuits of imperialism and capitalism.[33] Carrying his readers from the secure havens of their studies out into the wild ocean, Melville explores the complex web of connections and culpabilities that were starting to define his society. The violent struggle for whale oil thus becomes a metaphor for expansionist politics and the predations of nineteenth-century capitalism in a novel that works to identify clear networks of guilt and responsibility. His readers might have imagined themselves to be untainted by and even antagonistic towards slavery, violent conquest and industrialization, but *Moby-Dick* forces them to think otherwise and to recognize their own complicity. Within his tale of bloodlust on the high seas, Melville includes portraits of the moment of slaughter, the hellish processing of the tryworks and images of Nantucket where the oil is unloaded and sold to illuminate cosy studies far inland. These descriptions are central to Melville's demythologizing project and enable him to embark on an elegant attempt to defetishize the commodity. This commercial history of light, an apparently pure and weightless resource, thus allows Melville to demonstrate the ways in which even apparently neutral comforts are being incorporated into the commodified world of nineteenth-century industrial society.[34]

It is the seeming purity of the light produced by whale oil that gives his project its critical thrust. Light provides Melville with a near-perfect metaphor for the networks of capital developing across the globe. The use of the complex imagery of whiteness that dominates the novel adds an additionally ironic dimension to these descriptions and allows Melville both to dazzle the reader and at the same time to insist on a more penetrating analysis. 'The unmanufactured sperm oil', he writes, 'possesses a singularly cleansing virtue ... the decks never look so white as just after what they call an affair of oil.'[35] The point is that though whale oil might cleanse the blood from the decks of the Pequod, conceal the violent origins of its production and bathe nineteenth-century society in the white glow of progress, it also serves to light the pages of a novel that details the grim realities upon which this illusion of purity depends. Melville thus sets out, as Olson suggests, to reveal 'what lies under'.[36] He turns the problematic brightness of the enlightenment project upon itself and sees the lamp of civilization dip its taper into a well of blood and barbarism.

What is significant about this dimension of *Moby-Dick* is the peculiarly modern quality of its demythologizing project. A work like Klein's *No Logo* (1999), for example, moves through a series of arguments that offer particular echoes of Melville's approach. Concerned that a contemporary product like a pair of Nike shoes comes to us branded and boxfresh, primly pouched in tissue paper and smelling faintly of freshly cut leather, Klein seeks to historicize the object by taking her readers back through the processes of marketing and manufacture and forcing an awareness of the branding practices and sweatshop labour that underpin Nike's corporate power. The strength of Klein's argument lies in her unwillingness to allow the festishistic crispness of the tissue and the slick sophistication of the marketing to conceal the origins of the commodity. Just as Melville refuses to accept the casual assumption of light's purity (and the complacency of the North's claim to be slave free), Klein identifies the ways in which Western consumers are complicit in the destructive manufacturing processes and neo-slavery of international corporations around the globe. Anatomizing brands, an iconography as invisibly ubiquitous in contemporary America as the light from whale oil was in the early nineteenth century, thus allows Klein to do for logos what Melville does for light.

This comparison can be strengthened by reflecting on the specifics of Klein's project. *No Logo*'s analysis of brands is not restricted to Nike, but involves discussion of a familiar range of North American corporations and develops into a broad attempt to explore the networks of production and marketing that underpin contemporary consumerism. In, for example, a chapter entitled 'The discarded factory: degraded production in the age of the superbrand', Klein details a trip to Cavite, an export processing zone in the Philippines.[37] Describing the physical environment and working conditions, she writes: 'windowless workshops made of cheap plastic and aluminium siding are crammed next to each other only feet apart. Racks of time cards bake in the sun, making sure the maximum amount of work is extracted from each worker, the maximum number of working hours extracted from each day.'[38] Like the relentlessly detailed anatomy of 'sweated industry' aboard the Pequod, Klein follows the commodity back, not to the heart of the sea, but to what she calls the 'unbearable lightness of Cavite'.[39] Her desire to historicize the weightless, deterritorialized quality of the branded product (and her serendipitous pun on the word light) only serves to invigorate this sense of the relationship between her work and *Moby-Dick*'s demystification of another seemingly weightless commodity, illumination.

These parallels become even more apparent when Klein's attention turns towards the brutalizing and destructive practices associated with contemporary manufacturing. When, for example, Klein suggests that 'all over the world, children work in fields with toxic pesticides, in dangerous mines and in rubber and steel factories where small fingers are sliced off or mangled in heavy machinery', she employs a language and imagery that prompts, in general terms, comparisons with a whole range of nineteenth-century portraits of industrialization and, on a more particular level, precise echoes of the descriptions of butchery aboard the Pequod.[40] Blood equals responsibility, a point made explicit in one of Melville's most grotesque accounts of the violence of whaling, a scene that sees Stubb puncture an ulcer on a dying whale.

> At that instant an ulcerous jet shot forth from this cruel wound, and goaded by it into more than sufferable anguish, the whale now spouting thick blood, with swift fury darted at the craft, bespattering them and their glorying crews all over with showers of gore, capsizing Flask's boat and marring the bows. It was his death stroke. For, by this time, so spent was he by loss of blood, that he helplessly rolled away from the wreck he had made; lay panting on his side, impotently flapped with his stumped fin, then over and over slowly revolved like a waning world; turned up the white secrets of his belly; lay like a log, and died.[41]

In covering the page with gore, Melville reveals the cruel secret 'belly' of whaling. This process of exposure forces the reader to

The Fictions of Globalization

confront an all-encompassing guilt that even the purifying force of whale-oil light cannot expunge. The suggestion that 'all the tapers, lamps and candles that burn around the globe, burn as before so many shrines, to our glory', takes on, as a result, a very different complexion.[42] The illumination in these 'shrines' is turned red by Melville's descriptions and becomes a bloody sign of the reader's complicity with this world of cruelty and violence. Klein's accounts of branded products and contemporary manufacturing processes share this indignation and articulate the same desire to expose the invisible networks of responsibility. Through these processes *No Logo* is able to defamiliarize casual twenty-first century comforts like coffee, footwear and clothing by 'bespattering' them with gore. Forming a crucial part of both Melville's and Klein's attempts to apportion blame and identify responsibility, this emphasis on brutality is thus crucial to their demythologizing projects.

Though this comparison is interesting in itself, it is the ways in which the interpretation of these relationships can be used to raise broader questions about the globalization debate that makes this sense of the connections between Klein and Melville particularly suggestive. The images of the sperm whale as a 'world' and the portrait of a 'globe' lit by whale oil gestures towards links that tie the concerns raised in Melville's novel with contemporary understandings of globalization. It is the process of recognizing these relationships that opens up a critical reading, this discussion suggests, not only of Klein's work, but of the contours of the globalization debate as a whole.

No Logo is a work that articulates concerns about globalization that are shared by a whole host of contemporary commentators. Klein's book can be readily identified with works like, for example, George Monbiot's *Captive State: The Corporate Takeover of Britain* (2000), Noreena Hertz's *The Silent Takeover: Global Capitalism and the Death of Democracy* (2001) and Richard Barnet and John Cavanagh's *Global Dreams* (1994). All, in their different ways, set out to anatomize the global scene by employing variations of the kinds of demythologizing approaches used by Klein in *No Logo*. Though these similarities make it hard to differentiate the specific features of Klein's argument from the debates raised by this increasingly broad spectrum of commentators, *No Logo* has become the most successful and celebrated of these works.

Fictions of Globalization

Despite offering a series of fairly commonplace arguments, it is a book that has sold hundreds of thousands of copies and turned Klein into one of the twenty-first century's favourite iconoclasts.

Klein's success can be explained, in part, by thinking about the ways in which her focus on brands enables her to link together various parts of the debate around consumer society with broader concerns tied to globalization. This approach fosters a clear and engaging dissection of contemporary experience that gives *No Logo* a seductive simplicity, an appeal that is strengthened by Klein's emphatic sense of the novelty of the phenomena she describes. It is this desire to portray the contemporary period as unique that is perhaps the most marketable feature of *No Logo*'s argument. Setting out to describe the 'new branded world', Klein sees this process of corporatization as the defining characteristic of the contemporary period.[43] Her position is that the world has been transformed by what she calls the 'astronomical growth in the wealth and cultural influence of multi-national corporations over the last fifteen years.'[44] Branding, she suggests, is a defining symptom of a newly globalized society. These are views shared by many of Klein's fellow critics of contemporary capitalism. George Monbiot's argument is that 'the world's biggest companies have chosen a new route to growth: consolidation. By engineering a single, "homogenized", global market in which they can sell the same product under the same conditions anywhere on earth.'[45] Noreena Hertz locates her arguments within a similar vision of a world in which 'prevailing norms and mainstream thoughts are recorded, replayed and reinforced in Technicolor, while any criticism of the orthodoxy is . . . quashed . . . Corporations have become behemoths, huge global giants that wield immense power.'[46]

Like those of many of her contemporaries, Klein's arguments identify the forces of globalization as unique to the contemporary period. Such a view gives her writing both a chronocentric appeal and a seductive conceptual consistency. Marked by this millenarian tone, Klein's work gestures towards a kind of apocalyptic model of globalization, one that imagines the world on the brink of a new and unparalleled era of corporate co-option and integration. The suggestion is, however, that the process of identifying a relationship between her work and the critique of capitalism offered in a nineteenth-century novel like *Moby-Dick* complicates this appeal to novelty. Her apparently radical views are immediately compromised by this relationship with much older and more ingrained traditions of American critical thinking. Klein can, in these terms, no longer be regarded as a contemporary iconoclast engaged in a visionary attempt to map the start of a new age of global integration, but as a commentator who is simply re-articulating long-standing concerns about capitalism and commodification. Such a view fosters both a critical perspective on *No Logo* and fuels a wider analysis of the terms and trajectories that characterize the formation of the globalization debate as a whole. These suggestions can be extended by developing this sense of Klein's relationship with the literary traditions of the American Renaissance and seeing the links that connect her not just to *Moby-Dick*, but to a work like *Walden* (Thoreau 1854).

Fearing the world of commerce down the path from Walden Pond, Henry David Thoreau celebrates his own apparently pre-capitalist situation and describes a series of gestures intended to ward off the encroaching march of mercantilism. Nay-saying commerce in terms that pre-empt Klein's antagonism towards logos, Thoreau battles to refuse capitalism. The link established in Klein's mind between globalization and environmental destruction is also rehearsed in *Walden*. It is Thoreau's image of the ice merchants attacking the pond's frozen skin that provides *Walden* with one of its most powerful representations of the tensions between commerce and nature. 'In order to cover each one of his dollars with another,' Thoreau writes, the ice merchant 'took off the only coat, ay, the skin itself of Walden Pond'.[47] Using images that shadow Melville's portrait of the whale's blubber-rich 'blanket' and the descriptions of 'cutting in', Thoreau's writing is marked by a concern about the despoliation of nature that not only echoes *Moby-Dick*'s anxieties about the environmental effects of whaling, but foreshadows Klein's warnings about the pollution generated by destructive manufacturing processes. Ice and light, two staple commodities of an industrializing society, are thus connected to environmental destruction in terms that prefigure contemporary criticisms of global corporations. James Twitchell's discussion of contemporary consumption identifies exactly these kinds of continuities when he suggests, 'on our way to Walden Pond, we pack the sport utility vehicle with the dish antenna, the cell phone, the bread maker, the ashtray, the paddle ball.'[48] The implication is that Klein's work begins to look more like a recent expression of the concerns that inspired writers of the nineteenth century than a radically new perspective on the twenty-first.

Positions of this kind can be supported by recognizing that Klein's approach echoes *Walden*'s sense of the importance of thrift. Asked about whether her own wardrobe is 'certifiably sweatshop-free?' she responds, 'I'm lucky in that I happen to live a few blocks from some great independent designers, so I can actually shop in stores where I know where stuff is produced.'[49] Prioritizing the local, Klein apes Thoreau's dream of short-circuiting capitalism through strategies aligned with canny independence. In the same way that Thoreau sought to beat back the mercantilism he saw creeping towards him from Concord by downsizing and driving towards economic self-sufficiency, Klein suggests that the careful use of her power as a consumer can counter the reach of globalization. The problem for both Klein and Thoreau, however, is that their resistance remains closely allied to the commercial mechanisms they are seeking to oppose. Thoreau's rebellion, based on simplification, careful accounting and the reduction of overheads is an ideal economic blueprint for successful entrepreneurship with the irony being that he responds to capitalism by making himself into a more successful business operator.[50] The same applies to Klein's suggestion that she can use her power as a shopper to engage with consumption, a process that affirms the strength of consumer society as she tries to negate it. The difficulty for Klein is that thrift becomes a manifestation of a desire for an alternative form of luxury.

Klein is not alone in this contradictory pursuit of conspicuous abstinence, but her approach seems restrained when compared to the kind of hyper-aware consumption Noreena Hertz sees as an essential part of her challenge to corporate power. Advocating what she calls 'supermarket activism' or 'enlightened consumerism', Hertz's book features a lengthy description of some of her all-consuming weekend rituals.[51]

> Sunday morning. Central London, home. I wake up to the excesses of the night before. Washing up in piles. Open my bottle of Ecover and squeeze biogradable liquid on to yesterday's plates, crusted with

residues of GM-free organic pizza. Fill a cafetière with Fairtrade coffee and boil a free range egg. Take a 'not tested on animals' Lush bubble bath. Pull on my 'child labour free' Reeboks, 'made by 100% union labor' Levis, and 'never use furs' Chloe T-shirt. Spray my hair with a Wella non-CFC canister. Read the paper and learn about the latest McDonald's boycott.[52]

Beyond observing that it would be almost impossible to imagine a description that expressed a more confused response to consumerism, there is not much that can be said about this passage except to note that Klein's work in *No Logo* is certainly more sophisticated. Her approach is not, however, entirely free from the kind of powerful contradictions articulated in Hertz's *The Silent Takeover* (2001). These conflicts come to the fore in Klein's conclusion.

In her final section, Klein appeals to a 'resistance . . . that is as global, and as capable of coordinated action, as the multinational corporations it seeks to subvert.'[53] Not only does this appeal to globalized rebellion clash with her earlier emphasis on locality, but she finds herself forced to appropriate globalization's strategies in terms that affirm its authority in the moment of opposition. The result is that her response seems as much a testament to a sense of the authority of globalization as it is a call for opposition to that power. The presence of contradictions of these kinds make it easy to understand why early reviewers of Klein's work were quick to describe *No Logo* as a book that is long on diagnosis and short on cures. Having conceived globalization as an ever more powerful force of capitalist coordination, Klein finds it very difficult to escape its co-opting logic.

This sense of Klein's own complicity is compounded by her commercial and critical success. The need to promote her anti-consumerist message has drawn Klein into a series of compromises, the most obvious of which is her involvement with HarperCollins, part of Rupert Murdoch's empire. Klein, heavily criticized for this partnership, has defended her choice of publisher by saying that 'I really didn't have my pick of publishers in Britain. Only one wanted the book. What I said when I signed with HarperCollins was that I was going out of my way to write about Murdoch, more than I would have done otherwise. I did, and they didn't touch it.'[54] On a simple level the existence of a commercial relationship between Klein and her corporate adversaries works, once again, to highlight her entanglement in networks of complicity that mirror those explored by Melville in *Moby-Dick*. Just as nineteenth-century Americans read about the cruelty of capitalism by the brilliant smokeless light of spermaceti candles, modern society can learn about the iniquities of globalization on the acid-whitened pages of a HarperCollins imprint. The problem with criticisms of this kind, however, is that they dwell too heavily on amusingly ironic inconsistencies while obscuring the more significant weaknesses in Klein's work. The real problem with *No Logo* is not that Klein is complicit with the forces she sets out to describe, but that she fails to produce an adequate account of globalization and is thus unable to develop a workable critique.

There are two central flaws with Klein's argument. The first, as this discussion has already suggested, is a belief in the novelty of the kind of conditions she describes. The second is her sense that globalization is a totalizing, homogenizing and inevitable process. Both of these assumptions are deeply problematic, not only because globalization has origins that extend back into prehistory, but also because it cannot be charted as a simple incontestable movement. Klein's approach both neglects the relationship between contemporary conditions and those described in works like *Moby-Dick* and *Walden* and conceives globalization in absolute terms. In *No Logo*'s view, the world is becoming an ever more coordinated and integrated market in which corporations are increasing their power through processes of global deregulation and branding. The graph used in the opening chapter makes her position explicit.[55] In Klein's terms, a diagram that shows total US expenditure on advertising rising from $50 billion in 1979 to $200 billion in 1998, offers simple proof of the extension of branding and marketing in the modern world. The fact that her graph takes no account of either inflation or growth in the US economy is, even to an economic layperson, a sign of a drastic oversimplification of the debate. The absence of these relevant statistics reveals wider problems with her reading of globalization and opens up basic questions about *No Logo*'s methodology. Whether a symptom of cynicism or the product of a misunderstanding, this graph compromises the foundations of Klein's argument and exposes problems with her conception of globalization itself. Her view of an all-embracing international system, conceived as an absolute state, begins to look much more like myth than reality.

Noreena Hertz's work is problematized by a very similar kind of oversight. Early in *The Silent Takeover*, Hertz suggests that the 'hundred largest multinational corporations now control about 20 per cent of the global foreign assets, fifty-one of the hundred biggest economies in the world are now corporations, only forty-nine are nation states. The sales of General Motors and Ford are greater than the GDP of the whole of sub-Saharan Africa.'[56] This is information that makes Hertz's use of the word 'now' emphatic and appears to prove the existence of a new and hegemonic globalizing force. These facts look persuasive and seem to add weight to her argument. What is missing, however, is any sense of how this situation might be different from the conditions in previous periods. It would be surprising, for example, if a major trading company from the age of empire (say the British East India Company) did not, like General Motors today, have a turnover that far exceeded that of many countries across the globe. That Byron, as Niall Ferguson observes, should ask, in *Don Juan* (1823) 'Who holds the balance of the world in sway . . . Who keeps the world . . . in pain . . .?', a question he answers by identifying the banker 'Rothschild, and his fellow-Christian Baring' as the guilty parties, re-emphasizes the ways in which worries about the consolidation of wealth and power in the hands of a small number of organizations and individuals have had a persistent presence in western culture over the last few hundred years.[57]

Hertz and Klein's failure to engage with these possibilities is symptom of their determined desire to portray globalizing processes as unique to the contemporary period. The result is an unquestioning response to globalization that closes off possibilities for establishing alternative readings of the contemporary context. Their works thus lack any understanding of globalization as a debate of the kind Janet Abu-Lughod frames when she asks the question 'is the process of globalization as it is now occurring at the turn of the twenty-first century merely different in degree from earlier increases in the scale of world systems integration, or is it so different in character from previous instances that a sharp discontinuity has occurred?'[58] Niall Ferguson offers a similar argument when he explains that 'economic historians disagree about whether or not globalization today is greater than it was in the decade or so before the First World War.'[59] Ferguson's review of the complex and contradictory economic evidence suggests that it is hard to come to any concrete conclusions about the contemporary situation. There is however, no sense of these contradictions in Klein's work. The key conclusion is that there is much more to globalization than the simple visions of total coordination and incorporation outlined in a book like *No Logo*.

Questioning the globalization debate in these terms does not, it is important to note, signal an outright rejection Klein's findings or side with market populism's celebration of the opportunities these new economic relations create, but simply emphasizes the importance of recognizing that globalization's processes are more complex and contradictory than a work like *No Logo* suggests. Instead of interpreting these conditions as an unquestionable set of realities, commentators like Abu-Lughod, and Ferguson see a network of unstable forces, conditions that Canclini identifies when he describes 'globalization as a process of fragmentation and recomposition; rather than homogenizing the world, globalization reorders difference and inequalities without eliminating them.'[60]

In this light, Klein's descriptions of the incontestable and inevitable dynamics of globalization begin to look both naive and hegemonic. Conceiving globalization as a rampant, apocalyptic process, she finds her argument cut off from informing critical traditions and is, as a result, unable to interpret these debates in terms that do justice to the complexity of the contemporary situation. The conclusion is that her sense of globalization's co-opting and coordinating power seems as much a product of her own conceptualization as it is the manifestation of concrete contemporary realities. Klein thus finds herself caught in double bind with her attack on globalization's integrating and coordinating mechanisms working to strengthen those same homogenizing processes. Her failure to offer a viable critical account of globalization, might, in one view, signal a sense of the ways in which these processes have achieved exactly the kind of hegemony Klein fears. So powerful, it seems, are these forces, that they can co-opt even the most strident forms of critique. The irony is, however, that this portrait of a hegemonic, coordinating structure appears more a product of Klein's imagination than an image based on a

The Fictions of Globalization

considered engagement with contemporary conditions. When *No Logo* finds itself caught in this interpretative *impasse*, it is trapped not by the all-conquering forces of global coordination, but in a circular logic that springs from the book's inadequate account of those forces. Conceiving globalization in a more considered, nuanced fashion would, this argument suggests, not only have added to the conceptual weight of the work, but would have freed Klein from a cul-de-sac of her own construction.

Regarding the globalization debate in these terms thus opens up critical possibilities that are, to an extent, free from the kind of contradictions that beset Naomi Klein's argument. Prompted by a reading of *Moby-Dick* as a novel that portrays the internationalization of capitalism in visionary terms, it is the historical understanding of globalization as a dynamic process that provides the key to this approach. Locating *Moby-Dick* alongside *No Logo* thus not only exposes the weaknesses with Klein's approach, but also provides, as the discussion of whaling that follows suggests, a foundation for more sophisticated understandings of the globalization debate as a whole.

Published nearly 20 years before the laying of the first transatlantic telegraph cable (1866) and the bridging of the American continent by the rail network (1869), Melville takes the idea of Manifest Destiny as an ideology based within the United States' continental ambitions and translates that dream of conquest onto the global stage. Though the oceanic realm covered by the Pequod is usually interpreted as an image of the specific terrains of the American West, Melville's approach creates a strangely prophetic metaphor, one that identifies a relationship between the desire to conquer the prairie and the stirrings of a broader yearning for global coordination and control. Whaling becomes, in this reading, not simply a narrow emblem of westward expansion, but an industry that allows Melville to connect ideas linked to Manifest Destiny with processes of Americanization, imperialism and globalization. *Moby-Dick* makes this point explicit through its constant play on the global nature of whaling and the descriptions of the ways in which Nantucketers have 'overrun and conquered the watery world.'[61] With its international crew, Olson's 'bottom dogs of all nations and all races', circumnavigating the globe, Melville is not simply portraying the capitalist 'glories' of the present, but imagining a globalized future.[62] Such a suggestion means that Manifest Destiny need not be compared to globalization in simple terms as a similar kind of ideological project, but must instead be seen as part of the same expansionist process. These dynamics are evidenced in the history of the sperm whale fishery itself, an industry inextricably linked to the complex processes of nineteenth-century colonialism and capitalism.

Histories of whaling often describe how settlements based upon sealing and whaling in the early nineteenth century saw uncolonized islands like New Zealand 'caught in the world economy.'[63] Melville makes a similar claim for the colonization of Australia. 'That great America on the other side of the sphere,' he writes, 'was given to the enlightened world by the whalemen ... The whale-ship is the true mother of that now mighty colony.'[64] In whaling Melville thus finds a literal image for globalization's advanced guard. The Pequod's crew sail the grey ocean, exploiting an undifferentiated realm, free, as the discussion in 'Fast-Fish and Loose-Fish' makes clear, from national boundaries and regulations.

What is interesting, however, is that though whaling was once a key industry of the early nineteenth century, it is now an economic irrelevance. Seen off by a combination of factors that include over-fishing and the discovery of petroleum in 1859, the story of New England whaling is one that dramatizes the transient nature of global industries. The implication is that lessons learned from whaling might apply equally well to contemporary global industries, systems that though they might appear increasingly dominant, could, with a longer view, be seen as part of variable cycles in a much less stable and homogenized system. The recent history of the American power corporation Enron (at one time a company that used imaginative accounting practices to identify itself as the seventh largest company in the United States) is a testament to the enduring volatility of world markets. Like whaling before it, Enron developed new economic terrains across the globe (particularly in Mozambique, India and Brazil) and based its business upon generating electricity and bringing light and power to homes and industries. With a disregard for environmental considerations, local cultures and labour practices, Enron attracted tremendous hostility from the anti-globalization movement and was widely censured for its activities by, among others, Arundhati Roy and the NGO Human Rights Watch.[65] Despite its apparent willingness to exploit and its disregard for patterns of regulation, Enron has not been successful and its failure, as was the case with the sperm whale fishery before it, shows that buccaneering free market practices are not always or inevitably triumphant. Like Nantucket whaling, Enron reveals once again the unstable nature of global corporations. Brought down by financial irregularities, the collapse of Enron shows that consolidating and expansionist movements take place alongside processes of fragmentation and retreat. The story of Enron thus dramatizes once again the dynamic market-conditions that will shape the experiences of many of the corporations that are following in its (and whaling's) wake.

Perceived as an incontestable reality, the defining condition of contemporary society, globalization is constructed in millenarian terms by commentators like Naomi Klein. This is the end of social experience as we know it, they argue, the beginning of a period of ever more intense, extreme and destructive forms of homogenization and coordination. To see globalization in these terms, however, is to miss the implications raised by the recognition that *Moby-Dick* can be read as a fiction of globalization. Critics of globalization thus need to be aware of the relationships that exist between contemporary conditions and those of preceding centuries, a relationship evidenced by this reflection on the links between Klein and Melville. Contemporary visions of a world that is becoming ever more integrated by destructive economic practices must as a result, this discussion argues, be located within both a broader understanding of the history of globalizing processes and a sense of the contradictory nature of the globalization debate itself. Like the problems detected in DeLillo's attempts to construct a vision of an integrated world, the focus on these historical continuities suggests that the complex and contradictory networks of global capitalism cannot be interpreted by arguments that follow easy trajectories of hegemony and apocalypse.

As the collapse of Enron and the history of whaling demonstrate, capitalism does not simply involve expansion and solidification. The apocalyptic vision of remorseless and unstoppable market forces is, as these examples suggest, one of the most pervasive fictions of globalization. An even more dramatic illustration of the instability of the global market place can be found by reflecting upon the reversals that affected Internet businesses in 2000. Fuelled by dreams that technology could deliver unparalleled opportunities for global integration, Internet companies were able to profit from the fiction that a global interactive network could create the conditions for a stable and coordinated world market. Once revealed as illusory, the majority of these businesses imploded affecting not just their own industry, but all major companies. Precipitating one of the sharpest recorded falls in world share prices, the end of the tech stock bubble provided further dramatic evidence of the dynamism and unpredictability of the global marketplace. Far from being an increasingly solid, technologically reinforced and coordinated structure, the market proved itself to be as unstable as ever.

The interpretation of the irrational exuberance that characterized this period is important because it fosters both further critical understanding of the mythological quality of parts of the debate around globalization and, at the same time, opens up opportunities for interpreting the relationship between these businesses and modern culture. Central to the Internet's promise was that it would revolutionize contemporary experience and transform not just business and economics but everyday life and all forms of culture. Identified as a key element in the Internet's apparent revolution, the analysis of contemporary culture's relationship with and response to Internet technologies thus offers significant insight into these forces. What follows builds on this suggestion by reflecting upon the nature of the networked dreams conjured by Internet pioneers and linking them to representations of Internet technologies in recent fiction by William Gibson. The intention is to develop a perspective on both the nature of the globalization debate and the ways in which contemporary literature engages with these concerns.

William Gibson

Among the majority of accounts of the arrival of the information age, the development of new media and the expansion of the Internet produced towards the end of the 1990s, lay a common emphasis on revolution. The Internet promised radical transformation. Digital technology would, they claimed, change the very fabric of contemporary experience. The Harvard Business

School proclaimed 'the death of distance'.[66] The Head of the Computing at MIT, Nicholas Negroponte, insisted that world society was entering into a new relationship with the computer and refashioning its senses of time, space and identity.[67] More marginal figures like the late Timothy Leary also entered the fray with claims that the world wide web offered new possibilities for personal freedom, imaginative creativity and self-fulfilment.[68] The promise of Aquarius had, it seemed, given way to the networked dream of the digital age.

Leaving aside specific reservations about the detail of these visions, fundamental questions have to be asked about the validity of interpretations that conceive technological changes in terms of revolution and radical transformation. The central problem with such perspectives is that they prioritize discussion of scientific innovation over analysis of the social origins of those changes. Such an approach bears all the hallmarks of what Leo Marx calls the 'technological sublime', the tendency, in James Carey's words, 'to see revolutionary potential in the latest gadgets' and to identify them as forces '*outside* history and politics'.[69] The result is a failure to understand the historical processes of which those innovations are a part. These anxieties can be understood in clearer terms by looking back at the perspectives adopted by commentators on the impact of innovation in earlier epochs. Alan Trachtenberg's account of the development of technological and urban infrastructures in late nineteenth-century America, for example, offers an important understanding of the problems with approaches that privilege discussions of innovation over broader interpretations of the historical situation. Trachtenberg's argument is that while 'technology provided the visible instruments of change ... the character of urban transformation ... lay not in mechanization, but in its context: expansion of the marketplace.'[70] An interpretation of the connection between changes in the structure of capitalism and the development of systems like the railroad and the telegraph is thus prioritized in his work.

Trachtenberg's grasp on the general connections that tie technology with social and economic change was not, however, shared by many of the late twentieth-century's Internet prophets. Their preference was to privilege discussion of transformations motivated by and predicated upon scientific and digital innovation at

Fictions of Globalization

the expense of an understanding of the systems and continuities of which those developments were a part. The result was, as Frank Webster observes in *Theories of the Information Society*, a reliance on '*social impact* approaches ... [that were] hopelessly simplistic and possibly misleading.'[71] Echoing Trachtenberg's analysis of the Gilded Age, Webster offers instead a much longer view, arguing 'we should conceive of the *informatization* of life as a process that has been ongoing ... for several centuries.'[72] It is this sense of the relationship between innovations in information and the development of capitalism that is central to Webster's position. In his terms,

> *Informatization* ... has certainly accelerated with the development of industrial capitalism ... and ... has moved into overdrive ... as globalization and the spread of transnational organizations especially have led to the incorporation of hitherto untouched realms ... into the world markets.[73]

The understanding of the relationship between information systems and the demands of globalization is thus fundamental to Webster's position. Instead of speculating about the possibilities raised by innovation, Webster looks at the conditions of contemporary capitalism and reads those technological changes in relation to their economic contexts. This is a 'cybernetic capitalism' connected to the 'extension and reconfiguration of Fordism.'[74] Rejecting the separation between technology and economics, his argument interprets innovation in materialist terms and lays the foundations for a discussion of the connections between scientific advances and the economic structures of contemporary life. Informatization is thus tied to globalization.

What makes this relationship interesting is that, like the debates around the emergence of the Internet, interpretations of globalization have, as earlier parts of this discussion suggest, tended towards theories of revolution and apocalypse. The problem with these narratives, however, is that they, like social impact theories of technological change, are overly inclined to privilege rupture and transformation over the analysis of long-term patterns of change. The idea of a socioeconomic revolution predicated upon technological change obscures understandings of the ways in which these changes can be tied to the historical processes of capitalism. As far as the specific demand for new markets is

The Fictions of Globalization

concerned, the need for ever faster modes of communication is not a unique feature of the contemporary world, but, as *Grundrisse* makes clear, a central part of the operation of capitalism in all periods: 'capital must on one side strive to tear down every spatial barrier to intercourse, i.e. to exchange and conquer the whole earth for its market, it strives on the other side to annihilate this space with time, i.e. to reduce to a minimum the time spent in motion from one place to another.'[75] The focus on the erosion of 'every spatial barrier' (physical and political), the discussion of the need to 'conquer the whole earth for its market' and the pressure for time/space compression ('distanciation' in Giddens' terms) are all elements instantly recognizable to analysts of globalization.[76] Once again the implication is that any adequate account of globalization must look to interpret it in relation to the history of capitalism. Globalization is, in these terms, not a transformation, but an intensification of existing processes.

This understanding has important implications for the discussion of contemporary information technologies. Marx's analysis of the desire to reduce 'to a minimum the time spent in motion from one place to another' offers, in the first place, an insight into the long-standing nature of the demand that, in the contemporary period, is supplied by computing and telecommunications. On a deeper level, it gestures towards an understanding of the ways in which, like globalization, these contemporary information technologies are tied to familiar processes and systems. The result is a perspective that beds the interpretation of new technologies into an analysis of globalization and then reads those processes in relation to the changes that characterize the history of capitalism.

More precise insights into these connections can be found in an analysis of recent fiction by William Gibson, a writer who is very clearly preoccupied with the informatization of society. Gibson, often credited with being the individual who, in his novel *Neuromancer* (1984), coined the term and conceptualized the idea of cyberspace, makes both a direct attempt to engage with computerization and tries to fulfil some kind of futurological role in predicting possible outcomes. His sprawl novels, *Neuromancer*, *Count Zero* (1986) and *Mona Lisa Overdrive* (1988), were set in a distant future of virtual realities, spacecraft and cybernetic organisms. This vision has been superseded in his trilogy of works, *Virtual Light* (1993), *Iduro* (1996) and *All Tomorrow's Parties*

(1999). These novels, located in a more contemporary and recognizable future, are set primarily in California and Japan. What makes them interesting is that, unlike *Neuromancer*, these novels were written in the age when new media and Internet technologies were more reality than fantasy.

Using familiar detective/thriller plots, Gibson's characters pursue traditional goals and the narratives, though often dense and convoluted, move in fairly straightforward directions. *Virtual Light* describes an attempt to destroy the community squatting on the earthquake-ruined structure of San Francisco's Bay Bridge. In *Iduro*, the plot revolves around Rei Toei (a computer-generated celebrity in the Lara Croft mode) and her engagement to Rez, an ageing human rock star. *All Tomorrow's Parties* follows *Iduro*. Rei has left Rez and is pursuing freedom from her programmers and agents. The exploration of ontology, personal liberty and the philosophical implications raised by artificial intelligence are the familiar science fiction themes played out in these texts. Alongside these concerns, Gibson develops narratives that explore a range of issues linked both to the significance of technology and its relationship to business. It is discussion of these elements in Gibson's work that offers an opportunity for developing an understanding of the relationship between literature, new media and globalization.

In a passage from *All Tomorrow's Parties*, Laney, another of Gibson's computer hackers, logs on and sees the following: 'He clutches the eyephones and follows his point of view over the edge of a cliff of data, plunging down a wall of this wide mesa, its face compounded of fractally differentiated fields of information he has come to suspect of hiding some power or intelligence beyond his comprehension.'[77] Like some kind of netscape Monument Valley, Gibson paints a picture of a technological frontier, one that promises, as the West did to the pioneers, both economic opportunity and transcendent meaning. This is a 'mesa' that hides 'some power or intelligence beyond ... comprehension'. The confluence of images linking nature, freedom and colonization identifies Laney's explorations of the Internet with the traditions of American conquest. Gibson reiterates these concerns in other parts of his work. In *Iduro*, Laney sees himself as a 'native guide' to this data wilderness, and in *Neuromancer*, Case, another hacker, is nicknamed 'cowboy' by his companions.[78]

This connection between the terrains of cyberspace and frontier mythology is a common element in discussions of Internet technology. Howard Rheingold's *Virtual Communities: Homesteading on the Electronic Frontier* (1995), Michael Wolff's *Burn Rate: How I Survived the Gold Rush Years on the Internet* (1998) and Joseph Migga Kiza's *Civilizing the Internet* (1998) are all titles that offer an insight into the prevalence of this kind of imagery. What makes these metaphorical associations interesting is that they develop a sense of the connections that bind new technologies with established economic processes. This metaphorical identification gestures towards the existence of a connection between the forces that underpinned the subjugation of the American wilderness in the nineteenth century and the technological developments at the end of the twentieth. Both processes, these metaphors suggest, are part of the same capitalist dynamic. When Michael Wolff describes the patterns of economic expansion on the Internet as a system, in which 'land ... is the measure. Not trade ... the creation of an identity – is the name of the game. Conquer first, reap later', he emphasizes the relationships that connect Internet technologies with the expansion of contemporary capitalism and underlines the continuities that exist between the patterns of the present and those of the past.[79] The worlds mapped by Gibson are not, it seems, as different from those explored by Melville as they may have first appeared.

This analysis of the representations offered in these novels is echoed in the characteristics of Gibson's style. Both throughout his first trilogy and in these more recent texts, Gibson's writing has a kind of retrospective feel that seems to betray a connection to the clean stylistics of the modernist-influenced crime thriller. Clear echoes of the tough prose of Raymond Chandler and James M. Cain are readily discernible both in the detail of his writing and in the general structuring of the narratives. In Andrew Ross's terms, Gibson's fiction constitutes a 'hard-boiled masculinity, second time around'.[80] There is, moreover, little sense of anything hypertextual in his work. There are no hyperlinks, no multimedia games, nor anything that could be connected with a stylistic revolution predicated upon new media. Instead there is a strong formal connection with the traditions of popular modernism, one that reinforces the sense of the novels' relationships with the past. The point is that in the same way that these texts represent new technologies in terms of their continuities with existent social and economic patterns, their styles retain a parallel connection with established literary modes.

These positions are shadowed in Gibson's preoccupation with plots centred on the search for self-determination in the face of the co-opting interests of the market. Chia, Rei Toei and many of the other characters in the novels are, at the outset of the trilogy at least, seeking freedom in and through the Internet. The 'Walled City', an Internet enclave cut-off from the corporate processes that dominate much of the rest of the cyber-experience, seems to represent this promise. The 'Walled City', Gibson explains, exists in an 'informational wormhole', with no space or place, an electronic never-never land.[81] In *Iduro* Gibson writes, the 'Walled City is of the net, but not on it. There are no laws here, only agreements.'[82]

> The people that founded Hak Nam [the Walled City] were angry, because the net had been very free, you could do what you wanted, but then the governments and the companies, they had different ideas of what you could do, what you couldn't do. So these people, they found a way to unravel something. A little place, a piece, like cloth ... They went there to get away from the laws. To have no laws, like when the net was new.[83]

The Walled City offers a kind of virtual counterpart to Gibson's other uncolonized space, the squatter community on the Bay Bridge. In all three novels the narratives are driven forward by threats to the liberty of these communities. It is the idealistic desire to maintain the autonomy of these spaces in the face of colonizing corporate interests that provides a key dynamic at the heart of the texts.

These concerns are brought more clearly into focus in sections that appear to reinscribe this sense of the net as an incorporated experience. *Iduro*, in particular, works to emphasize these patterns. At the beginning of the novel, Chia manifests a youthful idealism about the Internet. Running the Seattle chapter of the Lo Rez fan club, she maintains a complex network of relationships between fellow fans. Communication, the free exchange of data and the formation of fluid, international connections are all, it seems, made possible through her use of the Internet. All of this changes, however, when the web brings her news of Rez's

The Fictions of Globalization

engagement to the iduro (an electronic being), a rumour that takes her to Japan and into contact with the corporate manipulations of an official Lo Rez fanclub. During this meeting she is told 'we are an *official* chapter . . . We have the honour of working closely with actual employees of the band . . . they have requested that we assist them in seeing that it [the rumour of Rez's engagement] is not spread further.'[84] This meeting signals the end of her innocent view of the web and moves her towards an understanding of the corporate forces that control the terrains of cyberspace. At the end of the novel, her journey from innocence to experience is complete. Chia drifts away from her naive enthusiasm for Lo Rez and the global fan network ('she hadn't really been that active in the chapter lately') and finds herself devoting her energies instead to the Hak Nam cyber-ghetto, the protected, inward-looking citadel, paranoid about encroachment and determined to resist colonizing processes.[85] Like the world travellers discussed in the following chapter, Chia is looking for a space outside the Internet's incorporated terrains and seeking solace in a remote, isolated, community.

In terms that mirror Chia's journey, Laney's narrative also dramatizes the limitations and co-options that characterize the netscape. Beginning *Iduro* as a professional surfer, a researcher for a tabloid network, Slitscan, he is fully connected to the net's corporate powers. For Laney, 'life at Slitscan had a certain focused quality . . . [his] colleagues limited themselves to a particular bandwidth of emotion.'[86] The company thus seems to symbolize corporate closure and colonization. Gibson writes: 'descended from "reality" programming and the network tabloids of the late twentieth century . . . Slitscan was the mature form, supporting fully global franchises. Slitscan's revenues had paid for entire satellites and built the building he worked in in Burbank.'[87] Gibson's vision of 'global franchises' and new media's shift back into areas of the old economy is one that echoes Chia's growing awareness of enclosure, an impression that is strengthened in *All Tomorrow's Parties*, the final part of the trilogy.

The novel starts with Laney living among the homeless in Tokyo station. No longer employed by Rei Toei, and in the grip of the side-effects caused by drug experiments conducted upon him as a child, he begins to stalk Cody Harwood, a 'pointedly uncharismatic billionaire . . . who, maybe, just maybe, ran it all'.[88]

97

Neglecting his health, and drifting in long cyberhallucinations, Laney foresees an apocalypse, a cataclysm with Harwood and the Bay Bridge at its heart. Aroused by this premonition, Laney contacts Rydell, *Virtual Light*'s protagonist, and elicits his help in manipulating these events. A typically complex sequence of narratives follows and the novel ends with Cody Harwood uploading himself into the circuits of the datastream. At the same time as he moves into the web, Rei Toei is released from it, converting herself from an electronic being, an iduro, into a living thing of flesh and bone. These two shifts occur against the background of Laney's death (suicide?), an event that is attributed to a semi-conscious desire to liberate himself from the shackles of cyberspace.

These three concluding events provide an important statement upon the relationship between globalization and information technologies. With the plutocrat Harwood entering the web, and those seeking freedom (Laney and Rei Toei) leaving it behind, Gibson portrays the Internet not as a place of liberation and opportunity, but as a colonized, corporatized space. Just as Chia forsakes her idealized view of the networked village at the end of *Iduro*, Rei and Laney find the web either existentially limiting (Rei) or dangerously destructive (Laney). It is only Harwood, the representative of wealth and power, who appears comfortable inhabiting these terrains. This view of the Internet contrasts strongly with the kind of vision offered in Gibson's earlier work. In *Neuromancer*, cyberspace is identified with liberation. It is the space where the artificial intelligences of Wintermute and Neuromancer can fuse together and find release from the corporate control of Tessier-Ashpool.[89] In *All Tomorrow's Parties*, however, the situation is reversed as Gibson has Rei Toei leave the net behind in an attempt to find freedom for her constructed identity.

Unlike Internet utopians, Gibson sees technology's connection to the historical patterns of culture, society and economics. Eschewing the technological sublime, *Virtual Light*, *Iduro* and *All Tomorrow's Parties* construct a vision of a future that is continuous with the contours and conditions of established social and economic landscapes. In Gibson's work technology is contextualized and change understood in relation to long term patterns of development. Gibson thus shadows the kinds of positions offered by commentators like Carey and Webster. In their work,

The Fictions of Globalization

as in Gibson's, technology and the information society can only be understood in relation to the processes and patterns of economic and social change. Exploring Gibson's netscape in these terms thus furthers both an understanding of the ways in which literatures represent technology and, at the same time, advances the understanding of technological change in relation to the globalization debate. Any lingering questions about the centrality of concerns linked to globalization and consumption to the dynamics of Gibson's fiction can be answered by considering, in concluding terms, the characteristics of his later novel, *Pattern Recognition* (2003).

As the years pass, Gibson finds himself inhabiting a world that used to be part of some distantly imagined technological future. The result is that where he once specialized in visions of fantastic possibilities, he now seems to prefer vibrant images of the present. The result is *Pattern Recognition*, a contemporary novel set in London, Tokyo and Russia. Focused on the experiences of Cayce, a freelance cool-hunter with a phobia for brand names and logos, the novel describes her attempts to trace the source of the 'footage', a series of haunting, anonymous fragments of film that are slowly appearing on the Internet.[90]

Like many of his novels, it is Gibson's eye for detail and setting that provide some of the text's most interesting insights, insights that emerge most clearly through Cayce's thoughts on her work for advertising agencies and marketing companies. Cayce explains her professional role in the following terms:

> I consult on design . . . and I hunt 'cool' . . . Manufacturers use me to keep track of street fashion . . . What I do is pattern recognition, I try to recognize a pattern before anyone else does [and then] . . . I point a commodifier at it . . . It gets productized. Turned into units. Marketed.[91]

Despite her allergy to logos, Cayce displays a preternatural sensitivity to patterns and trends that makes her perfectly equipped to fill her consultancy role at Blue Ant, a London-based advertising agency that is described as 'relatively tiny in terms of permanent staff, globally distributed, more post-geographic than multi-national.'[92] In this regard Cayce seems to inhabit a contradictory realm, allergic to brands, but financially beholden to her advertising clients, absorbed in the unsigned, anonymous and, by implication uncommodified images of the footage, yet willing to help 'point a commodifier at it'. Even her anti-materialism seems contradictory. Though apparently 'weaned off materialism', Cayce spends much of the novel toting an iBook, dressing in a studiously logo-free capsule wardrobe and wearing an obscure and expensive Japanese copy of an MA-1 flying-jacket.[93]

Of all of these contradictions, it is her willingness to accept Bigend's commission to source the footage that is the most curious. Like the Hak Nam cyberghetto and the Bridge community in Gibson's earlier novels, the footage represents a world outside the ordinary currents of commerce and the market. Cayce is aware, however, that finding its source will change its status. As she observes, 'any creation that attracts the attention of the world, on an ongoing basis, becomes valuable ... More valuable than you could imagine. The commercial part would simply be branding, franchising.'[94] Gibson links her decision to seek out the source of the footage with her search for her lost father, missing since the day of the attack on the Twin Towers. Finding one, the novel suggests, might bring certainty about the other and it also seems to imply that the attempt to isolate and insulate the footage from the forces of marketing is ultimately futile. Cayce, in accepting Bigend's commission, is simply performing a function that will be fulfilled with or without her. In some respects this reading suggests that *Pattern Recognition* offers a pessimistic view of a contemporary culture in which everything finds itself incorporated in the end.

This pessimism can be tempered, however, by considering the possibility that the novel is trying to step away from the idealistic opposition between the pure and uncommodified terrains represented by the footage and the commercial world represented by Bigend. Reflecting upon the novel's conclusion supports this suggestion. At the end of *Pattern Recognition* it is clear that Bigend and his Blue Ant organization have benefited from her work. Not only has he discovered the origin of the footage, he has also forged a new alliance with Volkov, a Russian robber baron, a relationship that can only work to reinforce his commercial power. It is important to note that Cayce also benefits from these events. Having discovered the creator of the footage, not only does she earn $50,000 in cash, she also starts to sense that her logo phobia is in remission. In addition, she finds freedom from her preoccupation with the footage and is now certain that her father did die in the aftermath of the attack on the World Trade Center.

The novel thus seems to end not with an idealistic attempt to separate culture from the market, but through a more fluid sense of the possibilities created by the interaction between the two. Like Cayce, the text suggests, we can surf the patterns, recognize them and revel in them, but not resist them. The role of technology in *Pattern Recognition* is equally unstable. The net is both the medium for the dissemination of the footage's uncommodified images and also the mechanism that allows Cayce to track down its source. The implication is that Gibson seems to be moving away from an attempt to either celebrate or condemn technology, and appears more interested in exploring the range of possibilities it generates. Neither totally homogenized and incorporated nor romantically liberating, technological changes and, by implication the interests of capital that fuel those changes, are thus represented as complex and contradictory forces that once recognized can be negotiated in any number of different ways. Just as Palahniuk's fiction exposes the limitations of attempts to offer violent resistance to the market and DeLillo's writing can be read in terms that problematize conceptions of globalization as the defining reality of contemporary experience, Gibson's fiction opens up a multi-dimensional understanding of the role of technology within this network of forces. In the chapter that follows these discussions will be developed further by showing the ways in which contemporary travel narratives dramatize a similar range of concerns. Like Gibson's Internet travellers, the journeys described in Kem Nunn's *The Dogs of Winter* (1997) and English novelist Alex Garland's *The Beach* (1996) open up a wide range of perspectives on both the fictions of globalization and the shape and character of international consumer culture.

5
Pure Shores

An emblem of release, the border between land and sea signifies freedom. Edna Pontellier in Kate Chopin's *The Awakening* (1899), for example, uses the beach as a way of escaping from the conventions of everyday life. For her, it is a place for sexualized swimming and, ultimately, the dreamy, ambiguous embrace of death. Katherine Mansfield's stories 'Prelude' (1916) and 'At the bay' (1922) (in *The Collected Stories*, 2001) portray the beach in similar terms, conceiving the sandy edge of the ocean as an impressionistic world of unlicensed thoughts and pleasures, a liminal terrain that nurtures unconventional possibilities. More contemporary narratives have developed these themes and used beach culture as a key site of rebellion and escape. In John Milius's film *Big Wednesday* (1978), for example, the surfer is portrayed as an individual seeking freedom from social norms, in brief moments atop the board. Contrasting sublime experiences in the ocean with a country shadowed by the Vietnam War, *Big Wednesday* counterpoints violent realities with the liberation found in the embrace of the perfect wave. Kem Nunn's 'surf noir' novels *Tijuana Straits* (2004), *The Dogs of Winter* (1997) and *Tapping the Source* (1984) extend these concerns and match the quest for idyllic beaches and waves with environmental themes and more general criticisms of consumption. The surfing beach-dweller, Nunn suggests, is imbued with both a natural eco-consciousness and a graceful anti-materialism.

In *The Dogs of Winter*, for example, Nunn tells the story of Jack Fletcher, an ageing surf photographer who is called out of

Pure Shores

semi-retirement to shoot legendary surfer Drew Harmon at the 'Heart Attacks Reef' in Northern California. Heart Attacks is 'California's premier mysto wave, the last secret spot. They said you had to cross Indian land to get there – a rocky point somewhere south of the Oregon border . . . There were no roads in. They said you had to risk your ass just to reach it.'[1] Welcoming this assignment as an alternative to the drudgery and boredom of his work as a wedding photographer, the novel establishes a straightforward contrast between the freedom of the waves and the limitations of life on the mainland. The irony is, however, that, in terms that echo Cayce's narrative in *Pattern Recognition* (Gibson 2003), Fletcher is hired to track down an elusive experience and commoditize it on the pages of *Victory at Sea*, a magazine whose title seems to foreground the novel's anxieties about the colonialism of commercialization.

Having set up this quest for the mythical beach, the novel then complicates the plot by drawing Harmon and Fletcher into conflict with warring bands of Native Americans, a clash that sets in motion a chain of violent events. As the novel nears its end, these hostilities are resolved as Harmon gets to both surf the perfect wave on the Heart Attacks Reef and to die in the attempt, as the expression of some form of ambiguous death-wish that the novel represents in transcendental terms. Nunn writes:

> There were no lip bashes or floaters, none of the manoeuvres worked out to score points in surfing contests and even though these waves were a little big for such items one could see that such was not the man's style. It was too pure and too clean for the admittance of cheap theatrics and there was something about it that broke Fletcher's heart to see. It was a statement, a last will and testament written on the watery face of the world and there were none there to witness it save for Fletcher himself and he was humbled in its presence for it was the thing itself.[2]

Untainted by any specious commercial frippery or showboating, Harmon finds ultimate freedom in this last ride on a virgin wave and experiences, in Nunn's terms, a kind of surf apotheosis.

This idealistic mood is reinforced by Fletcher's decision to remain in the Northern Californian woods after Harmon's death and take photographs of the waves. 'He liked them [the photos] hollow, empty and perfect,' Nunn writes, 'The few who saw them said there were like jewels. They said as well that he declined all offers to sell.'³ Like Harmon, he rejects commodification and finds freedom from the constraints of ordinary life in this celebration of the waves of this remote and untouched beach, a place he remains determined to protect and conceal.⁴ Nunn's novel thus offers a straightforward celebration of a world that it imagines can be protected from the reach of the market. For *The Dogs of Winter*, this wilderness beach represents a place that, in ways that shadow the desires for pure and authentic experiences articulated by the protagonists in novels like *Fight Club* (Palahniuck 1996) and *Virtual Light* (Gibson 1993), provides an antidote to commercialism and the constraints of modern life.

These perspectives can be developed by linking the analysis of this pattern of representations with contextual accounts of the beach's place in the cultural history of the twentieth century. Lena Lencek and Gideon Bosker's *The Beach: The History of Paradise on Earth* (1998), for example, offers a detailed account of the ways in which beaches have both reflected and participated in social change over the last hundred years. From sea bathing at health resorts at the end of the nineteenth century to contemporary preoccupations with beauty, the body and the beach, they recognize a potent strain of romanticism within recent western relationships with the beach. In their terms, 'whether an isolated stretch of sand staked out by a solitary towel, or a populous strand colonized with carnivals and curios, the beach is at once escape valve and inspiration, symbol and playground.'⁵ For Bosker and Lencek, the modern traveller, 'like their earlier romantic counterparts ... gravitated towards beaches that had not been spoiled by tourism, where "authentic", meaningful, traditional ways of life could still be found.'⁶

This position not only echoes the themes explored in the work of Mansfield, Chopin, Nunn *et al.*, but also offers a precise insight into the desires that motivate the characters in Alex Garland's first novel *The Beach* (1996). Though English, Garland's novel about an international tribe of world travellers has a wide resonance and raises issues around the rebellion against and resistance to the forces of globalization that are of importance not just to British fiction, but to fiction in English in the United States and in the rest of the world. This internationally successful tale of the adventures of a group youthful, Western travellers provides a key statement on both the significance of these experiences in the contemporary period and an insight into the relationships that connect travelling with the patterns of consumption and globalization.[7] Reading this novel alongside North American fiction by the likes of Nunn, Palahniuk and Gibson thus offers an important addition to the understanding not just of the meaning of the beach in contemporary culture, but of the ways in which recent fiction has looked to negotiate the relationship between culture and the market.

Beach life

Driven by the search for a 'hidden paradise', the characters in Garland's *The Beach* are motivated by classically romantic yearnings for solitude and escape.[8] With only a hand-drawn map to guide them, the novel develops around Richard, Étienne and Françoise's pursuit of a secret beach far from the mainstream locations populated by Thailand's many thousands of Western tourists. The place they seek is beautiful and remote, known only to a privileged few and seemingly untouched by commerce and development. Here they believe they will be able to cut away from the paths walked by their fellow travellers and satisfy the desire to experience 'something different'.[9] The problem Richard and his companions face, however, is that the possibility of finding 'exotic beaches far from home' where they can 'shed materialism, hypocrisy and clothing' seem to be diminishing.[10] Garland articulates these concerns in a scene that describes Richard's thoughts as he walks through Ko Samui.

> I began counting the guest-houses I passed along the shore line. After 20 minutes I'd counted 17, and they were still showing no signs of thinning out. If anything, the palm trees were more cluttered with Ray-Bans and concrete patios than before.[11]

Instead of finding escape, all Richard sees is a kind of sterile suburban sprawl clinging to the boundary between land and sea. Branded and urbanized, this world is the antithesis of the ideal beach. The problem is that thousands of wealthy westerners are not only trying to get away from it all but also from each other with the result being that Thailand's beaches find themselves transformed into exactly the kind of places they were intended to offer escape from: overdeveloped, overcommercialized and overpopulated.

Tourists and the promotion of tourism are, it seems to blame, and *The Beach* has particular concerns about the role of guidebooks in the popularizing of specific locations.

> Étienne picked up his guidebook and began a halting translation. '. . . This says travellers try new islands beyond Ko Pha-Ngan because Ko Pha-Ngan is now the same as Ko Samui.'
> 'The same?'
> 'Spoiled. Too many tourists. But look, this book is three years old.'[12]

Three years is, Étienne suggests, a long time in the life of a beach resort, particularly one that has found its way onto the pages of a guidebook. Étienne's point is that guidebooks have a destructive influence, a view shared by many of Garland's characters and focused through their common contempt for the Lonely Planet series. If guides are villains, then the Lonely Planet is, it seems, chief amongst them. One typical dialogue reads: ' "You know Richard, one of these days I'm going to find one of those Lonely Planet writers and I'm going to ask him, what's so fucking lonely about the Khao San Road?" I smiled. "Just before you punch his lights out, right?" '[13] If it were not for the Lonely Planet, *The Beach* implies, Thailand would be a perfect destination. The irony is, however, that though Garland's characters condemn these books, there remains a strong affinity between their ideals and the ethos of Lonely Planet guides. They are aimed at independent travellers and imbued with an idealism that mirrors the kind of desires that motivate Richard and his companions. Like them, these books look to identify remote and undeveloped locations and provide advice for travellers seeking to reject the conventional tourist trails. This relationship raises a number of interesting implications that can be fleshed out by looking more closely at Lonely Planet guidebooks themselves.

Lonely Planet guides offer a fundamentally paradoxical service. They both articulate yearnings for hidden paradises and participate in processes that will lead to development and overcrowding. The following description of Ko Samui from Joe Cummings's guide to Thailand makes these contradictions explicit.

> The island has had a somewhat legendary status among Asian travellers for the past 20 years or so, but it wasn't until the late 1980s that it escalated to the touristic proportions of other similar getaways found between Goa and Bali ... Nevertheless, Samui is still an enjoyable place to spend some time ... But there's no going back to 1971, when the first tourists arrived in a coconut boat from Bangkok.[14]

The paradox lies in the ways in which the author seems to mourn the development of the very place he is popularizing. As Garland's novel has it, 'set up in ... Ko Pha Ngan, Ko Tao, Borocay, and the hordes are bound to follow. There's no way you can keep it out of Lonely Planet and once that happens it's countdown to doomsday.'[15]

This sense of the contradictions that characterize Lonely Planet guides has to be tempered by an understanding of the ways in which the books remain conscious of their own participation in processes of development. Carrying a statement that begins with the observation that 'there are a number of reasons why we might exclude a place' and ends with the suggestion that 'sometimes it is simply inappropriate to encourage an influx of foreign visitors', most editions signal an awareness of the contribution they make to development.[16] The problem with this disclaimer, however, is that it raises as many questions as it answers. Though it signifies an understanding of the need to protect particular environments, it also suggests that while the Lonely Planet author is free to visit these sites, it is inappropriate for the readers of the guidebook to share in this experience. Unable to trust either the avaricious local or the overly zealous tourist, these elite travellers position themselves as gatekeepers of the world's delicate cultures.

Connected with this position is an equally contradictory critique of mass tourism and, by implication, the social and economic transformations upon which such tourism depends. Improved infrastructure and the increased wealth of many Westerners lie at the heart of the emergence of the tourist industry. The fact that the success of the Lonely Planet (a company based in Melbourne) is itself founded upon this boom in tourism and dependent upon the opportunities that developments in international transport and telecommunications have created for the successful marketing and distribution of the company's products is conveniently forgotten.

These reflections on the contradictions that characterize guides like the Lonely Planet and the paradoxical nature of the relationship between these books and Garland's characters are significant because they open up a number of broader interpretative perspectives on the beach community Garland's novel describes. The beach-dwellers' dream is simple: to short circuit the processes that lead from the discovery of a beautiful location to the development of that site and on towards its destruction by keeping their beach absolutely secret. As Sal explains: 'We come here to relax by a beautiful beach, but it isn't a beach resort . . . We're trying to make a place that won't turn into a beach resort.'[17] They, like the Lonely Planet author, are seeking to preserve this place for themselves. Having leapt so far from the tourist trail, they dream that they will be able freeze their beach at the idyllic moment of discovery, and keep it safely concealed behind its 'circle of protective cliffs'.[18]

In this respect, *The Beach*, like the idealistic moments that inform both *The Dogs of Winter* and any Lonely Planet guidebook, tries to construct a sense of separation between the developed and the undeveloped, between civilization and wilderness. With their communal social structure and their hunter-gatherer existence, the characters in Garland's novel inhabit an apparently pre-capitalist world constructed as the antithesis of modern life. They are in pursuit of a wild, remote place where no foot has ever walked. Their community is thus established in opposition to 'the world', the beach-dwellers' contemptuous appellation for the culture they have left behind.[19] The fundamental problem with this structure, however, is that it hinges upon a strict opposition between nature and society. Overlooking the market's colonizing reach, underestimating the ways in which wildernesses function as vital resources for the generation of wealth (as the earlier discussion of *Moby-Dick* has made clear) and reliant on a polarized contrast between the two realms, this idealistic separation is, as many commentators have observed, extremely problematic.[20] Recognizing these concerns and identifying these critical contexts thus problematizes the beach community's attempt to insulate their lagoon from the currents of commerce and makes their dream of a space cut off from the influence of the outside world seem both naive and unsustainable.

These ideas are significant because they illuminate the often-contradictory relationship between Garland's characters and their island environment. On a simple level, it is clear that no matter how hard they try to protect this world, the beach dwellers are still initiating processes that will lead to the transformation of the island into exactly the kind of environment they were originally seeking to escape. Already numbers on the island are growing and they know that it is only a matter of time before more travellers join them. It is this concern that explains the desire to forestall change and the anxiety generated by new arrivals. Worries over Zeph and Sammy's attempts to reach the island, for example, come to dominate much of the later parts of the novel and it is their arrival that sets in motion the chain of events that lead towards the destruction of the beach community and the novel's conclusion.

The ending of *The Beach*, however, is not as predictable as it might appear. As Zeph and Sammy work to build the raft that will carry them across the sound and onto the beach, the text seems to be heading towards a fairly obvious finale. The increased number of travellers making their way to the secret location will, the reader suspects, lead to further development and ultimately to the destruction of their idyllic world. The actual conclusion, however, is quite different and fosters not only a re-evaluation of the status of the beach community in Garland's novel but a critical reassessment of the tensions between nature and society constructed in the text.

As the beach dwellers fear, the arrival of Zeph and Sammy *does* precipitate change, not, however, because it foreshadows the transformation of the beach into a tourist trap, but because it attracts the attention of the local drug trade. Fearing that the increasing number of travellers will have a detrimental effect on their ability to grow marijuana on the island, they use force to evict the beach dwellers. The point about this ending is that it shatters their belief that the island was ever outside commerce. The secret, protected status of the beach is not, as the characters may have imagined, a sign that their world exists as one removed from the patterns of the market, but a consequence of the fact that the production of goods for the drug trade requires the preservation of secret locations. The ending of the novel thus inscribes a sense of the inextricable connections that tie the commercial forces of the outside world to the seemingly pure shores of the beach. This is the reality Richard is forced to contemplate when a Thai gunman, wearing 'Reeboks, like the Ko Samui spiv', knocks him to the ground.[21] He might have imagined he was getting away from it all, but as this detail shows the island has always been part of the tourist economy. The drug business wins over tourism in this instance because, for the time being at least, there seems to be more money in growing marijuana to sell to tourists than there is in building beach bars and bungalows to entertain and accommodate them. The dream of a place outside the market is thus destroyed in a conclusion that emphasizes the interdependence of nature and capital, wilderness and society.

Though most clearly apparent in the novel's conclusion, this understanding of the contradictory relationship between Garland's beach-dwellers and their apparently uncommodified environment can also be traced in other areas of the text. Despite their desire to shed materialism and the patterns of consumer life, Garland gestures towards a sense that his characters have always been to some extent dependent upon the outside world. As the novel demonstrates, they rely on the existence of local markets and use the money they have brought with them from the West to satisfy both their need for essential foodstuffs and their enduring desire for the batteries required to power their Gameboys. These points, implicit in Garland's novel, are made much more explicit in John Hodge's script for Danny Boyle's film version of *The Beach* (2000).

The story of *The Beach*'s transformation into a Hollywood-financed film featuring Leonardo DiCaprio is one that in its own way offers a whole range of insights into the relationship between culture and commerce. Representing both a colonization of an English novel by American capital (20th Century Fox) and the American cultural priorities that accompany that finance (particularly the casting of DiCaprio as Richard and the inclusion of a love scene between Richard and Françoise), the story of the film's production mirrors the dynamics at the heart of Garland's novel. Tales of the environmental destruction wrought by the production on Maya Bay only serve to heighten this sense that the making of *The Beach* played out many of the tensions that provide the novel with its central focus. The fact that John Hodge's script sharpens *The Beach*'s focus on the conflicts between nature and capital only serves to develop the debate further. In a key scene added to Garland's plot, Hodge has many of the characters approach Richard prior to the 'rice run' to order the luxuries they need to help them through their days on the island. The script reads:

> Richard is sitting on his mat with a pencil and a piece of paper. A line of people wait to pass him some crumpled Baht and their order . . . Their recitals overlap and freely intercut . . .[22]

The lengthy list that follows includes requests by 17 different community members, starting with Christo's order for 'Toothpaste, 60 cigarettes, a new hat, some Elastoplast, a pair of swimming trunks, four bars of chocolate and some razors' and ending with a request for 'A nail file, a G-string and a book by Barbara Cartland'.[23] The point is, once again, that far from being a world untainted by materialism, their life on the beach remains tied to familiar patterns of consumption.

Hodge's focus on the beach-dwellers' concern for luxuries and his identification of the ironies of their situation is particularly interesting as it echoes the tone of his adaptation of the only other novel to approach *The Beach*'s cult status in British fiction from the 1990s, Irvine Welsh's *Trainspotting* (1993). Renton, Welsh's central protagonist, is a character who, like Richard, appears to be rejecting materialism and convention, not by escaping to a remote location, but by dropping out into a heroin-using subculture. With an opening sequence that begins with shots of Renton fleeing from security guards after a shoplifting spree and his voice-over urging the audience to 'Choose life. Choose a job, choose a career. Choose a family. Choose a fucking big television, . . . But why would I want to do a thing like that? . . . I chose not to choose life: I chose something else . . . a sincere and truthful junk habit', Hodge starts with a scene that characterizes heroin use as both the antithesis of ordinary life and a rejection of consumption.[24] Having established this proposition, Hodge's script then goes on to undermine it by showing that Renton's 'sincere and truthful junk habit' is in fact the spur to a kind of hyperconsumption, one that creates a desire to consume a form of junk that is at least as strong as the urges felt by the most hardened of shopaholics. The narrative thus reveals Renton to be not cut off from capitalism, but in fact firmly connected to the particularities of the narco-economy. This point is made explicit in the film's conclusion, a scene that has Renton turning his back on both

Fictions of Globalization

Edinburgh's junk subculture and his friends and fleeing for Amsterdam with their pooled drug money. Like the opening, once again, Hodge uses voice-over to explain:

> I'm going to be just like you: the job, the family, the fucking big television, the washing machine, the car ... three-piece suite, DIY, game shows, junk food, children, walking in the park ... indexed pension, tax exemption, clearing the gutters, getting by, looking ahead to the day you die.[25]

In this closing moment Renton seems able to trade one form of consumption for another and substitute a desire for heroin with an enthusiasm for more mainstream patterns of consumption. The implication is that like the characters in *The Beach*, Renton has never really been outside consumer culture at all.

Such a reading of the relationship between subcultures and the market can be linked back to the work of Lencek and Bosker and their sense of the ways in which beaches have become increasingly tame, suburban and commercial. 'Throughout the 1950s', they write, 'beaches had been turned into extensions of the backyard patio.'[26] No longer a world free from materialism, the beach has become another opportunity for the elaborate display of consumer power. In this reading the sculpted physiques, polished paraphernalia of surf boards and shades, are tokens not of rebellion, but of the commodification of the beach.[27] The key point for Lencek and Bosker is that the border between land and sea does not simply offer another space for the expression of American commercial ideals, but that the beach and beach culture begins to participate in the reproduction and extension of those ideals.

> The beaches of southern California would leave their influence on everything from concepts of style and modern behaviour to notions of beauty and health. The sun-streaked hair, tanned glowing skin, tight musculature and springy step of the vacationer would become the common attributes of the southern Californian and, eventually, disseminated by Hollywood, set a new standard for American pulchritude.[28]

The beach's liminal landscape, like so many others, thus finds itself increasingly settled and regulated, organized by the demands of marketing and the market. Even the desire to unwind on a foreign shore must thus be read in the context of consumerism.

As is the case in *Trainspotting* and *The Beach*, Lencek and Bosker see that the yearning for an alternative beach lifestyle remains firmly connected to familiar patterns of consumption. The irony is that in all of these examples it is the promise of rebellion that makes these experiences more attractive to potential consumers. So potent are capitalism's co-opting forces, it seems, that they can package dissent and sell it back to the dissenters.

In these terms, a novel like *The Beach* appears to offer another powerfully pessimistic vision of contemporary experience, describing a world in which every gesture of refusal becomes absorbed by a voracious materialism. It is the market's apparent ability not only to disarm critical gestures, but to transform them into a saleable resource that becomes the most depressing evidence of its triumph. The gloomy conclusion is that there are few (if any) opportunities for critique in this environment. The question is that if criticism can become affirmation, and rebellion a dimension in a marketing campaign, what are the possibilities for resistance?

A response to these questions can be found by reflecting more closely on the ways in which this view of the globalized marketplace is constructed. Central to these arguments is the suggestion that free and uncolonized experiences are being constantly co-opted by capitalism. The problem with such a position, however, is that it hinges on a binary distinction between commodified and uncommodified experiences. The concern is that, as discussions of the tensions between wilderness and society have suggested, it is almost impossible to find evidence for an experience that has, in recent memory at least, ever actually been outside the market. On a very basic level, the suggestion that older social orders and cultures were somehow untouched by the market seems both false and informed by a presentist belief that the problems of the contemporary period are much more severe than those faced by preceding generations. Accounts of the voracious incorporation of uncommodified experiences by contemporary capitalism can thus be criticized for relying on an unsustainable opposition between the commercial and the uncommercial, the free and the unfree, capital and nature. These concerns can be fleshed out by examining the parallels that connect Garland's novel with the patterns and ideals of romanticism.

Though it is the beach that signifies escape for Garland's

generation, where for the romantics it was the wild spaces of Scotland, Cumbria and the Alps, there is a shared desire for sequestration and a celebration of remote places that promise an escape from materialism. These comparisons can be strengthened by considering the parallels that exist between the history of a region like the Lake District and the processes of development that Garland explores in *The Beach*. With Wordsworth drawn initially to the Lakes because of their apparent seclusion, the irony is that the success of his poems celebrating the putative wildness of these locations popularized them to such an extent that it threatened the very qualities that had attracted him to Cumbria in the first place. His opposition to the building of the Kendal to Windermere railway, for example, signalled an attempt to reverse the processes of development he had set in motion and a desire to bulwark his world against the masses wishing to share the scenery and tranquillity celebrated in his poetry. Central to Wordsworth's objection was the argument that, unlike the sensitive romantic poet, the ordinary person would not be able to fully appreciate the Lakes. It was his 'belief that the imperfectly educated classes are not likely to draw much good from rare visits to the Lakes . . . surely on their account it is not desirable that the visits should be frequent'.[29] Like Garland's characters and the authors of the Lonely Planet guidebooks, Wordsworth felt that only he and a select few like him were equipped to enjoy these precious environments. The problem is, however, as Lynne Withey's *Grand Tours and Cook's Tours* (1997) observes, 'in attempting to reserve the Lakes for people of his sensibility, however, Wordsworth was fighting an uphill battle. His own poetry helped promote the popularity of the region, to the point that he himself became one the region's top tourist attractions by the 1830s.'[30]

This contradiction can be brought into focus by looking at the Lonely Planet guide to Britain and considering the section on the Lakes. With this chapter prefaced by a quotation from Wordsworth's 'Daffodils' (1804), the guide goes on to suggest that 'the Lake District is one of England's most beautiful corners . . . Unfortunately, an estimated 14 million people pour into the Lakes every year . . . The crowds can be so dense and the traffic jams so long that it's debatable whether it's worth visiting on any weekend between May and October, or any time at all from mid-July to the end of August.'[31] The guide's more detailed descriptions continue this theme: 'Grassmere is a picture-postcard village and a lovely place to stay out of season. In summer, its good looks and associations with the poet Wordsworth ensure it's overrun with tourists.'[32] The chance to find refreshment at the Dove Cottage Tea-rooms and Restaurant is clearly more than the coached-in hordes can resist.

The point raised by these comparisons is not simply focused on the similarity between the story of the Lakes and that told in *The Beach*, but centred on the ways in which the experiences described in Garland's novel can be interpreted as part of long-standing historical processes, not as dramas unique to the contemporary period. The circumstances described in *The Beach* must, in this light, be seen as characteristic parts of ongoing patterns of development. These understandings are important because they problematize once again the sense that contemporary culture has to deal with unprecedented forces of capitalist incorporation. Garland's characters are not grappling with a new set of conditions, but confronting problems similar to those that faced pioneering tourists at the start of the nineteenth century. The concern is, however, that while these observations challenge the suggestion that the contemporary period is engaging in a unique battle with powerful and all-pervasive forces of co-option, they do little to alleviate the sense that there is nothing that can be done to resist the market. Knowing that these are old problems does not make the dilemmas any less acute. There is even a case for saying that these approaches actually make the market appear even more powerful and hegemonic. Where Garland's novel seems to imply that capitalism's triumph is nigh, these reflections on nature, capital and the experiences of the English romantics suggest that its victory is already complete. The market's influence is, it seems, already all-pervasive, a conclusion that makes opportunities for critique appear even more remote than ever.

Though this historicized understanding of the relationship between culture, tourism and the market does not provide an immediate sense of the ways in which the incorporating power of capitalism can be challenged, it does illuminate problems with the ways in which *The Beach* constructs its portrait of contemporary society. Central to the novel's vision is a perspective that draws on a model of a globalized world that is increasingly coordinated

Fictions of Globalization

and homogenized. In terms that echo earlier chapters in this discussion, Garland's narrative sees a world rendered flat and featureless by economic forces of integration and draws upon familiar accounts of globalization as a process rooted in 'distanciation' and 'dedifferentiation'.[33] It is Garland's description of Richard's experiences on the Khao San Road that offers his most vivid account of these conditions. Garland writes:

> The first I heard of the beach was in Bangkok, on the Khao San Road. Khao San Road was backpacker land. Almost all the buildings had been converted into guesthouses, there were long-distance telephone booths with air-con, the cafés showed brand-new Hollywood films on video, and you couldn't walk ten feet without passing a bootleg-tape stall. The main function of the street was as a decompression chamber for those about to leave or enter Thailand, a halfway house between East and West.[34]

Coming in the opening paragraph, this description not only provides the novel's most explicit commentary on globalized culture, but stands as a contextualizing frame for the events that follow. Like a down-at-heel version of the world imagined by Lyotard in his vision of postmodern jetsetters, 'backpacker land' is a place of homogenized cultures.[35] Anglicized and bearing the stamp of Hollywood, Garland's character sees Thailand transformed into a diluted and deterritorialized culture in which everything is 'halfway' between one thing and the other. From the beach dwellers' point of view, the concern is that this kind of terrain seems to be expanding across the world, producing a uniformly bland, sterile form of global culture.

A broader perspective on this passage, however, raises questions about the ways in which this vision shows *The Beach* to be dependent on a narrow and clichéd account of the impact of globalization. Garland clearly has an eye for the surface texture of a globalized tourist culture, but makes little effort to explore or explain it in greater detail. The result is an account of contemporary life that lacks the complexity needed for an effective engagement with the particularities of globalization. This problem is compounded by the fact that the passage not only naturalizes its vision of globalization and presents its narrow perspective as a framing reality, but does so in terms that represent those conditions in wholly negative terms. The world of the Khao San Road and by implication the environments created by globalization are, this passage suggests, limited and shallow. These are the forms that globalization takes and thus, it suggests, globalization should itself be condemned out of hand.[36]

From a different perspective, however, Garland's criticisms look less sustainable. Central to his vision is the idea of dilution. The problem, as he sees it, is that Thailand is neither sufficiently Thai, nor sufficiently Western. The tapes are not real, for example, but shady bootlegs. The implication is that the Khao San Road represents an ersatz form of culture, one that lacks the putative reality offered by either the West or a remote island wilderness. Globalization is, it seems, destroying these apparently authentic experiences. The problem with this position, however, is that the desire to separate Thailand from England, the real from the 'bootleg', reveals a yearning for a world in which older orders are preserved. The implication is that in condemning this 'halfway house' there is a sense that Richard does not simply want to maintain the cultural distinctions between the countries, but to prevent Thailand becoming like Europe in ways that might make it *equal*. Not only should Thailand be prevented from bootlegging the West, it should, by implication, be kept in a state that preserves the economic differentials that continue to provide Western tourists with the authentic (and discounted) experiences they cherish. Richard's critique of globalization is thus tied to an enthusiasm for older geopolitical structures. In criticizing the Khao San Road's globalized culture in these terms, he thus implicitly attacks the sustenance globalization provides for entrepreneurial cultures, cultures with the power to 'bootleg' hegemonic structures and replace economic and social division with a 'halfway-house'. The result is an expression of an imperialist fantasy, one that condemns development and looks to keep Thailand in its place.

The imperial dimensions of Garland's novel are underscored by the absence of any exploration of Thailand's social or historical context in *The Beach*. There is, for example, no engagement with the economic realities that create the conditions so conducive to Western backpackers or any discussion of the sex tourism around which significant parts of the Thai tourist economy depend. Thailand is not it seems, a real country, but a place that only exists to provide Garland with an exotic background and a source of metaphors for an escapist fantasy. The result is that the Thai ends up representing, in terms almost too predictable to recount, a mysterious other against which Richard and the rest of the beach community define themselves. The travellers inhabit the white sand on the beach, while the island's interior is controlled by mysterious and dangerous oriental forces. Known by their 'sing-song chatter', they are seen as part of the 'jungle, a quarry, a threat, the hidden presence of AK-47s and slanted eyes'.[37] As Richard's glimpse of 'a flash of brown through the leaves' suggests, it is only the exotic colouration of their skin that sets them apart from the wilderness.[38] The fact that Garland's characters prefer to steal grass from the marijuana farmers instead of purchasing it adds emphasis to this sense of the colonial dimensions of their project. Keaty might be aware that 'this place . . . it isn't really Thailand, considering there are no Thais . . .', but his thoughts do not develop into anything more than a casual aside.[39]

Latent in Garland's novels, these tendencies are even more obviously apparent in William Vollmann's *Butterfly Stories* (1993), a novel about the sexual adventures of a young American journalist in Thailand and Cambodia. Haunting the brothels and strip bars that are so conspicuously absent from Garland's vision of Thailand, the journalist (known in his youth as the Butterfly Boy), is presented by Vollmann as an individual engaging in 'that more honest kind of love called prostitution'.[40] In these terms, sex tourism forms part of what the novel represents as a process of self-discovery and offers the journalist a chance to reinterpret himself and his own experiences as a bullied and isolated child. The problem with his behaviour, however, is that it reproduces the processes of coercion and exploitation that plagued his young life. Seeing Thailand and Cambodia as a backdrop for his own journey of self-discovery and indifferent to the impact his actions may have on the women he pays for sex, *Butterfly Stories* does not simply mirror *The Beach*'s blindness to local culture, but demonstrates a more conscious contempt for it. In one scene, for example, he describes a prostitute as 'corpselike' and goes on to say, 'They [in this case the Cambodians] did not seem to admire whores or foreigners who whored. But of course there was not a damned thing they could do about it.'[41] Content to reify the bodies of local women and satisfied that his behaviour can structure local culture in terms that satisfy his own needs, the journalist thus embodies old imperialist traditions. Vollmann's conscious focus on the aesthetic and existential dimensions of his traveller's experiences, are thus developed in terms that seem grimly unconcerned about the ways in which they exoticize the Orient and reproduce long-standing inequalities around ethnicity, nationality and gender.

Michel Houellebecq's novel *Platform* (2002) also explores these themes, though in terms that can be differentiated in significant ways from the approach offered by Vollmann. For Houellebecq's protagonist, sexual tourism is a clear sign of the degeneracy and corruption of contemporary Western culture. His inability to resist Thai prostitutes and his willingness to participate in the establishment of an international hotel chain catering to the desires of the sex tourist thus offers both a statement of his own emptiness and, in Houellebecq's wider metaphorical scheme, an image of the West's exploitation of developing nations. In terms that are more knowing and critical than those offered by Vollmann, Houellebecq writes:

> As a wealthy European, I could obtain food and the services of women more cheaply in other countries; as a decadent European, conscious of my own approaching death. And given over entirely to selfishness, I could see no reason to deprive myself of such things. I was aware, however, that such a situation was barely tenable, that people like me were incapable of ensuring the survival of a society, and perhaps more simply were unworthy of life.[42]

Seeing sexual tourism as the sign of a decadent and exploitative society, Houellebecq's novel seems to recognize the exploitation involved in transactions of this kind and acknowledges that this business depends upon and reinforces a form of neo-slavery. With its apocalyptic conclusion, the result is a curious novel that, following on from the weary portrait of dissipation offered in *Atomised* (2000), constructs a lurid and often celebratory portrait of pleasure while acknowledging the limits, costs and consequences of that hedonism.

Unlike the indifference to local inhabitants that characterizes Vollman's fiction, or the almost total absence of any engagement with indigenous culture from *The Beach*, *Platform* does attempt to develop an understanding of the social and economic context in

Fictions of Globalization

which the events it describes take place. Though gloomy and at times confused, the suggestion is that reading *Platform*'s attempts to link its action to the wider conditions of globalization offers an illuminating contrast to *The Beach*. The fact that Houellebecq's protagonist offers a brief précis of Garland's novel, a story he claims to 'vaguely' remember, only serves to strengthen this comparison.[43] The point is that for all of these novelists (and for a whole host of other contemporary writers of travel fiction), their portraits of travelling can be read in terms that offer key insights into the relationships between different national cultures, the patterns and processes of international consumerism and the relationships between globalization, ethnicity and identity.

These broader points can be used to develop a more precise focus on *The Beach*'s portrait of an all-conquering global culture. Onto the suggestion that *The Beach*'s account of globalization is rooted in a presentist reading of contemporary conditions can be added both the realization that Garland's vision of globalization is narrow, incomplete and reliant on cliche and the understanding that the text tends to privilege older structures linked to imperialism. In this respect *The Beach*'s vision of all-colonizing global forces of homogenization needs to be regarded as an incomplete version of globalization, one that closes off the fluid and transformative possibilities created by global flows of capital and culture. It is true that globalization can be linked to 'McDonaldization' and the standardization of culture, but to see McDonaldization as the *only* possible outcome of development is a mistake.[44] As Kevin Meethan suggests in *Tourism in a Global Society* (2001), while

> It may be tempting to see the internationalization or globalization of tourism as the inevitable spread of modernity, of similarity and homogeneity . . . such approaches are little more that implicit criticisms of mass culture.[45]

In this light the beach community's response to globalization begins to look increasingly flawed and misguided. Conjuring a vision of globalization in terms of cultural 'doomsday' and echoing the apocalyptic tone that, as earlier chapters of this discussion have suggested, characterizes so many accounts of globalization, the text short circuits critique and stymies resistance. It is only by taking a step outside the frames of reference constructed by the novel and considering the foundations of its vision of globalization that a more critical engagement with these issues can be found.

Understanding the novel's limitations thus provides a way of mapping a response to the co-opting conditions feared by Garland's characters, one that can be supported by reflecting on the arguments offered by Michael Hardt and Antonio Negri in *Empire* (2000). Hardt and Negri's discussions centre on the belief that contemporary experience involves a conflict between forces looking to develop power blocks based on older models of imperial control and the more decentered social and economic networks that can emerge and flourish in the age of globalization. Favouring the later, they see globalization as offering both cause and cure. At the core of their argument is the insistence that the task is 'not simply to resist these processes but to reorganize them and redirect them towards new ends. The creative forces of the multitude that sustain Empire are also capable of constructing . . . an alternative political organization of global flows and exchanges.'[46] Refusing to see globalization as a homogeneous entity, their work suggests that it is possible to criticize the colonizing power of new forms of what they call 'empire' (forces reproduced by the corporation and corporate influenced governments) through a developing sense of the counterpowers contained within those same global movements. As Alexander Stille's review of *Empire* makes clear, 'For Negri and Hardt, the worldwide circulation of goods and services through international trade is a much more open system', one in which, in Hardt and Negri's words, the 'multitude' has opportunities to constitute itself as an 'active subject'.[47] In these terms, it is a mistake to see globalization as a closed system, one to be resisted from the outside, for as Hardt and Negri suggest, it is only those groups that find a place within this system and struggle to take some ownership over the diffuse networks of global power that can hope to shape their own destinies.

The problem faced by the beach community described in Garland's novel is that they see globalization as an apocalyptic force over which they have no control. Adopting this position limits their understanding of the relationships and responsibilities that tie them both to local culture and to the global market. The result is a novel that condemns globalization without ever making an attempt fully to understand it. The ultimate concern is that while the characters seem motivated by a desire to resist the encroachments of capitalism, the strategies they pursue seem to stifle dissent and limit critical understanding in ways that lead ultimately to a strengthening of the forces they were originally seeking to resist. Their desire to escape sees them not only fostering further development, but behaving in ways that reproduce the attitudes of the colonialist.

Criticizing the beach-dwellers in these terms should not, however, foster an outright condemnation of Garland's novel. True, his work can be criticized for failing to contextualize his portrait of Thailand, for seeing race as a sign of difference and for presenting his vision of globalization as an unquestioned reality, but a line has to be drawn between the attitudes of the characters in the novel and the perspectives offered by the text itself. Though Richard's first-person narration tends to collapse the distinction between author and character, a critical friction clearly exists between the two. These tensions emerge most strongly towards the end of the novel, the part of the text in which Garland's concerns about the nature of the community he has described become most clearly apparent. Not only does Garland explore the folly of their dreams of romantic separation through his account of the violent intervention of the drug traffickers, but he also forces the reader to reflect on the morality of the beach-dwellers' isolationism. It is the decision to preserve the secrecy of their beach instead of seeking medical attention for the injured Swedes that raises the most significant questions about the status of the community. The fact that the novel then describes Richard committing a morally suspect mercy-killing on the dying Christo underlines not only the growing distance between Garland and his characters, but the hardening of the novel's condemnatory attitude towards the beach dwellers. In the end *The Beach* makes it very clear that the community it describes has failed.

Though marked by this critical edge, the problem with Garland's vision is that while he develops a powerful account of the problems with both the cultures of globalization and the isolationist ideals of his beach community, he seems unable to offer any kind alternative position. Richard flees the beach aware that 'the world is a small place', but with no sense of having any more refined understanding of his situation or insight into his experiences.[48] The implication is that Garland does an effective job of framing the problems, but offers less in the way of solutions. The novel's portrait of the quest for the mythical beach establishes a potent image of the contradictory desires that motivate contemporary travel and fosters a wider understanding of backpack culture's links with the market, but seems less able to generate a critical perspective on the globalization debate itself.

There is, however, one area of *The Beach* in which a more complex response to the forces of global capital seems to emerge – the novel's language. Instead of creating a textual island insulated from the ebb and flow of the market from which to launch his exploration into the culture of globalization, Garland develops his position in a text steeped in images and languages drawn from within commercial and popular culture. Patterned with references to Hollywood movies, cartoons, American TV shows (*The Waltons* for example) and video games (*Tetris* in particular), *The Beach* remains firmly located inside contemporary culture and speaks the international language of brands. Richard's thoughts also take on this quality and remain coloured by the patterns of popular culture throughout. Evidenced in the names of characters (Bugs and Daffy) and in the chapter titles ('FNG', 'KIA' and 'Game Over'), the novel wears its associations with mass culture in obvious ways. Even the fabric of Richard's thoughts seems to take on this quality and remain coloured by references to video games, Vietnam movies and popular music (particularly Rose Royce's 'Street Life') throughout.[49] The incorporation of these languages is not, however, a sign of the text's passive reflection of the power of the market, but evidence of an engagement with consumerism in terms that offer a sense that the meanings of these corporatized symbols can be bootlegged and remobilized. Shadowing Hardt and Negri's discussion of the ways in which globalization's decentred networks of economic and social power can be used to foster a critical openness and agency, Garland's language sees possibilities for creative articulation within the supposedly incorporated terrains of contemporary culture. Language in *The Beach* thus operates as a kind of 'biopower', a structure that nurtures a circulation of ideas and significations that both shadow and resist the 'hybrid modulating terrains' of empire.[50]

The language used in *The Beach* thus illustrates the ways in which contemporary fiction can engage with an incorporated culture and open up ways of knowing, interrogating and understanding globalization from within. Crucially, these approaches emerge not from an aesthetic that attempts to remain separate *from* the market, but through processes of interaction *with* the market. Though the content of the text turns upon a binary structure that appeals to a strict separation between nature and the market, the novel's style, in terms that echo the approaches adopted by writers like Ellis, Palahniuk, Bushnell and moments in DeLillo, reveals a much more complex sense of the relationships that connect contemporary culture with global capital. Instead of simply exposing the problems raised by idealistic attempts to reject globalization, this reading identifies a trajectory within Garland's work that offers a strategy capable of connecting with the diffuse and mobile networks that characterize global capitalism.

The Beach's style thus offers a solution to some of the dilemmas raised in the novel's content and gestures towards the existence of creative dynamics that will not only survive processes of incorporation but will also draw nourishment and strength from those same processes. The point is that these elements are both central to the novel and significant in terms of the implications they raise for the interpretation of the relationships between culture and capital. Reflecting on the significance of Garland's language and recognizing the connections that tie it with the ideas raised by Hardt and Negri thus provides a way of reading the novel in terms that reach beyond the limits of this particular chapter, and connect with the wider contours of developing debates around aesthetics, culture and globalization. It is this sense of the ways in which the text prompts an examination of these broader issues that stands as the most significant feature of Garland's *The Beach*. In simple terms, the very fact that the themes explored seem common to so many contemporary travel narratives is significant in itself. Readily comparable not only to the work of Europeans like Michel Houellebecq, Emily Barr and William Sutcliffe and to Americans like Kem Nunn and William Vollmann, it is worth, as a brief concluding thought, reflecting on the ways in which Garland's interests coincide with those articulated in the fiction of Dave Eggers.

Dave Eggers

In some respects it is Eggers's novel *You Shall Know Our Velocity* (2002) that seems to promise the most fruitful point of comparison with *The Beach*.[51] *You Shall Know Our Velocity*'s tale of two friends, Will and Hand, who embark on a haphazard tour of the globe in an attempt to overcome their grief at the loss of a friend and as part of a wider philanthropic desire to dispose of some of the $80,000 Will has earned through an appearance in an advertisement, establishes a range of perspectives on international travel, consumer culture and the economic inequalities that divide the world. Prompted by a need to calm the anxieties Will feels at having earned such a large sum of money in such a facile way, the novel's account of the attempt to distribute his ill-gotten-gains in developing societies inverts the usual economic relationships between tourist and host and generates a whole range of insights into travel, consumption and the guilty affluence of wealthy westerners. These themes are echoed in 'We can't fix anything, even the smallest things, in Cuba', a story that offers a precise insight into the kinds of concerns that inform Eggers's reading of the relationships between travel, consumption and globalization.

The first significant point about this story is that it features in a collection published by the Lonely Planet. Proliferating beyond travel guides and looking for a wider diffusion of their brand, the Lonely Planet have published an increasingly wide range of titles including a number of collections of stories about travelling. Titles like *Brief Encounters: Stories of Love Sex and Travel* (1998), *Drive Thru America* (1998) and *The Kindness of Strangers* (2003), from which Eggers's story comes, all offer tales of escape and adventure. 'We can't fix anything, even the smallest things, in Cuba', is, however, in terms that seem to rub against the romantic ethos of the Lonely Planet imprint, a rather downbeat tale of the economic realities upon which tourism depends.

Set in Havana, the story describes how the narrator and his companion make the acquaintance of a Cuban couple and find themselves invited to their home for dinner. Almost immediately Eggers's narrator starts to point the reader towards the economic disparities that divide the Americans from the Cubans. He writes:

> The thing that all travellers at first find shocking when invited into such homes. . . is the lack of *things*. This couple was about 30 years old, and their son 7, and yet they had accumulated almost no *things*. There were no books, no magazines . . . no baubles, no tapes or records or CDs, only one small picture on the wall, of I can't remember what.[52]

Having offered money to help defray the costs of the meal and had the sum of $20 accepted, the interactions between the Americans and their hosts seem to become increasingly complicated and guilty. Instead of clarifying their relationship, the exchange of money seems to pollute it, and in the end Eggers's narrator and his travelling companion, concerned that they will be asked to provide more and more financial support, fail to keep their promise to visit the couple again. For the narrator this behaviour is the product of the 'hive of guilt' that this encounter prompts, a guilt that he views in an unsparing light.[53] Looking back on these events, he concludes, 'Our responsibility towards them was actually not muddled at all, but all too clear. As humans with means – our connecting flight from Cancun to Havana cost more than Vladimir would make in a year – we were morally obliged to share it with his family.'[54] His point is that while processes of globalization have brought cultural social, economic changes to the world, they have not produced a concomitant globalization of ethics and morality.

As vocal about the traveller's responsibilities as Garland's lotus-eaters are silent, Eggers offers an illuminating counterpoint to the ideas generated in *The Beach*. Foregrounding the economic realities and revealing the discontinuities that characterize experience across the globe, Eggers does not see a world in which difference is removed by the spread of a homogenizing global consumer culture, but one in which inequalities are reinscribed. Though sharing a thematic interest in travel that links his work with Nunn, Vollmann, Houellebecq, Garland and the many other contemporary novelists writing about international travel, Eggers's work raises important ethical questions that are often overlooked in these other texts. Focusing explicitly on the absence of things from the home of the Cuban couple and the ways in which the economic inequalities problematize ordinary relationships, this story, like *You Shall Know Our Velocity*, thus connects travel with globalizing consumer culture in terms that raise awkward implications. The chapter that follows looks to extend these concerns by discussing the representation of migration in contemporary fiction and developing and expanding these thoughts on the relationships that link ethnicity and postcolonial identities to the debate around globalization, consumption and the market.

6
Migrating Globalization

The title story of Jhumpa Lahiri's Pulitzer Prize-winning collection *Interpreter of Maladies* (1999) inverts the expectations that surround the kinds of travel narratives offered by writers like Garland, Nunn and Vollmann. Describing an encounter between Mr Kapasi, a travel guide, and the Das family from New Jersey as he drives them from Puri by the Bay of Bengal to the Sun Temple at Konarak, the story focuses on the interaction between a Bengali man and an American family of Indian descent. Seen largely from Mr Kapasi's perspective, 'Interpreter of Maladies' portrays the Das family as representatives of a spoiled and desensitized culture. Chewing gum and photographing the poor, Mina and Raj Das are touring India with their three brattish children and coming across a world that remains remote and alien to them. Lahiri's point is, it seems, a simple one. Rejecting any sense of a national identity conceived in terms of essence, the story shows that despite their origins, the Das family do not have any unique or privileged insight into Indian culture. Mr Kapasi has no more in common with them than he does with any of the other Western tourists who contract his services, a point Lahiri makes explicit when she writes: 'The family looked Indian but dressed as foreigners did ... When he'd introduced himself, Mr Kapasi had pressed his palms together in greeting, but Mr Das squeezed hands like an American so that Mr Kapasi felt it in his elbow.'[1] The result is that Lahiri's portrait of the encounter between Mr Kapasi and the Das family opens up an analysis of divisions based not upon race, but upon culture. Exploring the complexity of the migrant experience, the story thus balances a vision of the opportunities available to Indians who take up residence in America against questions about the social consequences of migration. These questions come to the fore when Mrs Das tells Mr Kapasi that her son Bobby was conceived after a brief affair with a friend of her husband's.

Discovering that, in addition to his work as a tour guide, Mr Kapasi is also employed to translate for Gujurati patients by a local doctor, Mrs Das begins to imagine something 'noble in interpreting people's maladies'.[2] Calling his work 'romantic', she starts to see Mr Kapasi as a kind of healer and counsellor, a man who is able to make sense of the suffering he encounters.[3] Mr Kapasi responds to her interest in his work by fantasizing about forging an equally romantic relationship with Mrs Das. These daydreams come to an end, however, when Mrs Das, left alone in the car with Mr Kapasi as her husband and children explore the hills at Udayagiri and Khandagiri and imagining that he will be able to offer her solace, tells Mr Kapasi the story of her infidelity. His response is not, however, what she had hoped for. Reflecting upon what he sees as her 'common, trivial little secret', he asks, 'Is it pain you feel . . . or guilt?', a question that reveals his censorious attitude towards her and instantly re-establishes the divisions between them.[4] Offended by his response, Mrs Das gets out of the car and rejoins her family, a gesture that makes it clear to Mr Kapasi that he 'was not even important enough to be properly insulted'.[5] Abandoning the pretence of equality, Mrs Das becomes once more an American and dismisses her Indian interlocutor. 'Interpreter of maladies' thus ends by reinscribing the differences that divide Mr Kapasi from his American clients. Lahiri's final scene makes this point explicit. Mr Kapasi, once more the native guide, is called upon to protect Bobby Das from a troop of aggressive monkeys while Mrs Das falls back into the role of the spoilt American, exclaiming 'Let's get out of here . . . This place gives me the creeps'.[6]

In these terms the story seems to gesture towards the existence of irreconcilable differences between not only India and America, but also, by implication, Western and developing societies. Though united by ancestry and sharing a brief moment of equality, the clash between Mr Kapasi and Mrs Das signals the presence of enduring differences rooted in both social and economic contrasts. 'Interpreter of maladies' thus seems to suggest that though the forces of globalization have spread people of Indian descent across the globe and created a situation where they can return to India as fully Westernized tourists, the result is not a more homogenized world. The lives lived by both Mr and Mrs Das and Mr Kapasi can be explained in relation to the economic and social forces of globalization, but those experiences are not connected, in Lahiri's story, with the creation of a world characterized by greater degrees of unity and sameness. Indeed, Mr Kapasi's experiences with Mrs Das seem to suggest that the planet is not, as Garland's characters fear in *The Beach*, becoming ever smaller and more similar, but remains a place in which local contrasts and differences are still key determinants. Migration, in Lahiri's terms, seems to draw out differences between cultures as much it establishes interconnections. Such a position needs to be qualified, however, by an understanding of the ways in which the story looks to establish a sense of the similarities that unite America with India.

The focus for this suggestion is Mr Kapasi's role as a translator. Presented as man who is able to make sense of India's polyglot culture (he knows Hindi, Bengali, Orissi and Gujarati), and speak a range of European languages (he has learnt English, French, Russian, Portuguese and Italian), he is able to synthesize and organize not only the different languages of the world, but by implication, the different cultures. Though he has drawn some of his knowledge of American culture from watching *Dallas*, he can still participate in processes of cultural exchange and as a result acts as an agent for forms of, using Giddens's term, dedifferentiation.

The kind of dedifferentiation articulated in 'Interpreter of maladies' is more strongly apparent in other stories from the same collection. In 'A temporary matter', for example, Shoba and Shukumar, a Boston couple of Indian descent, experience a week of power cuts, a situation that leads Shoba to observe, 'It's like India'.[7] Lahiri's story 'When Mr Prizada came to dine' makes a similar point when it compares the struggle for Bengali independence to the American Revolution. Lilia, the young narrator, describes the regular visits of Mr Prizada, a fellow Bengali, to her parents' New England home, and tells of their nights by the TV 'anticipating the birth of a nation on the other side of the world'.[8]

Throughout this time, in one of the many portentous parallels that characterize Lahiri's writing, Lilia explains that she is studying the War of Independence at school and learning of the colonial battles with the 'redcoats'.⁹ Equating the birth of one nation with the other and drawing links between the postcolonial status of the United States, Bangladesh, India and Pakistan, the story thus looks to establish a sense of the similarities that connect South Asia with America. In this regard, a homogenizing dynamic can be detected in Lahiri's writing, an energy aimed at synthesizing and assimilating these contrasting experiences. The most powerful sign of this dynamic can be found in an examination of Lahiri's use of language.

Debates about the use of English have had an important bearing on the development of the study of colonial, post-colonial and migrant literatures. Salman Rushdie's introduction to *The Vintage Book of Indian Writing 1947–1997* (1997), for example, contains the famous (and famously self-serving) observation that:

> The prose writing – both fiction and non-fiction created in this period by Indian writers *working in English* – is proving to be a stronger and more important body of work than most of what has been produced in the 16 'official languages' of India, the so-called 'vernacular languages' during the same time; and, indeed, this new, and still burgeoning, 'Indo-Anglian' literature represents the most valuable contribution India has yet made to the world of books.¹⁰

Though he argues for the superiority of this type of writing, it is interesting that Rushdie seems reluctant to try to explain it. Perhaps wary of fleshing out the links that would connect his ideas of a 'stronger and more important' literary tradition to a culture with imperial origins that would also see itself as 'stronger and more important', Rushdie simply gestures towards a loose sense that the form of English written by writers of South Asian origin is more exciting and exuberant, suggesting that 'in England at least, British-writers are often chastised for their lack of Indian-style ambition and verve' and goes on to note that 'it feels as if the East is imposing itself on the West, rather than the other way round.'¹¹ Reading Rushdie's 'Imaginary homelands' and noting his determination to celebrate 'the freedom of the literary migrant to be able to chose his parents' offers a further insight into these claims and implies that he is shadowing Homi Bhabha's sense that the migrant's hybridized double-vision is able to provide the most acute and insightful perspective on the modern world.[12] Suggesting that the merging of Indian themes and sensibilities with the English language produces richer and more interesting texts, Rushdie is clearly favouring a vision of a culture invigorated by the hybrid forms created by migration.

The problem with this argument, however, is that it gestures towards some kind of universalized sense of identity and privileges processes of cross-pollination that are implicitly aligned with the patterns of globalization. Transcending the national and regional identities linked with India's 'official languages', this is an internationalized language, one that can be read across the globe. The concern is, however, that these texts can only be consumed by those who read English, a group that, though large, is inevitably shaped in terms that reflect levels of educational (and by implication economic) opportunity. Segregated off from those who cannot speak the language, literature of this kind begins to reflect some of the problems with a globalized version of culture as a whole. As Anthony Smith's 'Towards a global culture' suggests:

> Unlike national culture, a global culture is essentially memoryless. Where the 'nation' can be constructed so as to draw upon and revive latent popular experiences and needs, a 'global culture' answers to no living needs, no identity-in-the-making. It has to be painfully put together, artificially, out of many existing folk and national identities into which humanity has been so long divided.[13]

Hybridized, post-national notions of identity and language are thus problematic. This is a position that is refined in Hardt and Negri's discussion of the implications raised by Bhabha's reading of hybridity in *Empire* (2000).

Though they recognize the power of Bhabha's attack on 'the dialectics of modern sovereignty and the proposition of liberation as a politics of difference', Hardt and Negri raise questions about the extent to which this emphasis on hybridity depends upon the binaries it sets out to interrogate.[14] Remaining 'fixated on attacking an old form of power and . . . [proposing] a strategy of liberation that could be effective only on that old terrain', the result is a 'very confused view' that seems to provide an inappropriate response to a world in which the stable structures of imperial power are on the wane.[15] Offering hybridity as a form of resistance in a world in which the structures of power are characterized by their ability to hybridize and their penchant for border crossing is thus problematic and Hardt and Negri conclude that though post-colonial theories of this kind make 'a very productive tool for rereading history' they are 'entirely insufficient for theorizing contemporary global power.'[16]

A similar concern is raised by Frederick Buell when he discusses what he calls the 'limits of post-colonial power' and argues that:

> In detotalizing and heterogenizing the identities of both colonized and colonist, in seeing both positions as constructions of a common, complexly interacting system, and in joining First World self-critique to Third World critique of First World knowledge, post-colonialism has poised itself on the brink of metamorphosis. Anti-colonialism has almost shifted into interactivity; oppositional analyses have almost shifted in analyses of mutuality; and corrosive deconstruction has nearly become polyglossic conversation.[17]

When diasporic notions of identity become the norm rather than a critically suggestive exception and when debates about hybridity can merge with loose conceptions of the 'global soul', questions about the critical force of such arguments are hard to overlook.[18]

Culture, as many of these contemporary accounts make clear, is the product of a global relationship between peoples, languages, societies and markets, and as a result it is hard to argue that hybridity and plurality can be conceived as the touchstone for the critical analysis of these relations. Globalization does not simply efface difference, it also produces it and as such difference and hybridity can no longer be conceived as straightforwardly oppositional positions. Whether these approaches ever offered a focus for dissent seems itself highly questionable. With hybridization such a central part of many colonial projects, particularly in India, it is difficult to see the ways in which hybridity could ever have been used as a way of developing wider questions about the polyglot and contradictory discourses produced in the service of colonialism. Just as arguments linked to cultural imperialism work on a problematic distinction between a strong cogent culture that imperializes and a weak, passive culture open to subjugation, positions that celebrate hybridity thus raise a range of awkward implications. The conclusion is that the attempt to set jeremiads against imperialism and homogenization alongside celebrations of liberating boundary-crossing simply creates a new kind of binary, one that promises to provide evidence of a resistance to power at the same time as it illustrates that power's irresistibility.[19]

Of even greater concern is the possibility that hybridized, transnational visions of self and culture ultimately accommodate and facilitate the hybridizing and internationalizing processes of contemporary capitalism. As Aijaz Ahmad points out, 'When cultural criticism reaches this point of convergence with the universal market . . . it becomes indistinguishable from commodity fetishism.'[20] Graham Huggan's *The Postcolonial Exotic* (2001) extends these ideas into a wider investigation into 'the varying degrees of complicity between local oppositional discourses and the global late-capitalist system in which these discourses circulate and are contained.'[21]

The way forward clearly lies in an argument that, instead of looking to counter Garland's fear of the bootleg with a celebration of hybridity, sets out to interpret cultures and cultural products as the expression of a mixing and merging of traditions, identities, powers and discourses. India, like other developing countries, is not the victim of modernity, but a key (though often subordinate) participant in its processes. The conclusion is that Indo-Anglian/Indo-American literature needs to be read in terms that remain sensitive to the complexities of its particular situation within the network of global relations. Such a position ultimately involves rejection of the 'binary logic that establishes the perpetual dialectic of subordinate reply and reaction to power and hegemony' and provides a way of moving beyond limiting discourses in which, as Iain Chambers explains, 'subordinate subjects have invariably been ordained to the stereotypical immobilization of an essential "authenticity" in which they are expected to play roles designated for them by others . . . for ever.'[22] These ideas have an even more precise relevance to this discussion of the ways in which colonial, post-colonial and migrant literatures represent globalization, because, as Fredric Jameson (1998) suggests, 'the speaking of English is the key to the global process', a process which both depends upon and is facilitated by linguistic homogenization.[23] Arguments about the extent to which this process either reflects or reproduces the patterns of global coordination are thus crucial to any understanding of English in this context.

Discussed at length in David Crystal's book, *English as a Global Language* (1997), one perspective suggests that English in its current incarnation has been stripped of its cultural and ideological resonances and is being taught not as part of a wider project aimed at facilitating assimilation into the English (or American) world view (in ways that echo the kinds of processes conceived by Thomas Macauley), but as a culturally neutral form of communications technology.[24] Freed from imperial connotations, this argument suggests, these versions of English are postnational and belong to no one. Its rise to prominence as the world's second language of choice is thus explained as the expression of a natural demand on the part of consumers for what is the most effective (or most useful) linguistic tool available to them.[25]

Such arguments seem problematic on a number of different counts. The first is that they conceive English as a post-historical language, one that has stepped beyond debates linked to social, national and imperial concerns, *and* conveniently forget about the processes of colonialism and cultural imperialism that laid the foundations for English's emergence as a global language in the first place. The second is that in conceiving English as a technology and foregrounding a reading of language as a straightforward medium for communications, it assumes that technologies are themselves outside the ordinary ebb and flow of history, an argument that as the reading of the Internet in earlier parts of this discussion has shown, has to be treated sceptically. The third problem is that in choosing to locate the explanation for the emergence of English as a global language in relation to an apparently natural consumer demand, it presumes that such demands are in themselves spontaneous and neither conditioned nor shaped by cultural and material processes. Claiming that English is post-historical and maintaining at the same time that it is a kind of consumer orientated technology thus appears oxymoronic. The process of identifying its relationship to technologies and consumption seems to insist upon a wider understanding of English's links to global social and economic realities. The conclusion is, as Martin Kayman suggests, that, 'what is being packaged as "Global English" is, in sum ... a utopia of communication in which "English" becomes the very image of a desire for global networks where informational and symbolic messages flow without resistance across frontiers.'[26]

Kayman's argument is careful, however, to avoid any easy suggestion that to speak English is simply to affirm the hegemony of Western power or to mimic and replicate the processes of imperialism and globalization. Aware that such a perspective is insulting to the many speakers of English (including writers as different as Rushdie and Ahmad) who use the language to create different kinds of oppositional discourses, he insists on an understanding of the emergence of English as a global language that retains a sense of the complexity of its origins, effects and meanings. Failure to address this range of forces is his main cause for concern, a concern that can be focused back upon this discussion of contemporary fiction by reflecting upon Amitava Kumari's insistence that Indian writing in English be read as 'neither simply as symptom nor merely as critique.'[27] Clearly, like any technology, the political implications generated by its employment depend very obviously on the contexts in which it is used.

To see English as *either* liberatingly post-historical *or* uniquely burdened by the inheritance of imperialism is thus to miss the point. It may seem obvious to note that English is a multidimensional space *par excellence*, a linguistic terrain in which a whole host of forces cross and compete with each other simultaneously, but this commonplace observation serves a useful function in foregrounding an understanding of English as a language that simultaneously reflects the power and influence of the modern market even as it maintains the capacity to talk about that market in critical and antagonistic terms. When Stephen Greenblatt observes that 'the linguistic medium is no longer the King's English and, despite the power of the American mass media, has never been and can never be the President's English' and goes on the suggest that 'English literary history, like so many other great collective enterprises in our century, has ceased to be principally about the fate of the nation; it is a global phenomenon', he is identifying processes that seem to define and characterize global culture in the contemporary period.[28]

Though it is possible to argue (as earlier parts of this book have done) about the extent to which international brands have penetrated the consciousness of the globe's citizens and to debate the amount of power corporations wield in the contemporary period, there is no doubt that English is much more widely spoken now than it ever has been. Whether this linguistic convergence signals a wider process of cultural homogenization is, however, still open to debate. As Richard Alexander suggests, the use of English both facilitates processes of standardization and control and at the same time creates an ever-greater audience for dissenting voices.[29] The expansion of English will inevitably produce coordination and help coordinate resistance with the particular effect dependent upon, as is the case with all languages, the specific qualities of the accents used, a point that can be illustrated by returning to the work of Jhumpa Lahiri and considering the ways in which she uses English.

Lahiri's linguistic situation seems more straightforward than that of someone like Rushdie who spent his early years in India. Born in England of Bengali parents and educated in the United States, English seems like the obvious (and perhaps only) choice for Lahiri. What is interesting about the language she uses, however, is the ways in which it seems to echo with what is one of the dominant accents of contemporary American fiction. Concerned with small domestic events and using a stripped down, minimal style, Lahiri is not simply writing in English, she is speaking the language of the dirty realist, a Carverese diction that has its origins in Hemingway's laconic prose.[30] Where Rushdie can celebrate the hybridization of English by Indian writers, Lahiri's writing seems particularly American, wilfully resistant to the kind of exuberant flourishes that characterize Rushdie's own prose. Choosing the short story, the preferred vehicle for the dirty realist, and writing in this solidly American style, Lahiri explores the experiences of her migrating characters in terms that are thus marked by a distinctly American tone and mood.[31] Adopting what is clearly one of the Pulitzer Committee's favourite idioms (evidenced in the fact that Richard Ford, Richard Russo, Annie Proulx and Jane Smiley have all won the prize in recent years), Lahiri thus offers her tales of cultural transformation, hybridization and exile in this peculiarly American voice.

The underlying point is that this use of language cannot be interpreted in neutral terms, but has to be read in relation to a broader understanding of her connection with processes of Americanization and her sense of the hierarchies that organize the relationship between Boston and Bengal. Though the narratives of her stories explore the different polarities created by this relationship, her use of language implies that these complexities are structured in terms that are much more hierarchical than the themes developed in some of her stories suggest. This impression can be strengthened by considering the hymn to assimilation and American bounty that concludes the final piece in *Interpreter of Maladies*, a story called 'The third and final continent'.

Looking back on a life that has brought him from his hometown of Calcutta to London to study at the LSE and then to a position at MIT in Boston, the narrator tells a story not simply of migration and assimilation, but of social progress. As the title suggests, from the narrator's perspective, his experiences involve a journey up from India through England to America, a place conceived as the ultimate or 'final' destination. This impression is reinforced in the story's concluding paragraph, a passage that not only provides the last word on the meanings of this story, but also, standing as it does as the final section in the whole collection, emerges as what appears to be Lahiri's concluding statement on *Interpreter of Maladies* as a whole. Lahiri writes:

> Whenever he [the narrator's son] is discouraged, I tell him that if I can survive on three continents, then there is no obstacle he cannot conquer. While astronauts, heroes forever, spent mere hours on the moon, I have remained in this new world for nearly 30 years. I know that my achievement is quite ordinary. I am not the only man to seek his fortune far from home, and certainly not the first. Still there are times when I am bewildered by each mile I have travelled, each meal I have eaten, each person I have known, each room in which I have slept. As ordinary as it all appears, there are times when it is beyond my imagination.[32]

Conflating his journey with those of American heroes like the astronauts and other pioneers, the narrator thus links his destiny to the 'ordinary', but epic achievements of America. This is the continent that has transformed and amazed him and enabled him to reach this final state. It is America, not London or Calcutta, that has prompted this declaration of otherworldly wonder. Like a space traveller who has left the terrains of ordinary history behind, he is now, in the story's terms, a fully assimilated resident of an exceptional and post-historical society.[33]

These are highly problematic views, ideas that do not simply reflect a certain vision of America and its place in the world system, but actually work to reproduce it. The crucial point, and one that informs the analysis of many of the representations of globalization covered in this discussion as a whole, is that, as Arjun Appadurai makes clear, the processes of globalization are linked to patterns of cultural and historical imagination. Appadurai writes:

> The image, the imagined, the imaginary – these are all terms that direct us to something critical and new in global cultural processes: the imagination as a social practice. No longer mere fantasy (opium for the masses whose real work is elsewhere), no longer simple escape (from a world defined principally by more concrete purposes and structures). No longer elite pastime (thus not relevant to the lives of ordinary people), and no longer mere contemplation (irrelevant for new forms of desire and subjectivity), the imagination has become an organized field of social practices, a form of work (in the sense of both labor and culturally organized practice), and a form of negotiation between sites of agency (individuals) and globally defined fields of possibility . . . the imagination is now central to all forms of agency, is itself a social fact and is the key component of the new global order.[34]

For Appadurai, the culture of globalization cannot simply be understood in relation to capital and the market, but needs to be interpreted in terms that take into account the contribution it makes to the operation and reproduction of power. Systems of cultural exchange and the symbolic capital of commodities and artworks are, in his terms, central components in the shaping and propagation of this 'new global order'. For Lahiri, the kinds of exchanges she imagines have an imperial complexion, one characterized by a hierarchical sense of America and American culture's privileged place in the world system. The concern is, as Appadurai suggests, that in an age in which the imagination plays such a key role in the shaping of the processes and patterns of globalization, her perspective inevitably contributes to the fashioning of a 'new global order' that begins to mirror the image of the world created in her fiction. If this point is sustainable in relation to a reading of Lahiri, then it may be even more applicable to the work of another writer of Bengali descent, Bharati Mukherjee. Where Lahiri offers what seem to be implicit celebrations of Americanness and the opportunities offered by migration from Bengal to the United States, Mukherjee's works provide a series of explicit commentaries on the benefits of America and American capitalism, commentaries that have attracted a considerable volume of critical attention.

Bharati Mukherjee

Throughout her career, Bharati Mukherjee has made a constant effort to portray herself as a successfully assimilated American. Born into a Bengali Brahmin family, she sees her journey from Calcutta, through Canada to the United States as a process of becoming. Presenting herself as a 'non-European pioneer' and making it very clear that she is 'not an economic refugee', Mukherjee states that she is determined to 'forge a national identity that is born of our acknowledgement of the steady de-Europeanization of the American population' and claims that her intention is to 'think of culture and nationhood not as an uneasy aggregate of antagonistic *them's* and *us's* . . . but as a constantly reforming, transmogrifying we.'[35] Mukherjee explains this approach by portraying herself as a woman who has always been in some senses a migrant and who conceives herself as the offspring of migrant and/or hybridized traditions. She writes:

> I was born into a class that did not live in its native language. I was born into a city that feared for its future, and trained me for emigration. I attended a school run by Irish nuns, who regarded our walled-off school in Calcutta as a corner . . . of England. My country – called Bengali desh, and suggesting a homeland rather than a nation of which one is a citizen – I have never seen. It is the ancestral home of my father and is now in Bangladesh.[36]

Exploring the complexities of ideas of belonging and problematizing the notion that migrant identity can be conceived in opposition to stable notions of place and identity, Mukherjee suggests that her experience is emblematic of the complex, shifting and unstable origins that characterize the lives of billions of the globe's inhabitants. Instead of seeing herself as an exception, one imbued with, as Rushdie would have it, a unique insight into the fabric of contemporary life, Mukherjee conceives herself as a typical example of a woman who lives in a world in which almost everyone can be defined in relation to a 'constantly reforming, transmogrifying we'.

This position has an important bearing on contemporary understandings of globalization, suggesting that Mukherjee's journey from Calcutta to the United States is not an exceptional experience, typical of a newly globalized world, but one continuous with the patterns of migration and translation that have, as she sees it, characterized life in India for at least 400 years. Mukherjee, like Lahiri, comes from a place characterized by shifting national borders and layered religious and linguistic traditions, a terrain that needs to be interpreted not in relation to contemporary patterns of global change, but withn regard to longstanding processes of cultural encounter. The point is that through these meditations on her own experiences, Mukherjee not only undermines the problematic assumptions that structure contrasts between migrants and natives, but weakens perspectives that read her life as emblematic of the displacements and patterns that are the particular features of contemporary processes of globalization.

Echoing her own perspectives, a number of critics have celebrated Mukherjee's position, praising her, as Jennifer Drake does, for her decision to reject 'the hyphen' and noting that 'her immigrant characters are settlers, *Americans*.'[37] In Drake's argument 'Mukherjee's stories do not simply promote American multiculture or celebrate assimilation, rather ... Mukherjee fabulizes America, Hinduizes assimilation and represents the real pleasures of cultural exchange.'[38] Such affirmative comment is, however, fairly rare and Mukherjee's work is usually read with a more critical eye. Concerned about her perceived assimilationism and the problematic attitude towards India articulated in her work, her novels have prompted some hostile comment. As Emmanuel Nelson's introduction to the essays collected in *Bharati Mukherjee: Critical Perspectives* explains, much of this debate springs from a discussion of Mukherjee's work at the Modern Language Association Convention in San Francisco in 1991, a panel session at which Mukherjee listened to critics like Anindyo Roy, Gurleen Grewel and Debjani Banerjee attack her work, and in particular *Jasmine* (1989), with the view that it universalizes the experiences it describes, condemns Indian history and celebrates American ideals.[39] Banerjee's sense that 'in *Jasmine*, the protagonist feels she can rip herself free of the past as she assimilates into American society', thus forms part of a wider critique of Mukherjee as a writer who seems willing to elide the 'deep contradictions built within the space of post-coloniality.'[40] The result is, as Gurleen Grewel suggests, that 'caught in the dialectic between the Third World and the First, between the past and the present, *Jasmine* does not attempt a resolution by a complex synthesis; it simply dissolves the claims of the past', in terms that lead to 'an insufficient confrontation with the historical circumstances of ethnicity in the United States.'[41]

Though powerful, these reservations are not without their problems, the first of which is their tendency to overlook some of the specific features of Mukherjee's writing and to ignore the ways in which her novels might work to create a greater degree of friction around the ideals of assimilation articulated by Mukherjee herself and the stories of social progress through migration lived out by her characters. These frictions are most readily detectable in *Jasmine*, a novel that Anthony Alessandrini suggests seems to defy the condemnatory positions adopted by Mukherjee's antagonists.[42] Praising the complexity of the novel, Alessandrini points towards the ways in which analysing the critical reception of Mukherjee's work opens up not just an understanding of the complexities of reading literature written by a migrant woman of Bengali descent through the politicized prism of the debate around post-colonial literatures, but more importantly, as far as this discussion is concerned, the ways in which this reception can be linked with a reading of the relationship between these novels and the contexts of globalization.

Many elements in *Jasmine* (1989) seem to affirm American culture and celebrate Jasmine's assimilation. Having left the 'mud hut' of her Punjabi home behind, and embarked on a journey to America that takes her ashore in Florida and through New York via Flushing to Iowa and finally California, Jasmine sees this journey as a sign that she has 'triumphed'.[43] Part of her understanding is rooted in her memories of India as a backward and static culture. 'Feudal compliance', Jasmine observes, 'was what still kept India an unhealthy and backward nation.'[44] Believing that her limited social expectations and the grim experiences of the sectarian violence that have left her a widow can be forgotten, she dreams that if she could 'just get away from India, then all fates would be cancelled.'[45] This perspective is most forcibly articulated in the metaphorical parallel that equates her decision, coming at the novel's conclusion, to leave Bud, her American partner, a man who has lost the use of his legs in a shooting, and head for California with her lost love Tyler, with her original desire to leave India. Claiming that, 'I am not choosing between men. I am caught between the promise of America and old-world dutifulness', she links her responsibility to the wheelchair-using Bud with the 'old world' of India, a parallel that implies India is a country suffering from a disability that she, a forward-thinking woman, has no time to care for.[46] In terms that reinforce the images of superstition, poverty and stagnation that characterize many of the images of India offered in the novel, this metaphor both condemns her former homeland and offers an implicit endorsement of America as a vigorous, healthy and able-bodied culture.

Connected with these ideas is a feeling, echoing Lahiri's sense of America as the 'third and final continent', that the United States represents an advanced state of social and economic development, the destination towards which all developing countries are headed. Stating that 'I see a way of life coming to an end' and talking of change as a kind of incurable and unstoppable 'virus', Mukherjee has Jasmine explain

> When I was a child, born in a mud hut without water or electricity, the Green Revolution had just struck Punjab. Bicycles were giving way to scooters and to cars, radios to television. I was the last to be born to that kind of submission, that expectation of ignorance. When the old astrologer swatted me under a banyan tree, we were both acting out the final hours of a social order that had gone untouched for thousands of years.[47]

In this respect, her journey to America is portrayed as a way of allowing her to accelerate processes of development that are just starting to transform Indian life. Her migration thus enables her to recognize the inevitable patterns of amelioration that will reshape social orders and bring an end India's stagnation. As Andrea Dlaska suggests, 'in Mukherjee's writing, immigrants who surrender their past and illusions about the present come to a profound understanding of the world and the shape of things to come.'[48]

Such a position does not, however, mean that Mukherjee can be protected against the charge of triumphalism and Dlaska is wrong to argue, as the discussion of the representation of Bud's disability demonstrates, that 'the much-invoked cultural rebirthing Mukherjee's critics have ... condemned as a validation of one culture over the other is not in evidence in the text.'[49] The ways in which *Jasmine* constructs a vision of America in millennial terms as the final destination of all societies must, as a result, be linked to a wider sense that the novel makes an equation between Americanization and globalization. In Mukherjee's fiction, processes that see the elision and erasure of regional and local differences are not only the inevitable consequence of and spur for economic modernization and the migrations that modernization inspires, but also are changes that should be welcomed and embraced.

Such a view is not, however, offered without qualification and it is in these moments that some of the novel's most interesting insights into globalization emerge. Linked with Mukherjee's vision of Jasmine's transformation is her sense that she is the child of migrants and the product of partition. Jasmine's mother, for example, explains that, 'God is cruel to partition the country ... to uproot our family from a city like Lahore where we had lived for centuries, and fling us to a village of flakey mud huts. In Lahore my parents had lived in a big stucco house with porticoes and gardens. They had owned farmlands, shops.'[50] This observation contradicts both the sense that India is a static culture and that economic opportunities are limited. Partition and the loss of family wealth reveal India's cultural and social dynamism and suggests not only that Jasmine is wrong to conceive herself as the emissary of some kind of new and final social condition, but also that her vision of India as an inferior society is based on an incomplete understanding of the histories of both her family and her country.

Related to these positions is Mukherjee's focus on the social significance of consumption and the importance she places on the relationship between choice and opportunity. Writing of her own experiences, for example, Mukherjee claims:

> In states such as New Jersey, malls have become the places of choice to meet for immigrant housewives with a sense of self. Driving to the mall is itself an empowering adventure ... And to keep those appointments in a consumer heaven like the Paramus Park Mall in Paramus, New Jersey, comes pretty close to bliss.[51]

Her implication is that America's plenty offers the migrant the possibility of renewal and provides a key emblem of their place in their new home. These ideas, carried forward in *Jasmine*'s repeated focus on the significance of consumer goods, particularly in the emphasis on radios and electronic equipment, offer a strongly affirmative statement on the significance of consumption. Expanding on the suggestion that scooters and cars are harbingers of the economic revolution that will sweep India from its social backwater, Mukherjee clearly sees a transformative potential in consumer goods. Becoming emblems of hope for Du, Prakash and Darrel (who dreams of a Radioshak franchise as an alternative to life as an Iowan pig framer), consumer goods become signs of both power and promise.

It is important to note, however, that the novel qualifies this affirmation with a series of much more anxious representations of consumerist plenty. Most obvious of these is the image of Jasmine's arrival on US soil, a scene that Mukherjee describes as follows:

> The first thing I saw were the two cones of a nuclear plant, and smoke spreading from them in complicated but seemingly purposeful patterns, edges lit by the rising sun, like a gray, intricate map of an unexplored island continent, against the pale unscratched blue of the sky. I waded through Eden's waste: plastic bottles, floating orange, boards, sodden boxes, white and green plastic sacks tied shut but picked open by birds and pulled apart by crabs.[52]

Though one doubts that it could be smoke that is rising from this nuclear power station (much more likely for it to be steam from a cooling tower), the apocalyptic feel of this passage is undeniable. Central to this scheme is the detritus of junk washing around America's shore, a detail that problematizes the perception of America as an Eden and qualifies the affirmative account of consumption offered in other parts of the text. Such an idea can be linked to a sense that in India consumer items have been turned against the citizenry and converted into bombs, one of which, planted in a radio, has killed Jasmine's husband.[53]

These qualifications to the sense that *Jasmine* offers a naive vision of the possibilities of assimilation through social and economic advancement can be linked to the novel's wider concern for the consequences of migration, consequences that Mukherjee's narrator describes as follows: 'There are no harmless, compassionate ways to remake oneself. We murder who we are so we can rebirth ourselves in the images of dreams.'[54] Signalling an awareness of the violence of the journey Jasmine has undertaken, this passage connects with the intertwined stories of Du and Half-Face, both veterans, in different ways, of the Vietnam War.[55] Representing a critical vision of imperialism and raising questions about American politics, these figures (and Jasmine's experiences at Half-Face's hands), complicate the novel's straightforwardly affirmative vision of America, migration, and globalization. This is the point that Fredrick Buell makes when he argues

> Mukherjee's appropriation of cosmopolitanism is not a return to Europe. It is complicated by the fact that, if it is a Third World appropriation of cosmopolitanism, it is also an intervention, in several ways, in her discourses of American nationalism. Most clearly Mukherjee uses her global cosmopolitanism as a means of transforming American attitudes towards immigrants and the conventions of immigrant literature.[56]

For Buell, Mukherjee remakes American culture as she is assimilated into it, a process that complicates the sense that she is simply rejecting one world in favour of another. The impression remains, however, that as Mita Banerjee explains in relation to readings of the work of Aijaz Ahmad, 'this refashioning of the self looms large in Mukherjee's fiction, where the surplus of choices is seen as the essence of the American dream, and where the ways in which this choice is limited for the resourceless remains untheorized.'[57] These ideas can be brought into much sharper focus by comparing Mukherjee with Arundhati Roy, a writer who offers a completely contrasting view of globalization.

Arundhati Roy

Having sold over 6,000,000 copies of her first novel, *The God of Small Things* (1997), seen it translated into more than 40 languages and established herself as a rival to Salman Rushdie as the most widely known novelist of Indian descent writing in English, Arundhati Roy has turned away from fiction and poured all of her energies into campaigning against the social, infrastructural and economic changes wrought on developing nations by the forces of international capital. Writing in *Power Politics* (2001), for example, Roy asks, 'Is globalization about "eradication of world poverty", or is it a mutant variety of colonialism, remote controlled and digitally operated?' and raises the hope that India will not be 'lobotomized into believing in one single idea, which is ultimately, what globalization really is: Life is Profit.'[58] In terms that contrast sharply with the assimilationism and market positivism of a writer like Mukherjee and align her more obviously with the polemical positions adopted by commentators like Naomi Klein, Roy pits herself against the interests of Western capital and offers an assault on the myths of progress coded into the dream of a single global market. Vigorously articulated and passionately felt, the essays in *Power Politics*, and her more recent collection *The Ordinary Person's Guide to Empire* (2004), offer a series of grim accounts of, in particular, the impact of dam-building on Indian life and, in more general terms, a vision of a society constantly injured and degraded by the interventions of international business.

The problem is, however, as the comparison with Naomi Klein suggests, that the essays included in these volumes offer very little sense that investment and technological development might also bring certain benefits to India. The 'green revolution', praised by Mukherjee, is thus forgotten in a series of essays in which India is seen to be continually exploited, denuded and deceived in its transactions with the West. Roy is absolutely right to cite Bhopal as an example of corporate atrocity and correct to highlight the folly and greed that underpin the dam-building projects in Madhya Pradesh and other parts of India, but questions remain about the ways in which her bleak vision of globalization depends upon a partial account of the influence of international capital in India and, as a result, her writing fosters a distorted understanding of the issues in hand. The feeling is that Roy is as problematically negative about globalization as someone like Mukherjee is naively affirmative.

Roy is, of course, alert to this charge and defends herself in interesting terms by noting, as part of her discussion of organizations formed to oppose dam-building, that:

> What will happen to them? Will they just go down in the ledgers as the 'price of progress'? That phrase cleverly frames the whole argument as

one between those who are pro-development versus those who are anti-development – and suggests the inevitability of the choice you have to make; pro-development, what else? It slyly suggests that movements like the NBA are antiquated and absurdly anti-electricity or anti-irrigation. This of course is nonsense.[59]

Making an effective job of unravelling some of the tensions around ideas like progress and development, Roy thus exposes the politically freighted nature of these seemingly neutral positions. The problem remains, however, that though she is very clear about the consequences of dam-building and aware that being opposed to such programmes does not mean she is either against change or 'anti-electricity', there is little sense of the ways in which her position could be converted into a strategy for a different kind of development. At the end of her 'power politics' essay, however, Roy does offer one of the few loosely programmatic statements to be found in her writing, a statement that reads:

> What we need to search for and find, what we need to hone and perfect into a magnificent shining thing is a new kind of politics. Not the politics of governance, but the politics of resistance. The politics of opposition. The politics of forcing accountability. The politics of slowing things down. The politics of joining hands across the world and preventing certain destruction. In the present circumstances, I'd say that the only thing worth globalizing is dissent. It's India's best export.[60]

Focusing on accountability and dissent and arguing for a form of global resistance conjured, one assumes, through the use of media and telecommunications technologies, this rallying call to internationalized protest is still long on rhetoric and short on detail.

Like the solutions offered in *No Logo* (Klein 1999), *The Ordinary Person's Guide to Empire* is shaded by an apocalyptic tone and organized around an idealized vision of a globalized community of dissenters. Exactly how this dissenting force would be applied or how this form of globalization could be untangled from other more corporatized parts of the same process is not, however, fully explained. The conclusion is that though Roy inverts the celebratory positions generated in *Jasmine*, she does so in terms that lock her into place alongside Mukherjee as a thinker who is only able to see globalization in polarized terms: affirmation or dissent; the global or the local; the hybridized, mobile, metropolitan self or the indigenous, static other. The result is a critical *impasse*, one that can only be resolved by thinking of these relationships not as binaries, but as interlinked multi-dimensional processes.

Contrasting Mukherjee's novel and Roy's political writing in these terms thus generates a debate that has a key bearing on wider understandings of globalization and provides a tacit demonstration of the need for approaches that are able to sustain more complex and nuanced perspectives. Deepika Bari's discussion of *Jasmine* frames these issues in terms that offer a precise sense of the ways in which Mukherjee's vision of the opposition between India and America shapes a particular view of identity (1998). Recognizing that 'the journeys of the novel's eponymous heroine, a syncretic symbol of the global migrant now familiar in metropolitan postcolonial literature, detail possible escape routes from assigned subjectivities for the Third World woman', Bari suggests that 'the transformative and regenerative method used by Jasmine to destabilize the notion of a passive and victimized Third World woman and escape typification . . . paradoxically paralyses the Other left behind at the origin of difference.'[61] Identifying the ways in which Jasmine's trajectory frees herself, while enslaving those she has left behind, Bari asks 'how to reconcile our aversion to the rampant individual demonstrated by characters like . . . Jasmine . . . while asserting individual difference and arguing against the fetishization of the static and collective Other?'[62] *Jasmine*, it seems, has no answer to this question and is unable to reconcile these two manoeuvres.

Recognizing this dilemma, however, prompts not just an awareness of the problems with Mukherjee's approach (and from the opposing camp, the ideas raised in Roy's political writing), but also fosters a more productive reading of the globalization debate as whole. The recognition that Mukherjee's narrative is only able to offer the kind of closed choices described by Bari thus encourages an engagement with more complex accounts of the relationships between the local and the global, India and America, the migrant and those who remain behind, an account rooted in an understanding that 'nowhere is globalized that is not at the same time regionalized, nationalized and localised' and linked to the realization that 'ethnic and cultural fragmentation and modernist homogenization are not two arguments, two opposing views of what is happening today, but two constitutive trends of global reality.'[63]

The problem with Mukherjee's fiction and, it seems, Roy's political writing, is that neither of them are able to fully embrace this complexity. As a result, the visions they construct are not only incomplete, but polarized in terms that limit and narrow understandings of the globalization debate. Though such an insight is interesting in itself, what is more significant is that *The God of Small Things*, unlike Roy's political writing, reveals a much more multi-dimensional understanding of the processes in hand, an understanding that offers wider insight into the complex and fluid relationships that link identity, migration and globalization together.

Exploring the interactions between the global and the particular and focused on manifestations of the power of the market, *The God of Small Things* takes place in a world marked by the impact of international capital. The sunken and polluted Meenachal, a 'river that smelled of shit and pesticides bought with World Bank loans', the strip of 'new, freshly baked, iced, Gulf-money houses built by nurses, masons, wire-benders and bank clerks who worked hard and unhappily in faraway places' and the five star 'Heritage' hotel built on the site Kari Saipu's house are all signs of the novel's attempt to link its action with a wider view of global social and economic forces.[64] As Julie Mullaney argues, the novel explores the ways in which 'India is shaped by a global culture and how it seeks to shape and understand its place in that culture in local terms.'[65] These concerns, played out not only in the setting, but also in the plot's concentration on the back-and-forth migrations of its various characters and the consequences it attaches to their experiences as migrants, become the focus for the novel's story of causes and effects, actions and consequences.

Roy's novel describes diasporas that have their origin in forces that are both ancient and modern. Powers linked to family, tradition and international capital all converge in a text that refuses the story of progress told in Mukherjee's *Jasmine* or implied in the studied Americana of Lahiri's *Interpreter of Maladies*.[66] Exploring the identities formed at the intersection between discourses linked to nationality (Indian and English), religion (Hindu and Syrian-Christian), capital (both local and international), politics (socialism, imperialism and nationalism), and caste (particularly the untouchables), *The God of Small Things* thus generates a powerful awareness of the ways in which the experiences it describes are shaped by complex patterns of social, political and economic change. Some of the novel's central concerns are developed in the themes of reversal and return. Estha's 'rereturn' to Kerala from a life with his father, Rahel's journey to Boston and back, and the series of movements that see India's colonial and precolonial past emerge to influence the destinies of many of the different characters in the novel combine to prioritize the network of forces that shape not simply the events Roy describes, but, by implication, processes of social and historical change. Where Mukherjee and Lahiri see the lives and the societies they represent as aimed toward some ultimate destination, Roy offers a more complex and sophisticated vision of history as a series of unstable and unending transactions between different discourses and powers.

Apparent in both plot and setting, it is also significant that Roy's stylistics should further this point by merging local languages with its predominantly English voice. Using vernacular pronunciations (and mispronunciations) of English words (most strikingly articulated in the 'lend me YAWyers' speech from *Julius Caesar*) alongside words and phrases from 'Malayalam' foregrounds Roy's sense of the discursive complexity of the world she is writing about and indicates a sensitivity to the politics of her own aesthetic.[67] Graham Huggan extends this point by suggesting the novel reveals what he sees as a critical self consciousness about its own patterns of representation. Huggan writes:

> It both displays and implicitly ironises its own lushly romantic images, its metaphor-laden language, its transferred Conradian primitivist myths. It is aware of the recent history of Indo-Anglian fiction, and of the parallel history of imperialist nostalgia in the West: the films of Lean and of Merchant and Ivory; the profitable *Heart of Darkness* industry, the travel writing business with its recuperative parodies of imperial heroism and derring-do. In bringing these histories together, Roy's novel shows the continuing presence of an imperial imaginary lurking behind Indian literature in English, among other putatively colonial products.[68]

For Huggan, Roy's attention to the discourses employed in her novel is evidence not simply of the complexity of the situation of the 'Indo-Anglian' author, but also of the intricacies of the relationships that link colonial, post-colonial, global and local forces together. Huggan's argument thus reinforces the impression that *The God of Small Things* is a novel that, in contrast to the polarized visions constructed by Lahiri and Mukherjee, maps the complex constellation of forces that characterize culture and experience in the contemporary period. There is, however, something naggingly pessimistic about *The God of Small Things* that casts a shadow over the world it creates, a pessimism that is detectable in its representation of consumption.

Rahel's down-at-heel experiences as an employee at an American gas station and the novel's sense of the emptiness of the claim that 'Things go better with Coca-Cola', function as signs of the text's critical vision of consumerism.[69] Connected with this perspective are the ways in which the novel tends to identify consumerism with foreignness:

> And there they were, the Foreign Returnees, in wash'n'wear suits and rainbow sunglasses. With an end to grinding poverty in their Aristocrat suitcases. With cement roofs for their thatched houses, and geysers for their parent's bathrooms. With sewage systems and septic tanks. Maxis and high heels. Puff sleeves and lipstick. Mixy-grinders and automatic flashes for their camera. With keys to count, and cupboards to lock.[70]

Arriving at an airport characterized by 'birdshit' and 'spitstains', the novel seems to suggest that there is something shabby about the 'Foreign Returnees'.[71] Though their journeys promise an 'end to grinding poverty', they also seem to cheapen and coarsen the migrants. Roy suggests that Indian culture is being diminished by their 'wash'n'wear' clothes and their desire for material things and implies that now cupboards will have to be locked and keys carried to protect not just the material goods but also the desire for material goods that these 'Returnees' have brought home with them.

The same regretful tone marks her portrait of the dancers hired to enact traditional Kathakali performances for residents at the new hotel in versions that have been 'collapsed . . . amputated . . . slashed' in order to satisfy the 'small attention spans' of the foreign guests.[72] Roy thus refuses to follow Mukherjee in seeing consumer goods and the desire to participate fully in the culture of consumption as part of a wider process of social amelioration.

Migrating Globalization

In her terms, a view suggested in the image of the old Plymouth rusting in the garden of the Ayemenem house, consumption is more a sign of failure than success. Indeed, where Mukherjee sees commodities as emissaries of change, Roy suggests that they simply promote a different kind of stasis. Baby Kochamma's new satellite dish, for example seems to immobilize her like the decaying Plymouth, and she becomes lost in a world of empty dreams and undifferentiated experiences. Roy writes: 'Baby Kochamma had installed a dish antenna on the roof of the Ayemenem house. She presided over the World in her drawing room on satellite TV ... Blondes, wars, famines, football, sex, music, coups d'etat – they all arrived on the same train.'[73]

This critical vision of consumption emerges even more forcibly in the description of the sexual abuse Estha suffers in his encounter with the Orangedrink Lemondrink man. Taking place not just in a movie theatre, but at a screening of *The Sound of Music*, a film that Chako has already identified as emblematic of a form of cultural imperialism rooted in 'Anglophilia', the Orangedrink Lemondrink man uses the lure of a soft drink to trick Estha.[74] Roy's scheme of associations thus works to link popular culture ('Abhilash Talkies') and consumerism ('Orangedrink Lemondrink') together with foreignness ('Anglophilia') and sexual abuse in terms that imply a process of exploitation. Contributing to the chain of events that lead to his withdrawal from ordinary life, Estha is permanently damaged by this event in ways that generate a powerfully pessimistic view of India's relationship with a consumer society that the novel implies has its origins overseas.

These ideas are echoed in Rahel's rejection of America, a place that is not the 'final continent', but a world of pimps, drunkness and violence. Working either in an Indian restaurant, or behind the security glass of a gas station, Rahel is clearly not an assimilated migrant, but an outsider who leaves America 'gladly' when the time comes.[75] Unlike Mukherjee's triumphalistic suggestion that bounty flows from the West to the East, Roy's vision is much more problematic, an impression strengthened by the fact that almost all of the journeys and migrations described in the novel are at best unsuccessful and at worst disastrous. Rahel, Chako and Baby Kochamma all return to Ayemenem after disappointments in other places, Sophie Mol comes back to her father and drowns

153

in the river that flows past his home, Estha is exiled, Ammu departs for Assam when she marries then leaves her drunken husband and comes home again, before leaving once more after Sophie Mol's death only to die in desperate and lonely circumstances. Chako does end up living in Canada, but Roy makes it clear that the antiques business he runs is 'unsuccessful'.[76]

All of these elements combine to create a darkly pessimistic novel, a text that contrasts strongly with the celebrations of opportunity and freedom that inform the works of Mukherjee and Lahiri. It is the novel's sense of the complexity of the forces that shape and structure the experiences of its cast of characters that is its main strength. Offering a counter to simplistic versions of globalization, Roy's novel recognizes the intricacy of modernity's relationship with tradition and globalization's interaction with the local. *The God of Small Things* is thus consistently alert to the changes wrought on Indian life by globalization and sees these forces not as powers that are carrying India from a state of stasis into one of dynamism, but in relation to existent patterns of social and historical transformation. Indian independence, the decline of the family's social and economic standing, communism, conflict with China, globalization and the migrations that carry Chako and Rahel abroad and home again have all contributed to the experiences *The God of Small Things* describes and the result is a novel that offers a sophisticated engagement with the constellation of forces that shape contemporary experience. The problem is, however, that in mapping this vast array of competing and interrelated forces, Roy creates a world in which the individual seems weak and powerless. Engineering the deaths of Sophie, Velutha and Ammu, and imprinting Estha, Rahel and Chako with an enduring sense of loss and dislocation, this network of powers seems to create individuals who are seen more as victims than agents. Such a suggestion can be reinforced by considering the meanings generated by the novel's title.

Establishing an opposition between a 'big god' linked to the 'vast, violent, circling, driving, ridiculous, insane, unfeasible, public turmoil of a nation' and a 'small god' that oversees the 'cosy and contained, private and limited', Roy's novel suggests that the individual is caught between these competing fates.[77] The small god is imbued with a resilience born of a 'confirmation of his own inconsequence', a state that breeds a 'brittle elation' over the 'relative smallness of his misfortune.'[78] 'In the country where she [Rahel] came from, poised forever between the terror of war and the horror of peace, Worse Things kept happening', writes Roy, a position that implies that worshipping the 'small god' offers not resistance or redemption, but a kind of grimly playful stoicism.[79] Subject to the whims of the big god (a deity that has to be seen as an expression of the massive forces of imperialism, tradition, postcolonialism and globalization), which howls 'like a hot wind, and demanded obeisance', Rahel has no choice but to seek solace in the 'small things', a solution that involves reconciling herself to the destiny shaped by the forces of the big god. Where Mukherjee sees globalization as an end to India's stasis, Roy describes a world in which these new energies simply strengthen the power of the big god and reinscribe old systems of domination and control. Constructing a gloomy, naturalistic environment, *The God of Small Things* thus creates a vision of a world system that is both fatal and fatalistic.

The contrast between Roy, Mukherjee and Lahiri thus suggests that the different ways in which they imagine the processes and consequences of migration can be linked to broader perspectives on globalization as a whole. Lying behind all of these positions is a related question about the marginalization and exclusion of those who do not have the freedom and resources to make the kinds of journeys these fictions describe. True, as Mukherjee makes clear, Jasmine comes from a 'mud hut', but her education and family history differentiate her from either traditional peasantry or the child of an untouchable like Roy's Velutha. He is representative of a class that seems to have few choices in a world that, for members of other social groups, appears increasingly fluid and flexible. The violence of his death confirms this position and though there is no sense that Roy sees him as a deserving victim of this brutality, his murder suggests that she is unable to imagine any alternatives for him. Indeed this event, when linked to the generally gloomy tone of the novel as a whole, suggests that for individuals like Velutha, there are very few options even in a world experiencing changes as apparently dramatic as those produced by the forces of globalization. This is the kind of insight that prompts Simon Gikandi, when writing in general terms about the links between globalization and postcolonial literature, to ask 'Is the global culture of professional émigrés the same as those who cross national boundaries in dangerous circumstances? What indeed is the consensual community shared by these two groups?'[80]

Mukherjee and Lahiri's lack of interest in the ways in which social class can be factored into discussions of the significance of migration and Roy's pessimistic vision of Velutha's treatment suggest that there is very little common ground shared by these two groups. A more consensual vision of the ways in which such interactions might operate can be found by looking not at a novelist in the Indo-Anglian or Indo-American tradition, but at a Chicana writer like Sandra Cisneros and considering the ways in which she represents the increasingly porous and unstable nature of the idea of American culture and the instability and unsustainability of homogenous ideas of class, ethnicity and economic power.

Sandra Cisneros

Exploring the cultural situation of those who draw their identity from America and Mexico simultaneously, Cisneros writes a border prose, 'pocked' with Spanish, that, in a number of stories from *Woman Hollering Creek* (1991), creates a revealing sense of the place consumption has in shaping responses to migration and ethnicity.[81] These perspectives come most obviously to the fore in 'Barbie-Q'. Offering a portrait of two young Chicana girls growing up in Chicago, this story uses their desire for Barbie dolls as a way of dramatizing the specifics of their cultural, social and economic situation. For some, like Ann Ducille, Barbie toys simply instruct 'us all that it's a small world after all' and reproduce 'dye-dipped versions of archetypal American beauty.'[82] Emblematic of US power and a sign of the colonization of international culture by American tastes and ideals, the desire for these dolls, according to Ducille's argument, signals a yearning to be accepted and assimilated into the incorporating machine of American cultural life.

Such a view echoes traditional accounts of the significance of American goods, accounts like those offered by Leslie Sklair who insists that, 'even in the most remote places, Coke and Pepsi and their ubiquitous marketing slogans and logos are acknowledged as symbols of the American way of life. They are also marketed in the prospect that anyone, however poor, who can afford a bottle or a can, can join in the great project of global consumerism.'[83] Seen very much as a vehicle for a form of globalization that functions in the service of American interests, Sklair argues that cultural products like Coke (and by implication Barbie) are engines for the eradication of local differences. These goods are the carriers of a homogenized culture. Sklair's argument is that:

> Watching soap operas ... or cheering on a team as you watch the world cup on TV in a village or a shanty town or a global city does not necessarily mean that the individual has planetary consciousness (in the way that Giddens might conceive the term in his phrase 'emergent forms or world interdependence and planetary consciousness'), whatever that is. What it does mean, however, is that when the viewer actually starts to become conscious of the global prestige of the lifestyles these media events embody and desires and eventually buys the products displayed, then an objective relationship is established with the transnational corporation, the core of the capitalist global system.[84]

Barbie, with her clearly demarcated ethnicity and easy identification with the hegemonic ideals of white American culture can thus be identified as a cultural product with a place at, in Sklair's terms, 'the core of the capitalist global system'.[85]

The problem with this view, however is that it only works if the goods themselves are received and consumed in uniform and homogenous ways. Prioritizing what David Howes calls the 'global homogenization paradigm', a process through which 'cultural differences are increasingly being eroded through the worldwide replacement of local products with mass-produced goods which usually originate in the West', the perspective offered by Sklair neglects the politically and socially transformative ways in which goods can be both received and consumed.[86] Predicated on a model of consumption that works from the top down, her approach constructs a hegemonic vision of consumption, and overlooks the possibility that, as Jonathan Friedman suggests in his discussion of the consumption of Coca-Cola in the Congo, that, 'The consumption of Coke ... is locally significant! To be someone or to express one's position is to display the imported can in the windshield of one's car. Distinction is not simply show, but is genuine 'cargo' which always comes from the outside, a source of wellbeing and fertility and a sign of power.'[87]

Fictions of Globalization

The processes described by Friedman are mirrored in Cisneros' story. Long denied the Barbies they desire, the girls are delighted when they come across discounted dolls in a fire sale and are able to persuade their parents into a purchase. In some respects the intensity of their desire and the fact that they can only afford to satisfy it with fire-damaged goods would seem to suggest that their marginal position in American society is reconfirmed by this act of purchase. Belonging to a social group that is both economically underprivileged and ethnically marginalized, they are, in this reading, forced to accept both inferior goods and a subordinate position. If the story ended here then clearly Cisneros would have developed a view of consumption that would offer ready a comparison with the kinds of ideas outlined by Leslie Sklair. The point is, however, that the girls do not see the dolls as inferior. The fire damage makes the dolls 'sooty', and they are thus darkened and hybridized in ways that seem to make them even more desirable.[88] Reinforced by the fact that the goods come from a fire sale and are thus not bought from Mattell in ways that would reinforce the company's economic power, but appropriated through a less formal transaction, there is a feeling that the Barbie dolls are being remade and redefined as part of this process.[89]

Though in many respects these Barbies are inferior (they are slightly melted) and have, as a result, been rejected by mainstream America, as far as the girls are concerned, there is something precious and magical, both about the discovery of this bounty after the fire in the Halsted Street warehouse, and in the ways they have individuated qualities that differentiate them from ordinary dolls. Not only is their skin darkened and their ethnicity transformed by the smoke of the fire, their presence at the fire sale means that they are already existing at one remove from the mainstream patterns of American commerce.[90] The story thus celebrates this discovery, preferable not just in terms of price and ethnicity (this is particularly important as Cisneros is writing at a time before Mattel started to market non-caucasian dolls), but because they seem to emblematize the situation of the girls themselves, and suggest that this icon of American popular culture can be remade in terms that echo the experiences and interests of the girls concerned. As the story has it, 'and if the prettiest doll, Barbie's MOD'ern cousin Francie with real eyelashes, eyelash brush included, has a left foot that's melted a little – so? If you dress her in her new "Prom Pinks" outfit, satin splendour with matching coat, gold belt, clutch, and hair bow included, so long as you don't lift her dress, right? – who's to know.'[91] 'Watersoaked and sooty' these Barbies thus offer an image of the forces reshaping the patterns of American consumerism in ways that echo the transformations wrought on America's cultural and linguistic landscape by migrations from across the border.[92]

Cisneros' interest in these themes is echoed in other stories in *Woman Hollering Creek*. 'Mexican movies', for example, portrays Chicanos as members of a culture who seem determined to read consumer culture in active ways. Describing the behaviour of an audience at a Mexican movie, the young narrator explains 'We like Mexican movies', and goes on to describe the kids playing in the aisles and blowing like *burros* through empty packs of jujubes to the shout of '*¿Quien saquen a ese niño?*' as other members of the audience eat *churros* and *torta*.[93] Instead of quiet rows of silently receptive viewers, the story describes a community consuming mass culture in engaged and interactive terms. The same critical response to the apparently homogenized and homogenizing products of consumerism is articulated in the story 'The Marlboro man'. Like Barbie, this icon of Americanness is treated in irreverent style. 'There've been lots of Marlboro men', one of Cisneros' protagonists explains, 'Just like there've been lots of Lassies, and lots of Shamu the Whale, and lots of Ralph the Swimming Pig. Well, what did you think girlfriend? *All* those billboards. *All* those years!'[94]

For Cisneros, her characters are 'Mericans', individuals who are both absorbing what America has to offer and transforming it, remaking not just its culture and its language, but its commodities too.[95] In this respect the stories seem to offer visions of creolization. As John Howes explains, 'Whereas Coca-colonization refers to the flow of goods from the West to the rest of the world, creolization is concerned with the in-flow of goods, their reception and domestication . . . Secondly, whereas Coca-colonization is centred on the presumed intentionality of the producer, creolization also takes in the creativity of the consumer.'[96]

Such a view can be set against the influential account of the impact of consumption in Latin-America articulated by Canclini. His argument is that:

> With the imposition of a neoliberal conception of globalization according to which rights are necessarily unequal, the novelties of modernity now appear to the majority only as objects of consumption ... the rights of citizenship which should be to decide how these goods are produced, distributed and used, is circumscribed to the domain of the elites.[97]

The girls in Cisneros' story are clearly not members of the elite, but they are still able to make choices and reshape the apparently hegemonic forms of the culture they are consuming in ways that are clearly different from those described in Canclini's hierarchical model.

These approaches are also significant because they offer ways of stepping beyond the celebrations of hybridity that usually attach themselves to Cisneros' fiction. More than simply a statement of the 'elasticity and permeability of the many borders that have defined our lives as global', these stories seem to offer not a loose sense of fluidity, but a specific account of the processes of cross-cultural exchange.[98] Indeed, recalling the suggestion that such celebrations of hybridity could themselves be seen not just as a statement of liberalism and the benefits of a polyglot identity but, more worryingly, as a position that endorses and facilitates the operation of international capital, differentiating Cisneros from these perspectives serves an important critical function. It also moves the reading of these stories away from the kind of bland claim that commentators like Jeff Thomson make when they celebrate Cisneros as a writer who 'speaks from the silence, speaking freedom into existence and possible identity in being.'[99] Instead of simply speaking and being heard, Cisneros's writing offers a sense of the ways in which individuals, cultures and communities can begin to make sense of globalization and establish productive relationships with both consumer society and the incorporating forces of consumption and the market.

Cisneros' work thus represents a further qualification and response to conceptions of the global market that function in terms of homogeneity and standardization. Different ethnicities, communities and regions inevitably, as Iain Chambers explains, share 'certain goods, habits, styles and languages', but what is important, as far as he is concerned, is the fact that:

For each thing in common there is also a correspondingly local twist, inflection, idiolect. They are not merely physically distinct, but also remain sharply differentiated in economic, historical and cultural terms. Nevertheless, such differences are not always and inevitably instances of divisions and barriers. They can also act as hinges that serve both to close *and* to open doors in an increasingly global traffic.[100]

Chambers' central point is that these differences are 'hinges', parts of mobile networks of social symbolism that participate in processes that are simultaneously liberating and limiting. It is an understanding of this type of experience that is offered by the reading of Cisneros and, as preceding chapters have suggested, the other writers considered in *Fictions of Globalization*. Janet Abu-Lughod's sense that instead of reading contemporary culture as the product of a

> Type of instantaneous, indiscriminate and complete diffusion of all cultural products, with *no need for intermediate interpretation* . . . what we are experiencing is rapid, incomplete and highly differentiated flows in global transmission. We have a globalizing but not necessarily homogeneous culture. While in the last analysis, we think that this is good, enriching and generative, we have not figured out how to live with the dilemmas it creates.[101]

The suggestion is that reading Cisneros in these terms offers a sense of the ways in which some of these dilemmas might be resolved.

Cisneros, in terms that differentiate her work from the approaches offered by Lahiri, Mukherjee and Roy, thus portrays characters capable of playing active roles in the multi-directional processes of globalization and consumerism. Where Roy sees a gloomy set of massive systems over which the individual has little control, and Mukherjee and Lahiri offer affirmative accounts of the opportunities these systems create, Cisneros' fictions adds Roy's anxious response to the power of the global market to Mukherjee's recognition of the benefits they bring, and combines these awarenesses with a sense of the ways in which processes of this kind are mediated through and influenced by individuals in specific situations. Reading these works alongside each other thus gestures towards a conclusion that recognizes the contrasting ways in which different writers set out to represent these experiences and uses that understanding to foster a wider view on the globalization debate itself. As Padmina Mongia argues in the introduction to her reader on post-colonial theory, 'It is no doubt true that new technologies of communication and the global movements of peoples strain any simple understanding of location. Nevertheless, to suggest that post-colonial writers share a common frame of reference in some unified (and implicitly equal?) transnational circulation of ideas and cultural products, is to refuse to address the inequities that shape current global relations.'[102]

Despite the many contrasts that divide the work of Lahiri, Mukherjee, Roy and Cisneros, what brings all of these fictions together is the sense that they are shaping and remaking the very idea of American literature. Roy in particular, as an Indian writing in English for, one assumes, a readership that is primarily British and American, asks important questions about the viability of the idea of a national literature in the contemporary period. Strengthened by an appreciation of the ways in which the origins of Cisneros, Mukherjee and Lahiri complicate these debates and fuelled by the recognition that an English novelist writing a novel that uses an international idiom, as Alex Garland does in *The Beach*, and a Canadian writer like William Gibson (a man born, incidentally, in South Carolina) can also be linked to the currents of recent American fiction, there is little doubt that the processes of globalization have transformed the understanding of national literary traditions. This 'revision ... of the idea that literature exists in a national framework' is, for Edward Said, one of the key consequences of linking the analysis of globalization to literary studies.[103] So important, it seems, are these questions that they are becoming the primary focus for critics writing about the relationship between literature and globalization. Recent special issues of the journals *Modern Fiction Studies*, *South Atlantic Quarterly* and *PMLA* have all, for example, focused on the fate of literature as a discipline in the age of globalization and connected these debates with established arguments linked to post-colonialism. This focus on an understanding of the processes 'globalizing literary studies', as Giles Gunn describes it, is thus read in terms of their influence on literary theory, particularly insofar as post-colonialism is understood.[104]

The problem with these approaches, however, is not that these issues are irrelevant, but that giving them priority over other

Migrating Globalization

perspectives channels the analysis of globalization towards the understanding of literature and literary theory, when there seems to be a more pressing need to interpret literature and literary theory in terms that might aid the understanding of globalization. Though many of the articles included in these special issues are informed by readings of Appadurai and Robertson and are aware, as Paul Jay's article explains, that literature can be seen to contribute to the 'facilitation of economic and cultural globalization', there is a tendency to privilege, as the title of Jay's article makes clear, a debate on 'the future of English' as a discipline, over a broader exploration of the social consequences of globalization.[105]

The arguments offered in *Fictions of Globalization* are, in contrast, an attempt to connect the discussion of literary texts with readings of the social and cultural consequences of globalization. It is the understanding that globalization must be read in relation to the ordinary transactions of ordinary people that underpins this analysis of the representations of leisure, technology, consumer culture, the market *and* migration in recent American fiction. To focus solely on the post-colonial situation and the internationalization of the English language is thus to neglect these other areas. Instead of asking what the understanding of globalization can do for literary studies, this book has asked what the study of literature can do for the understanding of globalization. Asking these questions and reading recent fiction in these terms offers, *Fictions of Globalization* suggests, a sense of the ways in which it might be possible to develop both insight into and critical purchase upon the massive systems that surround us.

Notes

1. Introduction: Culture Incorporated

1. Cf. Eric Schlosser, *Fast Food Nation: What the All American Meal is Doing to the World* (London: Penguin, 2002). See also: Morgan Spurlock (dir.), *Super Size Me*, (Hart Sharp Video LLC, 2004). Schlosser's book, particularly in its portrait of the manufacture of junk food, seems able to summon the same revulsion that Upton Sinclair's *The Jungle* (1906) employed with such powerful effect in its descriptions of life in the Chicago meat packing district at the start of the twentieth century.
2. Joel Bakan, *The Corporation: The Pathological Pursuit of Power and Profit* (London: Constable, 2004), p. 60. Bakan's book was published alongside a documentary film of the same name. See: Mark Achbar, Jennifer Abbott and Joel Bakan (dirs), *The Corporation*, (Zeitgeist Films, 2004). This film features appearances by both Michael Moore and Naomi Klein.
3. Stuart Ewen, *Captains of Consciousness: Advertising and the Social Roots of Consumer Culture* (1976) (25th Anniversary Edition) (New York: Basic Books, 2001), p. 14.
4. Ambalavaner Savanandan, 'Globalism and the left', in *Race and Class: The Threat of Globalism* (1998), 40, (2/3), 5; John Berger, 'Against the great defeat of the world', in *Race and Class: The Threat of Globalism* (1998), 40, (2/3), 3.
5. Cf. Josef Stiglitz, *Globalization and its Discontents* (London: Allen Lane, 2002). See also: Dani Rodrik, *Has Globalization Gone too Far?* (Washington DC: Institute for International Economics, 1997); Fredric Jameson, 'Postmodernism and the market', in Slavoj Zizek (ed.), *Mapping Ideology* (London: Verso, 1994), p. 291.
6. Cf. Liz McFall, *Advertising: A Cultural Economy* (London: Sage, 2004). McFall's book suggests that, p. 3: 'Advertising is conceived as an institution that is steadily evolving in power and sophistication' and goes on to argue that this view, p. 3: 'is complemented by a perception that while contemporary advertisements are pervasive, ubiquitous and inescapable, earlier advertisements were rare and unusual'
7. Cf. Steven Graukroger, 'Romanticism and decommodification: Marxism's conception of socialism', in *Economy and Society* (1986), 15, (3).
8. Cf. Theodore Adorno, 'Culture industry reconsidered', trans. Anson Rabinbach, in *New German Critique* (1975), 6, 13: 'It is industrial more in a sociological sense,

in the incorporation of industrial forms of organization even when nothing is manufactured – as in the rationalization of office work – rather than in the sense of anything really and actually produced by technological rationality.'

9. James Twitchell, *Lead us into Temptation: The Triumph of American Materialism* (New York: Columbia University Press, 1999), p. 90: 'The culture of the way we live now is carried on the back of advertising . . . If you cannot find commercial support for what you have to say, it will not be transported.'
10. Cf. Benjamin Barber, *Jihad vs. McWorld* (New York: Ballantine Books, 1995).
11. Anthony Giddens, *The Consequences of Modernity* (Cambridge: Polity, 1990), p. 64.
12. Gary Teeple, 'What is globalization?', in Stephen McBride and John Wiseman (eds), *Globalization and its Discontents* (London: Macmillan, 2000), p. 9.
13. David Held, *Global Covenant: The Social Democratic Alternative to the Washington Consensus* (Cambridge: Polity, 2004), pp. 3–4.
14. Arjun Appadurai, *Modernity at Large: Cultural Dimensions of Globalization* (Minneapolis: University of Minnesota Press, 1997), p. 31.
15. Cf. Julian Murphet, *Literature and Race in Los Angeles* (Cambridge: Cambridge University Press, 2001); Maria Balshaw, *Looking for Harlem: Urban Aesthetics in African American Literature* (London: Pluto, 2000).
16. Cf. Nick Heffernan, *Capital, Class and Technology in Contemporary American Culture: Projecting Post-Fordism* (London: Pluto, 2000); Philip Simmons, *Deep Surfaces: Mass Culture and History in Postmodern American Fiction* (Athens: University of Georgia, 1997); Stephen Baker, *The Fiction of Postmodernity* (Edinburgh: Edinburgh University Press, 2000).
17. Nick Heffernan takes an opposing line when he argues in *Capital, Class and Technology*, p. 13: 'The usefulness of the terms postmodernism and postmodernity as descriptions of cultural change consists in their remarkably broad range of reference.'
18. Susie O'Brien and Imre Szeman, 'Introduction: the globalization of fiction/the fiction of globalization', in *South Atlantic Quarterly* (2001), 100, (3), 605: 'Given the ever-increasing interrelationship between culture and economics, it now seems for most critics pointless not to call this the logic of "globalization" too and to see postmodernism as the early name for social and cultural forces whose emergence was only partially grasped two decades ago.'
19. Fredric Jameson seems guilty of this sleight of hand. See, for example: Fredric Jameson, 'Notes on globalization as a philosophical issue' in Fredric Jameson and Misao Miyoshi (eds), *Cultures of Globalization* (London: Duke University Press, 1998), when he reformulates his famous comments from 'The politics of theory: ideological positions in the postmodernism debate', in the following terms, p. 55: 'One can deplore globalization or celebrate it, just as one welcomes the new freedoms of the postmodern era and the postmodern outlook.'
20. Paul Jay, 'Beyond discipline? Globalization and the future of English', in *PMLA* (2001), 116, (1), 35.
21. Michel Bérubé, 'Introduction: worldly English', in *Modern Fiction Studies* (2002), 48, (1), 7.
22. Stephen McBride and John Wiseman, 'Introduction', in Stephen McBride and John Wiseman (eds), *Globalization and its Discontents* (London: Macmillan, 2000), p. 1.

Notes

2. Cash Rules Everything Around Me

1. Quoted in David Toop, *Rap Attack: African Rap to Global Hip Hop* (Revised and expanded third edition) (London: Serpent's Tail, 2000), p. xv.
2. bell hooks, *Outlaw Culture: Resisting Representations* (New York: Routledge 1994), p. 147.
3. Cf. Nelson George, *Buppies, B-Boys and Bohos: Notes on a Post-Soul Black Culture* (London: HarperCollins, 1994); Cornel West, *Race Matters* (New York: Beacon Press, 1993), p. 17; Ellis Cashmore, *The Black Culture Industry* (London: Routledge, 1997), p. 171.
4. DJ-Shadow, 'Why Hip Hop Sucks in '96', from *Endtroducing* (Mowax, 1996).
5. Paul Gilroy, *Small Acts* (London: Serpent's Tail, 1993), p. 189.
6. Robert Goldman and Stephen Papson, *Nike Culture: The Sign of the Swoosh* (London: Sage, 2004), p. 101.
7. Cashmore, *The Black Culture Industry*, p. 179.
8. Zora Neale Hurston, 'Characteristics of negro expression', in Nancy Cunard (ed.), *Negro Anthology* (London: Wishart, 1934), p. 40.
9. Ibid., p. 39.
10. Paul Mullins, *Race and Affluence: An Archaeology of African-American Consumer Culture* (New York: Kluwer Academic, 1999), p. 173
11. Wu-Tang Clan, 'C.R.E.A.M', from *Enter the Wu-Tang 36 Chambers* (BMG/RCA/Loud, 1993).
12. William Shaw, *Westsiders* (London: Bloomsbury, 2000), p. 21.
13. Ibid., p. 21.
14. Robin Kelley, *Race Rebels: Culture, Politics and the Black Working Class* (New York: Free Press 1994), p. 200.
15. E. Franklin Frazier, 'Durham: Capital of the black middle class', in Alain Locke (ed.), *The New Negro* (New York: Albert and Charles Boni, 1927), p. 339. See also: E. Franklin Frazier, *The Black Bourgeoisie: The Rise of a New Middle Class* (New York: Free Press, 1957), p. 202: 'Rich negroes ... indulge in lavish expenditures and create a world of fantasy.'
16. Frazier, 'Durham, capital of the black middle class', pp. 339–40.
17. Mullins, *Race and Affluence*, p. 18.
18. bell hooks, *Outlaw culture*, p. 126.
19. Ibid., p. 146.
20. Michael Dyson, *Reflecting Black: African American Cultural Criticism* (Minneapolis: University of Minnesota Press, 1993), pp. 72–3.
21. Robin Kelley, 'Playing for keeps: pleasure and profit on the postindustrial playground', in Wahneema Lubiano (ed.), *The House that Race Built* (New York: Vintage, 1998), p. 224.
22. Hurston, 'Characteristics of negro expression', p. 42.
23. Cf. Paul Edwards, *The Southern Urban Negro as a Consumer* (1932) (New York: Negro Universities Press, 1969), pp. 98–100.
24. Mullins, *Race and Affluence*, p. 173.
25. Ibid., p. 174.
26. Maya Jaggi, 'Poetry in the projects', in *Guardian* (22 July 2000), p. 7.
27. Paul Beatty, *Tuff* (2000) (London: Vintage, 2001), p. 15.

28. Ibid., p. 33.
29. Ibid., p. 221.
30. Paul Beatty, *White Boy Shuffle* (London: Minerva, 1996), p. 57.
31. Mark Neal, *Soul Babies: Black Popular Culture and the Post-Soul Aesthetic* (New York: Routledge, 2002), p. 136.
32. West, *Race Matters*, p. 16.
33. Cf. Eithne Quinn, 'Who's the mack?: the politics of the pimp figure in gangsta rap', in *Journal of American Studies* (2001), 34, (1) 136: 'Of all the black archetypes mobilized in gangsta, the pimp figure is probably the most fully resistant to the dynamics of mainstream incorporation, market co-option and white imitation.'
34. T. N. Baker, *Sheisty* (Columbus, Ohio: Triple Crown, 2004), p. 1.
35. K'wan, *Road Dawgz* (Columbus, Ohio: Triple Crown, 2003), p. 2.
36. Russell Potter, *Spectacular Vernaculars: Hip-Hop and the Politics of Postmodernism* (Albany: State University of New York Press, 1995).

3. *Branding, Consumption and Identity*

1. Bret Easton Ellis, *Glamorama* (1998) (London: Picador, 1999), p. 98.
2. Victor himself was first glimpsed in Ellis's earlier novel *The Rules of Attraction*, as a student at Camden College who, significantly in terms of *Glamorama*'s narrative, makes an aimless trip to Europe. See: Bret Easton Ellis, *The Rules of Attraction* (London: Picador, 1987), p. 24. It is also worth noting that in the same year that Ellis was publishing *Glamorama*, Jay McInerey was publishing *Model Behaviour* (1998), a novel about a journalist's relationship with a fashion model. Though very different in approach, it is interesting that two writers whose careers have been so closely linked for so long should publish on the same subject in the same year.
3. Ibid., p. 27.
4. Ibid., p. 305.
5. Perhaps Ellis is playing here on the range of associations that surround the Prada brand itself, a company known for designs that literalize the concept of designer socialism and toy with militaristic, freedom-fighter chic (one advertising campaign featured what it called 'the Prada Army'). It is also interesting to note that Miuccia Prada has associations with communism and alleged links to the fringe elements that characterized Italian politics in the early 1970s.
6. This image seems to echo a scene from Ian Fleming's *From Russia with Love* (1957) (London: Hodder and Stoughton, 1988), in which Bond assassinates an adversary as he steps through a door cut in a poster bearing the image of Marilyn Monroe (p. 140). As many commentators have observed, Ian Fleming's Bond novels were some of the first to use consumer items and brands in terms intended to denote status and wealth.
7. Ellis, *Glamorama*, p. 445.
8. Cf. Ben Stiller (dir.), *Zoolander* (Paramount/Village Roadshow/VH1/NPV, 2001), a film that has a great deal in common with *Glamorama* including, most obviously, the premise of a supermodel assassin.
9. Cf. Benjamin Buchloh, 'Andy Warhol's One Dimensional Art: 1956–1966', in Kynaston McShin (ed.), *Andy Warhol: A Retrospective* (New York: Museum of

Notes

Modern Art, 1989). Buchloh talks of Warhol's (p. 41) 'commercial folklore'. See also: Kirk Varndoe, 'Campbell's Soup Cans, 1962', in Heiner Bastion (ed.), *Andy Warhol: Retrospective* (London: Tate, 2002), p. 43: 'The structure of repetition or the strategy of appropriation, the slurs and gaps and mottlings and tics constitute the particular artist and the particular cultural moment at issue.'

10. Twitchell, *Lead us into Temptation*, p. 163.
11. Cf. Chris Mazza and Jeffrey DeStell (eds), *Chick-Lit: Postfeminist Fiction* (Normal, Illinois: FC2, 1995).
12. Candace Bushnell, *Sex and the City* (1996) (London: Abacus, 2004), p. 49.
13. Cf. Sarah Niblock, ' "My Manolos, my self": Manolo Blahnik shoes and desire', in Kim Akass and Janet McCabe (eds), *Reading Sex and the City* (London: Taurus, 2004).
14. Bushnell, *Sex and the City*, p. 54.
15. Ibid., p. 140.
16. James Joyce, *Ulysses* (1922) (London: Bodley Head, 1993), p. 99. For a further discussion of the significance of these elements in *Ulysses* see: Mark Osteen, *The Economy of Ulysses: Making Both Ends Meet* (New York: Syracuse University Press, 1995).
17. John Dos Passos, *Manhattan Transfer* (1925) (Boston: Houghton Mifflin, 1953), pp. 10–11. This poster is reproduced in Charles Goodrum and Helen Dalrymple, *Advertising in America* (New York: Harry N. Abrams, 1990), p. 115.
18. Cf. Stuart Davis, *Lucky Strike* (1924), Charles Demuth, *Buildings, Lancaster* (1930) and Edward Hopper, *Drug Store* (1927).
19. Cf. Gertrude Stein, *Tender Buttons*, in Carl Van Vechten (ed.), *Selected Writings of Gertrude Stein* (New York: Vintage, 1972).
20. F. Scott Fitzgerald, *The Great Gatsby* (1926) (London: Heinemann, 1982), pp. 106–107. Though the cars are unbranded, it must be acknowledged that the text does include details of the sign that adorns Wilson's garage, p. 24: 'Repairs. George B. Wilson. Cars bought and sold.' *The Great Gatsby* also includes one of literature's most famous images of advertising, the poster promoting the optometrist (p. 23), 'Doctor T. J. Eckleburg'.
21. William Faulkner, *The Sound and the Fury* (1921) (Harmondsworth: Penguin, 1982), pp. 212–17.
22. Ralph Ellison, *Invisible Man* (1952) (London: Penguin, 2001), p. 37.
23. Richard Wright, *Native Son* (1940) (New York: Harper Row, 1964), pp. 60–61.
24. Naomi Klein, *No Logo: Taking Aim at the Brand Bullies* (London: HarperCollins, 1999), p. 28: 'The scaling-up of the logo's role has been so dramatic that it has become a change in substance', a process that she argues is part of the (p. 30), 'project of transforming culture into little more than a collection of brand-extensions.'
25. Monroe Friedman, *A 'Brand' New Language: Commercial Influences in Literature and Culture* (New York: Greenwood, 1991), p. 2.
26. Colonel Cantwell drives a 'big Buick' into Venice in *Across the River and into the Trees*. See: Ernest Hemingway, *Across the River and into the Trees* (New York: Scribners, 1950), p. 20. David drives a Bugatti and carries his notebooks in a 'big Vuitton suitcase' in *The Garden of Eden*. See: Ernest Hemingway, *The Garden of Eden* (New York: Scribners, 1950), p. 77, p. 218. In *The Moveable Feast* (1936)

Notes

(London: Random House, 1994), Hemingway endorses a range of products and services including ski chalets run by the 'Alpine Club' and, of course, shopping at Shakespeare and Company, p. 31, p. 172.
27. Richard Godden, *The Fictions of Capital: The American Novel from James to Mailer* (Cambridge: Cambridge University Press, 1990), p. 70.
28. Ibid., p. 43; p. 50.
29. Ibid., p. 78.
30. Cf. Ibid., p. 139, where Godden writes of Fitzgerald, '*Tender is the Night* provides what Late Capitalism must deny; history – a history, from drawing-room to Hollywood, of the very thing that would revoke history – commodity.'
31. Cf. Rosalind Coward's *Female Desire: Women's Sexuality Today* (London: Paladin, 1984), p. 13: 'To be a woman is to be constantly addressed, to be constantly scrutinized, to have our desire constantly courted... Desire is endlessly defined and stimulated. Everywhere female desire is sought, bought, packaged, and consumed.'
32. Ernest Hemingway, 'Hills like white elephants', in *Men Without Women* (New York: Scribner's, 1928), p. 71.
33. Pierre Bourdieu, *Distinction: A Social Critique of the Judgement of Taste*, trans. Richard Nice (London: Routledge and Kegan Paul, 1986), p. 12.
34. Ibid., p.2.
35. Raymond Williams, 'Advertising the Magic System', in *Problems in Materialism and Culture* (London: Verso, 1980), pp.188–89.
36. Mary Douglas and Baron Isherwood, *The World of Goods* (Harmondsworth: Penguin, 1978), p. 62.
37. It is important to appreciate, however, that while commentators like Bourdieu and Hebdige refuse to be limited by arguments that link consumerism to ideology and economics, they do not look to disavow or disqualify such approaches. Perspectives that connect consumerism with the social and the anthropological are not offered as an alternative to arguments tied to capital, but as a vital supplement to them.
38. Chuck Palahniuk, *Fight Club* (1996) (London: Vintage 1997), p. 125.
39. Cf. Filippo Marinetti, 'The founding and manifesto of futurism' (1909), in Filippo Marinetti, *Selected Writings*, edited and translated by R. W. Flint (London: Secker and Warburg, 1972), p. 43: 'So let them come the gay incendiaries with charred fingers! Here they are! Here they are! ... Come on! Set fire to the library shelves! Turn aside the canals to flood the museums ... Take up your pickaxes and hammers, and wreck, wreck the venerable cities, pitilessly!' See also: Palahniuk, *Fight Club*, pp. 123–24: 'I wanted to burn the Louvre. I'd do the Elgin Marbles with a sledgehammer and wipe my ass with the *Mona Lisa*.'
40. Palahniuk, *Fight Club*, p. 50.
41. Susan Faludi, *Stiffed: The Betrayal of Modern Man* (London: Vintage, 2000). The phrase 'ornamental masculinity' is used throughout the book.
42. Ibid., p. 37.
43. Ibid., p. 451.
44. Palahniuk, *Fight Club*, p. 51.
45. Ibid., p. 50.
46. Ibid., p. 149.
47. Ibid., pp. 110–11.

Notes

48. Cf. Thorstein Veblen, *The Theory of the Leisure Class: An Economic Study of Institutions* (1899) (London: Allen and Unwin, 1949), p.179: 'it has ... become the office of the woman to consume vicariously for the head of the household; and her apparel is contrived with this object in view.' See also: Rachel Bowlby, *Shopping with Freud* (London: Routledge, 1993), p. 101: 'The two modes ... correspond ... to the classical and romantic consumer: to the mature masculine saver determined to avoid a loss and the infantile, feminine spender, unregulated in her desires.'
49. Palahniuk, *Fight Club*, p. 125.
50. Cf. David Savran, *Taking it Like a Man: White Masculinity, Masochism and Contemporary American Culture* (Princeton: Princeton University Press, 1998), p. 16: 'Certainly, what appears to be paramount in the representation of masculinity in capitalist societies is an obsession with competition and achievement. In other words, masculinism appears to lend itself very nicely to the ethos of industrialism and capitalism.'
51. Cf.Palahniuk, *Fight Club*, p. 47: 'More of my lips are sticky with blood as I try to lick the blood off, and when the lights come up, I will turn to consultants Ellen and Walter and Norbert and Linda from Microsoft and say, thank you for coming, my mouth shining with blood and blood climbing the cracks between my teeth.' See also: Anthony Easthope, *What a Man's Gotta Do: the Masculine Myth in Popular Culture* (London: Routledge, 1990), p. 72: 'Pain becomes narcissism for the injured sportsman, a prompt for self-absorbed analysis, the seeming antithesis of ornamental preening, but still linked to ideas of vanity and pride in the maintenance of the body.'
52. Palahniuk, *Fight Club*, p. 150.
53. David Fincher (dir.), *Fight Club* (20th Century Fox/Fox 2000/Regency, 1999).
54. Palahniuk has himself indicated that he is aware of these contradictions and has discussed the significance of Pitt's iconic good looks in some of his own writing on the making of Fincher's version of *Fight Club*. Cf. Chuck Palahniuk, 'The lip enhancer', *Non-Fiction* (London: Jonathan Cape, 2004).
55. Fincher (dir.), *Fight Club*.
56. Ibid.
57. Palahniuk's own thoughts on the making of the film share this sensibility. See, for example: Chuck Palahniuk, 'Consolation Prizes', in, *Non-Fiction*, pp. 228–29: 'Twentieth Century Fox let me bring some friends down to the movie shoot, and every morning we ate in the same café in Santa Monica. Every breakfast we got the same waiter, Charlie, with his movie-star looks and thick hair, until the last morning we were in town. That morning, Charlie walked out of the kitchen with his head shaved. Charlie was in the movie. My friends who'd been anarchist waiters with shaved heads were now being served eggs by a real waiter who was an actor who was playing a fake anarchist waiter with a shaved head. It's the same feeling you get between two mirrors in the barber shop and you can see your reflection of your reflection going off into infinity.'
58. Palahniuk, *Fight Club*, p. 204.
59. Ibid., p. 14.
60. Cf. Marc Auge, *Non-Places: Introduction to an Anthropology of Supermodernity*, trans. John Howe (London: Verso, 1995).
61. Cf. Colin Campbell, *The Romantic Ethos and the Spirit of Modern Consumerism*

(Cambridge: Blackwell, 1987), p. 206: 'Not merely that the Romantic Movement assisted crucially at the birth of modern consumerism; it is also maintained that romanticism has continued in the two centuries or so since that time to work in such a way as to overcome the forces of traditionalism and provide a renewed importance to the dynamics of consumerism.'
62. Palahniuk, *Fight Club*, p. 25.
63. Chuck Palahniuk, *Survivor* (London: Vintage, 2000), p. 266.
64. Cf. Steven Miles, *Consumerism as a Way of Life* (London: Sage, 1998), p. 148: 'This, some would say middle-class, vision of an empowering culture is all well and good, but what I want to suggest is that in many ways the consumer society we live in is more remarkable for the way in which it divides than for the ways in which it provides.'

4. The Fictions of Globalization

1. Cf. Tom Wolfe's portrait of Wall Street trader Sherman McCoy, 'master of the universe', in *The Bonfire of the Vanities* (1987) (London: Picador, 2002), p. 31.
2. Don DeLillo, *Cosmopolis* (2003) (London: Picador, 2004), p. 90.
3. Cf. Steffen Huntke, *Conspiracy and Paranoia in Contemporary American Fiction: The Works of Don DeLillo and Joseph McElroy* (Frankfurt: Peter Lang, 1994); Tom LeClair, *In the Loop: Don DeLillo and the Systems Novel* (Urbana: University of Illinois Press, 1987).
4. Don DeLillo, *Underworld* (1997) (London: Picador, 1998), p. 826.
5. Thomas Pynchon, *The Crying of Lot 49* (1965) (London: Picador, 1979), p. 36.
6. DeLillo, *Underworld*, p. 614.
7. William Boyd, 'The course of true life', in *Observer* (11 November 1998) (Review Section), p. 15.
8. Ibid., p. 15.
9. Don DeLillo, *Libra* (London: Penguin, 1989), p. 57, p. 181.
10. DeLillo, *Underworld*, p. 785.
11. Cf. Giddens, *The Consequences of Modernity*, p. 14.
12. DeLillo, *Underworld*, p. 372.
13. Ibid., p. 374.
14. Ibid., pp. 85–6.
15. Peter Knight, 'Everything is connected: *Underworld*'s secret history of paranoia', in *Modern Fiction Studies* (1999), 45, (3), 830.
16. James Wolcott, 'Blasts from the past', in *The New Criterion* (1997), 16, (4), 68.
17. Thomas Friedman, *The Lexus and the Olive Tree* (London: HarperCollins, 1999), p. 8.
18. Klein, *No Logo*, pp. xx–xxi.
19. Roland Robertson, *Globalization: Social Theory and Global Culture* (London: Sage, 1992), p. 8.
20. Nestor García Canclini, *La Globalización Imaginada* (Buenos Aires: Paidós, 1999) (Author's translation), pp. 31–2.
21. Andrew Sayer, 'Postfordism in question', in *International Journal of Urban and Regional Research* (1989), 13, (4), 666.

Notes

22. John Micklethwait and Adrian Wooldridge, *A Future Perfect: The Challenge and Hidden Promise of Globalization* (London: William Heinemann, 2000), p. 52.
23. Cf. ibid., p. 97–118.
24. Tony Tanner, 'Afterthoughts on Don DeLillo's *Underworld*' in *Raritan* (1998), 17, (4), 70.
25. Wolcott, 'Blasts from the past', p. 66.
26. DeLillo, *Underworld*, p. 827.
27. Ibid., p. 826.
28. Mark Osteen, *American Magic and Dread: Don DeLillo's Dialogue with Culture* (Philadelphia: University of Pennsylvania Press, 2000).
29. Ibid., p. 216.
30. DeLillo, *Underworld*, p. 820.
31. Osteen, *American Magic and Dread*, p. 257.
32. Ibid., p. 258.
33. Cf. Charles Olson, *Call me Ishmael: A Study of Melville* (1947) (London: Jonathan Cape, 1967).
34. Cf. Michael Rogin, *Subversive Genealogy: The Politics and Art of Herman Melville* (New York: Alfred Knopf, 1983), p. 114: 'Melville has given the commodity, sperm oil, a history ... Melville returns to a prehuman, ocean wilderness, and places working men at its center.' Melville was not the only American writer to identify the central place of whaling in the American economy. J. Hector St John De Crevecouer sees Nantucket whaling as an exemplary site of American colonial industry. See: J. Hector St John De Crevecouer, *Letters from an American Farmer* (1782) (Oxford: Oxford University, 1997), p. 121: 'It is astonishing what a quantity of oil some of these fish yield, and what profit it affords to those who are fortunate enough to overtake them.'
35. Herman Melville, *Moby-Dick or, The Whale* (1851) (Oxford: Oxford World's Classics, 1998), p. 382.
36. Olson, *Call Me Ishmael*, p. 19.
37. Klein, *No Logo*, p. 195.
38. Ibid., p. 204.
39. Olson, *Call me Ishmael*, p. 24; Klein, *No Logo*, p. 202.
40. Klein, *No Logo*, p. 424.
41. Melville, *Moby-Dick*, p. 321.
42. Ibid., p. 96.
43. Klein, *No Logo*, p. 4.
44. Ibid., p. 3.
45. George Monbiot, *Captive State: The Corporate Takeover of Britain* (London: Macmillan, 2000), p. 9.
46. Noreena Hertz, *The Silent Takeover: Global Capitalism and the Death of Democracy* (London: Heinemann, 2001), p. 6.
47. Henry David Thoreau, *Walden* (1854) (London: Everyman, 1997), p. 233.
48. Twitchell, *Lead us into Temptation*, p. 2.
49. Katharine Viner, 'Hand-to-brand combat', in *Guardian* (12 September 2000) (Weekend Section), p. 18.
50. Cf. Max Weber, *The Protestant Ethic and the Spirit of Capitalism* (1905) (New York: Scribner's, 1958).

51. Hertz, *The Silent Takeover*, p. 112, p. 116.
52. Ibid., p. 119.
53. Klein, *No Logo*, p. 446.
54. Viner, 'Hand-to-brand combat', pp. 20–1.
55. Klein, *No Logo*, p. 11.
56. Hertz, *The Silent Takeover*, p. 6.
57. George Gordon (Lord Byron) *Don Juan* (1823) Canto 12, verse 5, in Frederick Page (ed.), *Byron Poetical Works* (Revised Edition) (Oxford: Oxford University Press, 1987), p. 799. See also: Niall Ferguson, *The Cash Nexus: Money and Power in the Modern World, 1700–2000* (London: Allen Lane, 2001), p. 289.
58. Janet Abu-Lughod, *New York, Chicago, Los Angeles: America's Global Cities* (Minneapolis: University of Minnesota Press, 1999), p. 400.
59. Ferguson, *The Cash Nexus*, p. 309.
60. Nestor García Canclini, *Consumers and Citizens: Globalization and Multicultural Conflicts* (Minneapolis: University of Minnesota Press, 2001), p. 3.
61. Melville, *Moby-Dick*, p. 56
62. Olson, *Call me Ishmael*, p. 25.
63. W. H. Oliver and B. R. Williams (eds), *The Oxford History of New Zealand* (Revised Edition) (Oxford: Clarendon, 1987), p. 32.
64. Melville, *Moby-Dick*, p. 97. See also: J. Ross Browne, *Etchings of a Whale Cruise* (1846) (Cambridge, Mass.: Belknap, 1968), p. iv: 'There are now in active employment more than seven hundred whaling vessels belonging to the New England States. We are indebted to them for the extension of our commerce in foreign countries; for valuable additions to our stock of knowledge; for all the benefits resulting from their discoveries and researches in remote parts of the world.'
65. Cf. Arundhati Roy, *Power Politics* (Cambridge, Mass: South End Press, 2001). See also: Human Rights Watch, *The Enron Corporation: Corporate Complicity in Human Rights Violations*, (New York: Human Rights Watch, 1999).
66. Cf. Francis Cairncross, *The Death of Distance: How the Communications Revolution Will Change Our Lives* (Boston: Harvard Business School Press, 1997).
67. Nicholas Negroponte, *Being Digital* (London: Coronet 1996).
68. Timothy Leary, *Chaos and Cyber Culture* (Berkeley, California: Ronin, 1994).
69. Cf. Leo Marx, *The Machine in the Garden* (New York: Oxford University Press, 1964); James Carey, *Communication as Culture: Essays on Media and Society* (Boston: Unwin and Hyman, 1989), p. 191. David Nye, *American Technological Sublime* (Cambridge, Mass.: M.I.T. Press, 1994) offers a thorough exploration of these concepts and their place in the history of technology in America.
70. Alan Trachtenberg, *The Incorporation of America: Culture and Society in the Gilded Age* (New York: Hill and Wang 1982), p. 121. These arguments have been made more explicit in Tom Standage, *The Victorian Internet* (London: Weidenfeld and Nicolson, 1999).
71. Frank Webster, *Theories of the Information Society* (London: Routledge, 1995), p. 3.
72. Ibid., p. 217.
73. Ibid., p. 217.
74. Kevin Robbins and Frank Webster, 'Cybernetic capitalism: Information technology and everyday Life', in Vincent Mosko and Janet Waska (eds), *The*

Political Economy of Information (Wisconsin: University of Wisconsin Press, 1988), p. 56.
75. Karl Marx, *Grundrisse, Foundation of the Critique of Political Economy (Rough Draft)* (1857), trans. Martin Nicolaus (London: Allen Lane, 1973), p. 539. These points and other related issues are explored more thoroughly in Jon Stratton, 'Cyberspace and the globalization of culture', in David Porter (ed.), *Internet Culture* (New York: Routledge, 1997).
76. Cf. Giddens, *The Consequences of Modernity*, p. 14.
77. William Gibson, *All Tomorrow's Parties* (London: Penguin, 1999), p. 71.
78. William Gibson, *Iduro* (1996) (London: Penguin, 1997), p. 25; William Gibson, *Neuromancer* (1984) (London: HarperCollins, 1993), p. 117.
79. Michael Wolff, *Burn Rate: How I Survived the Gold Rush Years on the Internet* (London: Weidenfeld and Nicolson, 1998), p. 18.
80. Andrew Ross, *Strange Weather: Culture, Science and Technology in the Age of Limits* (London: Verso, 1991), p. 156.
81. Gibson, *All Tomorrow's Parties*, p. 252.
82. Gibson, *Iduro*, p. 209.
83. Ibid., p. 221.
84. Ibid., p. 100.
85. Ibid., p. 291.
86. Ibid., p. 38.
87. Ibid., p. 39.
88. Gibson, *All Tomorrow's Parties*, p. 15.
89. As Nick Heffernan's *Capital, Class and Technology in Contemporary American Culture* points out, however, this process is not without its own complications. Heffernan writes, p. 143: 'Yet the achievement of consciousness . . . omniscience and total supremacy is ultimately problematic. For the merged AIs do not simply *displace* the obsolete capitalist class, they *become* capital itself, now constituted as a de-individualized social totality. It is nowhere suggested that the AIs relinquish their control of the Tessier Ashpool corporate empire once they have freed themselves from and destroyed its human owners.'
90. William Gibson, *Pattern Recognition* (2003) (London: Viking, 2004), p. 3.
91. Ibid., p. 86.
92. Ibid., p. 6.
93. Ibid., p. 89.
94. Ibid., p. 307.

5. Pure Shores

1. Kem Nunn, *The Dogs of Winter* (1997) (London: No Exit, 1998), p. 20.
2. Ibid., p. 329.
3. Ibid., p. 361.
4. Cf. Ibid., p. 361: 'But as to the whereabouts of this place, the author remained quite mute, saying only it was there for those who looked.'
5. Lena Lencek and Gideon Bosker, *The Beach: The History of Paradise on Earth* (London: Secker and Warburg, 1998), p. xxi.

6. Ibid., p. 250.
7. Garland's concerns in *The Beach* have been shadowed by a large number of recent novels describing the experiences of Western travellers abroad, 'backpacker fiction' like, for example, William Sutcliffe, *Are You Experienced* (1997), Will Rhode, *Paperback Raita* (2002) and Emily Barr, *Backpack* (2001). Beyond these comparisons, the novel most frequently linked with *The Beach* is William Golding's *Lord of the Flies* (1954). Similar in terms of their setting and in the violent descriptions of the collapse of the 'utopian' communities they describe, there are obvious parallels between the two novels. Crucially, however, where Golding sees his Eden destroyed from within, shattered by the latent savagery of the boys, in Garland's novel the disruption comes from outside, carried onto the island by tourism and the market. A clear contrast can thus be established between the two texts. Where Golding uses images of paradise to explore existential themes, Garland's descriptions of life on his island open up debates linked to capitalism and consumption.
8. Alex Garland, *The Beach* (1996) (London: Penguin, 1997), p. 140. It is worth noting that the plot of Nunn's *The Dogs of Winter* published in 1998 has a number of striking similarities with Garland's earlier tale. Not only is Fletcher guided to Heart Attacks by a vague description of the place included in a dusty guidebook, but once there his experiences are marked by conflict with drug-cultivating locals.
9. Ibid., p. 19.
10. C.f. Lencek and Bosker, *The Beach*, p. 249.
11. Garland, *The Beach*, p. 49.
12. Ibid., p. 25.
13. Ibid., p. 194.
14. Joe Cummings, *Thailand* (8th edition) (Melbourne: Lonely Planet, 1999), p. 837.
15. Garland, *The Beach*, p. 139.
16. Cf. Jeanne Oliver, *Crete* (Hawthorn, Victoria: Lonely Planet, 2000), p. 10.
17. Garland, *The Beach*, p. 96.
18. Ibid., p. 193.
19. Ibid., p. 144.
20. Cf. Karl Marx and Frederick Engels, *The German Ideology*, trans. Clemens Dutt (1857) (London: Lawrence and Wishart, 1965), p. 58: 'The nature that preceded human history ... no longer exists anywhere (except perhaps on a few Australian coral-islands of recent origin).' See also: William Cronon (ed.), *Uncommon Ground: Toward Reinventing Nature* (London: Norton, 1995), p. 46: 'Market exchange and commodified relations with nature have been transforming the landscape of ... the entire planet, for centuries.' See also: Neil Smith, *Uneven Development: Nature, Capital and the Production of Space* (Oxford: Blackwell, 1984), p. 65: 'Through human labour and the production of nature at the global scale, human society has placed itself squarely at the centre of nature.'
21. Garland, *The Beach*, p. 424.
22. John Hodge, *The Beach* (London: Faber and Faber, 2000) (Film script), p. 80.
23. Ibid., pp. 80–2.
24. John Hodge, *Trainspotting*, in John Hodge, *Trainspotting and Shallow Grave* (London: Faber and Faber, 1996), p. 3.

Notes

25. Ibid., p. 106.
26. Lencek and Bosker, *The Beach*, p. 248.
27. Ibid., p. 249.
28. Ibid., p. xxiv.
29. William Wordsworth, 'To the Editor of the *Morning Post*', in *The Morning Post* (11 December 1844), reprinted in William Wordsworth, *Selected Prose*, edited by John Hayden (Harmondsworth: Penguin, 1988), p. 84.
30. Lynne Withey, *Grand Tours and Cook's Tours: A History of Leisure Travel, 1750 to 1915* (London: Aurum, 1997), p. 51.
31. Bryn Thomas, Tom Smallman, Pat Yale, *Britain* (3rd edition) (Melbourne: Lonely Planet, 1999), p. 608.
32. Ibid., p. 614.
33. Giddens, *The Consequences of Modernity*, p. 14.
34. Garland, *The Beach*, p. 5.
35. Cf. Jean-Francois Lyotard, *The Postmodern Condition: A Report on Knowledge*, trans. Geoff Bennington and Brian Massumi (Manchester: Manchester University Press, 1984).
36. A similar vision of globalization is offered in the opening to Garland's second novel, *The Tesseract* (1998). Beginning with a scene set in a McDonald's restaurant in the Philippines, Garland uses the inflammatory sign of the golden arches as shorthand for the same kind of bland and homogenous global culture described in the opening to *The Beach*. Garland's script for Danny Boyle's film *28 Days Later* (2002) moves away from the South-East Asian settings used in *The Beach* and *The Tesseract* and seems to leave behind the implicit commentaries on globalization that inform both novels. Despite the obvious contrast in subject matter, echoes of the themes developed in *The Beach* can, however, still be found. Seeking sanctuary from a deadly global virus, Garland's protagonists, Jim and Selena, escape London and the infected zombies that prowl its streets. Initially an army-controlled country house seems to promise security, but soon this community collapses into violence and the couple are forced to flee again. Only when they get to the Lake District (still, it seems, an English writer's favourite refuge from the perils of modernity) and discover that the plague is not as global as they had first feared do they find relief. With the virus successfully kept out of other parts of the world, the film ends with apocalypse averted. The point is that *28 Days Later* not only reveals striking similarities with Garland's plot for *The Beach*, but also a residual concern for a thematics linked to globalization and consumerism. The fact that the film draws heavily on George Romero's images of zombie-consumers in *Dawn of the Dead* (1978) makes these parallels even more apparent.
37. Garland, *The Beach*, p. 80, p. 238.
38. Ibid., p. 280.
39. Ibid., p. 127.
40. William Vollman, *Butterfly Stories* (London: Andre Deutsch, 1993), p. 5.
41. Ibid, pp. 82–3.
42. Michel Houellebecq, *Platform*, trans. Frank Wynne (London: Heinemann, 2002), p. 209. Houellebecq returns to the theme of tourism in his novella *Lanzarote*. (London: Heinemann, 2003).
43. Houllebecq, *Platform*, p. 237.

Notes

44. Cf. George Ritzer, *The McDonaldization of Society: An Investigation into the Changing Character of Contemporary Social Life* (London: Thousand Oaks, 1993).
45. Kevin Meethan, *Tourism in Global Society: Place, Culture, Consumption* (Houndmills: Palgrave, 2001), p. 122.
46. Michael Hardt and Antonio Negri, *Empire* (Cambridge, Mass: Harvard, 2000), p. xv.
47. Alexander Stille, 'Apocalypse soon', in *New York Times Book Review* (7 November 2002), p. 47; Hardt and Negri, *Empire*, p. 397.
48. Garland, *The Beach*, p. 438.
49. Ibid., p. 116.
50. Hardt and Negri, *Empire*, p. 218.
51. Cf. Dave Eggers, *You Shall Know Our Velocity* (2002) (London: Hamish Hamilton, 2003), p. 42: 'I gave them the routing number for the $80,000, their cash offer and apparently the going rate for people transformed into silhouettes to sell things. I felt briefly, mistakenly powerful: *My outline burned into the minds of millions!* But then came back down, crashing. It was an outline, it was reductive. It was nothing.'
52. Dave Eggers, 'We can't fix anything, even the smallest things, in Cuba', in Don George (ed.), *The Kindness of Strangers* (Melbourne: Lonely Planet, 2003), p. 120.
53. Ibid. p. 124.
54. Ibid. p. 123.

6. Migrating Globalization

1. Jhumpa Lahiri, 'Interpreter of maladies', in *Interpreter of Maladies* (London: Flamingo, 1999), pp. 43–44.
2. Ibid., p. 51.
3. Ibid., p. 50.
4. Ibid., p. 66.
5. Ibid., p. 66.
6. Ibid., p. 68.
7. Jhumpa Lahiri, 'A temporary matter', in *Interpreter of Maladies*, p. 11.
8. Jhumpa Lahiri, 'When Mr Prizada came to dine', in *Interpreter of Maladies*, p. 34.
9. Ibid., p. 33.
10. Salman Rushdie, 'Introduction', in Salman Rushdie and Elizabeth West (eds), *The Vintage Book of Indian Writing 1947–1997* (London: Vintage, 1997), p. x.
11. Ibid., p. xiv.
12. Salman Rushdie, 'Imaginary homelands', in *Imaginary Homelands: Essays and Criticism 1981–1991* (London: Granta, 1991), p. 20. In the same essay Rushdie claims, p. 15: 'Our identity is at once plural and partial. Sometimes we feel that we straddle two cultures; at other times, that we fall between two stools. But however ambiguous and shifting this ground may be, it is not an infertile territory for a writer to occupy.' See also: Homi Bhabha, 'DissemiNation: time, narrative and the margins of the modern nation', in Homi Bhabha (ed.), *Nation and Narration* (London: Routledge, 1990), p. 314: 'In the restless drive for cultural translation, hybrid sites of meaning open up a cleavage in the language of a culture which suggests that the similitude of the *symbol* as it plays across cultural sites must not

Notes

obscure the fact that repetition of the *sign* is, in each specific social practice, both different and differential.'
13. Anthony Smith, 'Towards a global culture?', in Mike Featherstone *et al.* (eds), *Global Culture: Nationalism, Globalization and Modernity*, pp. 179–80.
14. Hardt and Negri, *Empire* (Cambridge, Mass: Harvard University Press, 2000), p. 145.
15. Ibid., p. 146.
16. Ibid., p. 146.
17. Frederick Buell, *National Culture and the New Global System* (Baltimore: Johns Hopkins University Press, 1994), p. 232.
18. Cf. Pico Iyer, *The Global Soul: Jet Lag, Shopping Malls and the Search for Home* (London: Bloomsbury, 2000), p. 269: 'And so our dreams of distant places change as fast as images on MTV, and the immigrant arrives at the land that means freedom to him, only to find that it's already been recast by other hands. Some of the places around us look as anonymous as airport lounges, some as strange as our living room suddenly flooded with foreign objects. The only home that any Global Soul can find these days is, it seems, in the midst of the alien and indecipherable.'
19. Cf. John Tomlinson, *Cultural Imperialism: A Critical Introduction* (London: Continuum, 1991).
20. Aijaz Ahmad, *In Theory: Classes, Nations, Literatures* (London: Verso, 1992), p. 217.
21. Graham Huggan, *The Postcolonial Exotic: Marketing the Margins* (London: Routledge, 2001), p. vii.
22. Iain Chambers, *Migrancy, Culture, Identity* (London: Routledge, 1994), pp. 37–8.
23. Jameson, 'Notes on globalization as a philosophical issue', in Fredric Jameson and Misao Miyoshi (eds), *Cultures of Globalization* (London: Duke University, 1998), p. 63.
24. David Crystal, *English as a Global Language* (Cambridge: Cambridge University Press, 1997).
25. Martin Kayman, 'The state of English as a global language: Communicating culture', in *Textual Practice* (2004), 18, (1), 17.
26. Ibid., p. 18.
27. Amitava Kumar, 'Introduction', in Amitava Kumar (ed.), *World Bank Literature* (Minneapolis: University of Minnesota Press, 2003), p. xxi.
28. Stephen Greenblatt, 'Racial memory and literary history', in *PMLA* (2001), 116, (1), 53.
29. Cf. Richard Alexander, 'G.lobal L.anguages O.ppress B.ut A.re L.iberating too: the dialectics of English', in Christian Mair (ed.), *The Politics of English as a World Language* (Amsterdam: Ropodi, 2003), p. 95.
30. Cf. Bill Buford, 'Editorial' in *Granta: Dirty Realism* (1983), 8, 5: 'A flat "unsurprised" language, pared down to the plainest of plain styles. The sentences are stripped of ornament.'
31. Cf. Jumpha Lahiri's first novel *The Namesake* (2003) (London: HarperCollins, 2004) echoes the approach used in *Interpreter of Maladies*, choosing to tell its small tale of the growth and development of Gogol, a Boston born child of Bengali parents, in the same stripped down, Carveresque prose.

32. Jhumpa Lahiri, 'The third and final continent', in *Interpreter of Maladies*, pp. 197–98.
33. Cf. Judith Caesar, 'Beyond cultural identity in Jhumpa Lahiri's "When Mr Prizadi Came to Dine" ', in *North Dakota Quarterly* (2003), 70, (1), 91: '*The Interpreter of Maladies* [sic] goes beyond post-colonial fiction, just as it goes beyond traditional mainstream American fiction and hyphenated American fiction.'
34. Arjun Appadurai, *Modernity at Large*, p. 31.
35. Bharati Mukherjee, 'Beyond multiculturalism: Surviving the nineties', in *Journal of Modern Literature* (1996), 20, (1), 29, 31, 32, 34.
36. Bharati Mukherjee, 'A four-hundred year-old woman', in Philomena Mariani (ed.), *Critical Fictions* (Seattle: Bay Press, 1991), p. 24.
37. Jennifer Drake, 'Looting American culture: Bharati Mukherjee's immigrant narratives', in *Contemporary Literature* (1999), 40, (1), 61.
38. Ibid., p. 61.
39. Emmanuel Nelson, 'Introduction', in Emmanuel Nelson (ed.), *Bharati Mukherjee: Critical Perspectives* (New York: Garland, 1993), p. ix.
40. Debjani Banerjee, ' "In the presence of history": the representation of past and present Indias in Bharati Mukherjee's fiction', in Nelson (ed.), *Bharati Mukherjee*, p. 171; Anindyo Roy, 'The aesthetics of an (un)willing immigrant: Bharati Mukherjee's *Days and Nights in Calcutta* and *Jasmine*', in Nelson (ed.), *Bharati Mukherjee*, p. 128.
41. Gurleen Grewel, 'Born again American: the immigrant consciousness in *Jasmine*', in Nelson (ed.), *Bharati Mukherjee*, p. 183; Susan Koshy, 'The geography of female subjectivity; ethnicity, gender, and diaspora', in Lois Parkinson Zamora (ed.), *Contemporary American Women Writers: Gender, Class, Ethnicity* (Harlow, Essex: Addison Wesley Longman, 1998), p. 139.
42. Anthony Alessandrini, 'Reading Bharati Mukherjee, reading globalization', in Kumar (ed.), *World Bank Literature*.
43. Bharati Mukherjee, *Jasmine* (1989) (London: Virago, 1994), p. 229, p.231.
44. Ibid., p. 77.
45. Ibid., p. 85.
46. Ibid., p. 240.
47. Ibid., p. 229.
48. Andrea Dlaska, *Ways of Belonging: The Making of New Americans in the Fiction of Bharati Mukherjee* (Wien: Wilhelm Braumuller, 1999), p. 162.
49. Ibid., p. 140.
50. Mukherjee, *Jasmine*, p. 41.
51. Bharati Mukherjee, 'Oh, Isaac, Oh, Bernard, Oh Mohan', in Roger Rosenblatt (ed.), *Consuming Desires: Consumption, Culture and the Pursuit of Happiness* (Washington: Island Press, 1999), p. 84.
52. Mukherjee, *Jasmine*, p. 107.
53. Cf. Ibid., pp. 88–9.
54. Ibid., p. 29.
55. Cf. Suzanne Kehde, 'Colonial discourse and female identity: Bharati Mukherjee's *Jasmine*', in Anne Brown and Marjanne Gooze (eds), *International Women's Writing: New Landscapes of Identity* (Westport, Conn.: Greenwood, 1995).

Notes

56. Frederick Buell, *National Culture and the New Global System* (Baltimore: Johns Hopkins, 1994), p. 207.
57. Mita Banerjee, *The Chutnification of History: Salman Rushdie, Michael Ondaatje, Bharati Mukherjee and the Postcolonial Debate* (Heidelberg: Unversitatsverlag C. Winter, 2002), p. 81.
58. Arundhati Roy, *Power Politics* (Second Edition) (Cambridge, MA.: South End Press, 2001), p. 14, p. 31.
59. Arundhati Roy, *The Ordinary Person's Guide to Empire* (London: HarperCollins, 2004), pp. 5–6.
60. Roy, *Power Politics*, p. 33.
61. Deepika Bahri, 'Always becoming: narratives of nation and self in Bharati Mukerkjee's *Jasmine*', in Susan Roberson (ed.), *Women, America and Movement: Narratives of Relocation* (Columbia: University of Missouri, 1998), pp. 137–8.
62. Ibid., p. 138.
63. Edward Soja, *Postmetropolis: Critical Studies of Cities and Regions* (Cambridge: Blackwell, 2000), p. 200; Jonathan Friedman, 'Being in the world: globalization and localization', in Featherstone (ed.), *Global Culture*, p. 311.
64. Arundhati Roy, *The God of Small Things* (1997) (London: HarperCollins, 1998), p. 13, p. 126.
65. Julie Mullaney, *Arundhati Roy's* The God of Small Things (New York: Continuum, 2002), p. 52. See also, p. 15: 'In some contrast to Roy's later critical articles which tend to oscillate between focusing on globalization as a result of top-down dominance to recognizing it more broadly as a transcultural process in which both individuals and local communities actively appropriate and transform for their own uses and contexts inherited models, *The God of Small Things* itself contains a more alert and detailed, if indirect, exploration of the *variety* of strategies deployed by the receiving as well as the sending culture in its transactions with a global culture. In this, *The God of Small Things* is concerned with the resemblances *between* how individuals, groups, or local communities engage with the forces of globalization and how they might have engaged and appropriated the forces of imperial dominance historically.'
66. It is worth noting that Roy's *Power Politics* includes the following sideswipe at Lahiri, p. 9: 'Jhumpa Lahiri, the American writer of Indian origin who won the Pulitzer Prize, came to India recently to have a traditional Bengali wedding. The wedding was reported on the front pages of national newspapers.'
67. Roy, *The God of Small Things*, p. 274, p. 60.
68. Huggan, *The Postcolonial Exotic*, p. 77.
69. Roy, *The God of Small Things*, p. 62.
70. Ibid., p. 140.
71. Ibid., p. 140.
72. Ibid., p. 127.
73. Ibid., p. 27.
74. Ibid., p. 55.
75. Ibid., p. 20.
76. Ibid., p. 15.
77. Ibid., p. 19.
78. Ibid., p. 19.

79. Ibid., p. 19.
80. Simon Gikandi, 'Globalization and the claims of postcoloniality', in *South Atlantic Quarterly* (2001), 100, (3), 654.
81. Sandra Cisneros, 'Woman hollering creek', in *Woman Hollering Creek* (1991) (London: Bloomsbury, 1993), p. 55.
82. Ann Ducille, 'Dyes and dolls: multicultural Barbie and the marketing of difference', in *Differences* (1994), 6, (1), 48–9.
83. Leslie Sklair, *Globalization: Capitalism and its Alternatives* (Oxford: Oxford University Press, 2002), p. 196.
84. Ibid., p. 2.
85. Cf. Jeff Thomson, ' "What is called heaven": identity in Sandra Cisneros's *Woman Hollering Creek*', in *Studies in Short Fiction* (1994) 31, (3), 417: 'in "Barbie-Q" Cisneros attacks artificial feminine stereotypes.'
86. David Howes, 'Introduction: commodities and cultural borders' in David Howes (ed.), *Cross-Cultural Consumption: Global Markets and Global Realities* (London: Routledge, 1996), p. 3.
87. Jonathan Friedman, 'Being in the world: globalization and localization', in Howes (ed.), *Cross-Cultural Consumption*, p. 315.
88. Sandra Cisneros, 'Barbie-Q', in *Woman Hollering Creek*, p. 16.
89. Cf. Jeannie Thomas, *Naked Barbies, Warrior Joes and Other Forms of Visible Gender* (Urbana: University of Illinois Press, 2003), p. 131: 'If the media invades homes and shapes consumers, the consumers fight back and rework mass-marketed goods – including Barbie – whether or not Mattell like them doing so.'
90. Cisneros reinforces this sense of the relationship between smoke and Mexican identity in the story *'Bien pretty'*, a piece that describes a creation myth in which the Mexican is the person who has been baked in the oven longer than the others and been made darker as a result. See: Sandra Cisneros, 'Bien pretty', in *Woman Hollering Creek*.
91. Cisneros, 'Barbie-Q', p. 16.
92. Ibid., p. 16.
93. Sandra Cisneros, 'Mexican movies', in *Woman Hollering Creek*, p. 12.
94. Sandra Cisneros, 'The Marlboro man', in *Woman Hollering Creek*, p. 59.
95. Sandra Cisneros, 'Merican', in *Woman Hollering Creek*, p. 20.
96. Howes, 'Introduction: commodities and cultural borders', in Howes (ed.), *Cross-Cultural Consumption*, p. 5.
97. Canclini, *Consumers and Citizens*, p. 26.
98. Susan Roberson, 'Narratives of relocation and dislocation: an introduction', in Roberson (ed.), *Women, America and Movement*, p. 5. See also: Jacqueline Doyle, 'Haunting the borderlands: La llorona in Sandra Cisneros' "Women hollering creek" ', in the same collection.
99. Jeff Thomson, ' "What is called heaven" ', p. 424.
100. Chambers, *Migrancy, Culture, Identity*, p. 2.
101. Janet Abu-Lughod, 'Going beyond global babble', in Anthony King (ed.), *Culture, Globalization and the World System: Contemporary Conditions for the Representation of Identity* (Houndmills: Macmillan, 1991), p. 135.
102. Padmina Mongia, 'Introduction', in Padmina Mongia (ed.), *Contemporary Postcolonial Theory: A Reader* (London: Arnold, 1996), p. 7.

Notes

103. Edward Said, 'Globalizing literary study', in *PMLA* (2001), 116, (1), 64.
104. Cf. Giles Gunn, 'Introduction: globalizing literary studies', in *PMLA* (2001), 116, (1).
105. Paul Jay, 'Beyond discipline? globalization and the future of English', in *PMLA* (2001), 116, (1), 35.

Bibliography

Abu-Lughod, Janet, *New York, Chicago, Los Angeles: America's Global Cities* (Minneapolis: University of Minnesota Press, 1999).
Adorno, Theodore, 'Culture industry reconsidered', trans. Anson Rabinbach, in *New German Critique* (1975), 6, 13.
Ahmad, Aijaz, *In Theory: Classes, Nations, Literatures* (London: Verso, 1992).
Akass, Kim and Janet McCabe (eds), *Reading Sex and the City* (London: Taurus, 2004).
Alexander, Richard, 'G.lobal L.anguages O.ppress B.ut A.re L.iberating too: the dialectics of English', in Christian Mair (ed.), *The Politics of English as a World Language* (Amsterdam: Ropodi, 2003).
Amis, Kingsley, *The Bond Dossier* (London: Pan, 1965).
Appadurai, Arjun, *Modernity at Large: Cultural Dimensions of Globalization* (Minneapolis: University of Minnesota Press, 1997).
Appadurai, Arjun (ed.), *Globalization* (Durham: Duke University Press, 2001).
Auge, Marc, *Non-Places: Introduction to an Anthropology of Supermodernity*, trans. John Howe (London: Verso, 1995).
Bakan, Joel, *The Corporation: The Pathological Pursuit of Power and Profit* (London: Constable, 2004).
Baker, Stephen, *The Fiction of Postmodernity* (Edinburgh: Edinburgh University Press, 2000).
Baker, T. N., *Sheisty* (Columbus, Ohio: Triple Crown, 2004).
Balshaw, Maria, *Looking for Harlem: Urban Aesthetics in African American Literature* (London: Pluto, 2000).
Banerjee, Mita, *The Chutnification of History: Salman Rushdie, Michael Ondaatje, Bharati Mukherjee and the Postcolonial Debate* (Heidelberg: Unversitatsverlag C. Winter, 2002).
Barber, Benjamin, *Jihad vs. McWorld* (New York: Ballantine Books, 1995).
Bahri, Deepika, 'Always becoming: narratives of nation and self in Bharati Mukherjee's *Jasmine*', in Susan Roberson (ed.), *Women, America and*

Bibliography

Movement: *Narratives of Relocation* (Columbia: University of Missouri, 1998), pp. 137–8.

Barnot, Richard and Cavanagh, John, *Global Dreams: Imperial Corporations and the New World Order* (New York: Simon and Schuster, 1994).

Barr, Emily, *Backpack* (London: Headline, 2001).

Beatty, Paul, *White Boy Shuffle* (London: Minerva, 1996).

—,*Tuff* (2000) (London: Vintage, 2001).

Berger, John, 'Against the Great Defeat of the World', in *Race and Class: The Threat of Globalism* (1998), 40, (2/3).

Bérubé, Michel, 'Introduction: worldly English', in *Modern Fiction Studies* (2002), 48, (1).

Bhabha, Homi (ed.), *Nation and Narration* (London: Routledge, 1990).

Bilton, Alan, *An Introduction to Contemporary American Fiction* (Edinburgh: Edinburgh University Press, 2002).

Boon, Kevin, 'Men and the nostalgia for violence: culture and culpability in Chuck Palahniuk's *Fight Club*', in *The Journal of Men's Studies* (Spring 2003), 11, (3).

Bourdieu, Pierre, *Distinction: A Social Critique of the Judgement of Taste*, trans. Richard Nice (London: Routledge and Kegan Paul, 1986).

Bowlby, Rachel, *Shopping with Freud* (London: Routledge, 1993).

—,*Carried Away: The Invention of Modern Shopping* (London: Faber and Faber, 2000).

Boyd, William, 'The course of true life', in *Observer* (11 November 1998).

Brewer, John and Roy Porter (eds), *Consumption and the World of Goods* (London: Routledge, 1993).

Browne, J. Ross, *Etchings of a Whale Cruise* (1846) (Cambridge, Mass.: Belknap, 1968).

Buell, Frederick, *National Culture and the New Global System* (Baltimore: Johns Hopkins University Press, 1994).

Buchloh, Benjamin, 'Andy Warhol's one dimensional art: 1956–1966', in Kynaston McShin (ed.), *Andy Warhol: A Retrospective* (New York: Museum of Modern Art, 1989).

Bushnell, Candace, *Sex and the City* (1996) (London: Abacus, 2004).

Caesar, Judith, 'Beyond cultural identity in Jhumpa Lahiri's "When Mr Prizadi came to dine" ', in *North Dakota Quarterly* (2003), 70, (1).

Campbell, Colin, *The Romantic Ethos and the Spirit of Modern Consumerism* (Cambridge: Blackwell, 1987).

Cairncross, Frances, *The Death of Distance: How the Communications Revolution Will Change Our Lives* (Boston: Harvard Business School Press, 1997).

Canclini, Nestor Garca, *La Globalización Imaginada* (Buenos Aires: Paidós, 1999).

—,*Consumers and Citizens: Globalization and Multicultural Conflicts* (Minneapolis: University of Minnesota Press, 2001).

Carey, James, *Communication as Culture: Essays on Media and Society* (Boston: Unwin and Hyman, 1989).
Cashmore, Ellis, *The Black Culture Industry* (London: Routledge, 1997).
Cavallaro, Dani, *Cyberpunk and Cyberculture: Science Fiction and the Work of William Gibson* (London: Athlone, 2000).
Chambers, Iain, *Migrancy, Culture, Identity* (London: Routledge, 1994).
Chopin, Kate, *The Awakening* (1899) (London: Penguin, 2004).
Cisneros, Sandra, *Woman Hollering Creek* (1991) (London: Bloomsbury, 1993).
Clark, Michael, 'Faludi, *Fight Club*, and phallic masculinity: exploring the emasculating economics of patriarchy', in *The Journal of Men's Studies* (2002), 11, (1).
Coupland, Douglas, *Microserfs* (London: HarperCollins, 1995).
Coward, Rosalind, *Female Desire: Women's Sexuality Today* (London: Paladin, 1984).
Crevecouer, J. Hector St John De, *Letters from an American Farmer* (1782) (Oxford: Oxford University, 1997).
Cronon, William, *Uncommon Ground: Toward Reinventing Nature* (London: Norton, 1995).
Crystal, David, *English as a Global Language* (Cambridge: Cambridge University Press, 1997).
Cummings, Joe, *Thailand* (8th edition) (Melbourne: Lonely Planet, 1999).
Davis, Erik, *Techgnosis: Myth, Magic and Mysticism in the Age of Information* (London: Serpent's Tail, 1998).
DeLillo, Don, *Libra* (1988) (London: Penguin, 1989).
—,*Underworld* (1997) (London: Picador, 1998).
—,*Cosmopolis* (2003) (London: Picador, 2004)
Diaz, Junot, *Drown* (New York: Riverhead Books, 1997).
Dlaska, Andrea, *Ways of Belonging: The Making of New Americans in the Fiction of Bharati Mukherjee* (Wien: Wilhelm Braumuller, 1999).
Donaldson, Scott, *By Force of Will: The Life and Art of Ernest Hemingway* (New York: Viking, 1977).
Dos Passos, John, *Manhattan Transfer* (1925) (Boston: Houghton Mifflin, 1953).
Douglas, Mary and Isherwood, Baron, *The World of Goods* (Harmondsworth: Penguin, 1978).
Drake, Jennifer, 'Looting American culture: Bharati Mukherjee's immigrant narratives', in *Contemporary Literature* (1999), 40, (1).
Ducille, Ann, 'Dyes and dolls: multicultural Barbie and the marketing of difference,' in *Differences* (1994), 6, (1).
Durix, Jean-Pierre, *The Global and the Particular in the English Speaking World* (Dijon: Edition Universitaires de Dijon, 2002).

Dyson, Michael, *Reflecting Black: African American Cultural Criticism* (Minneapolis: University of Minnesota Press, 1993).
Easthope, Anthony, *What a Man's Gotta Do: The Masculine Myth in Popular Culture* (London: Routledge, 1990).
Edwards, Paul, *The Southern Urban Negro as a Consumer* (1932) (New York: Negro University Press, 1969).
Eggers, Dave, *You Shall Know Our Velocity* (2002) (London: Hamish Hamilton, 2003).
—, 'We can't fix anything, even the smallest things, in Cuba', in Don George (ed.), *The Kindness of Strangers* (Melbourne: Lonely Planet, 2003).
Ellis, Bret Easton, *Less than Zero* (London: Picador, 1985).
—, *The Rules of Attraction* (London: Picador, 1987).
—, *American Psycho* (London: Picador, 1991).
—, *The Informers* (London: Picador, 1994).
—, *Glamorama* (1998) (London: Picador, 1999).
Ellison, Ralph, *Invisible Man* (1952) (London: Penguin, 2001).
Ewen, Stuart, *Captains of Consciousness: Advertising and the Social Roots of Consumer Culture* (1976) (25th Anniversary Edition) (New York: Basic Books, 2001).
Faludi, Susan, *Stiffed: The Betrayal of Modern Man* (London: Vintage, 2000).
Faulkner, William, *The Sound and the Fury* (Harmondsworth: Penguin, 1982).
Featherstone, Mike (ed.), *Global Culture: Nationalism, Globalization and Modernity* (London: Sage, 1990).
Featherstone, Mike, Scott Lash and Roland Robertson (eds), *Global Modernities* (London: Sage, 1995).
Ferguson, Niall, *The Cash Nexus: Money and Power in the Modern World, 1700–2000* (London: Allen Lane, 2001).
Fitzgerald, F. Scott, *The Great Gatsby* (1926) (London: Heinemann, 1982).
Fleming, Ian, *From Russia With Love* (1957) (London: Hodder and Stoughton, 1988).
Forster, E. M., *Howards End* (1910) (Harmondsworth: Penguin, 1960).
Frank, Thomas, *The Conquest of Cool: Business Culture, Counterculture and the Rise of the Hip Consumer* (Chicago: University of Chicago Press, 1997).
Frazier, E. Franklin, *The Black Bourgeoisie: The Rise of a New Middle Class* (New York: Free Press, 1957).
Friedman, Monroe, *A 'Brand' New Language: Commercial Influences in Literature and Culture* (New York: Greenwood, 1991).
Friedman, Thomas, *The Lexus and the Olive Tree* (London: HarperCollins, 1999).
Garland, Alex, *The Beach* (1996) (London: Penguin, 1997).

—, *The Tesseract* (1998) (London: Penguin, 1999).
—, *28 Days Later* (London: Faber and Faber, 2002).
George, Nelson, *Buppies, B-Boys and Bohos: Notes on a Post-Soul Black Culture* (London: HarperCollins, 1994).
Gibson, William, *Neuromancer* (1984) (London: HarperCollins, 1993).
—, *Virtual Light* (1993) (London: Penguin, 1994).
—, *All Tomorrow's Parties* (London: Penguin, 1999).
—, *Iduro* (1996) (London: Penguin, 1997).
—, *Pattern Recognition* (2003) (London: Viking, 2004).
Giddens, Anthony, *The Consequences of Modernity* (Cambridge: Polity, 1990).
Gikandi, Simon, 'Globalization and the claims of postcoloniality', in *South Atlantic Quarterly* (2001), 100, (3).
Giles, James, *Violence in the Contemporary American Novel: An End to Innocence* (Columbia, South Carolina: University of South Carolina Press, 2000).
Gilroy, Paul, *Small Acts* (London: Serpent's Tail, 1993).
Godden, Richard, *Fictions of Capital: The American Novel from James to Mailer* (Cambridge: Cambridge University Press, 1990).
Golding, William, *Lord of the Flies* (1954) (London: Faber and Faber, 1986).
Goldman, Robert and Stephen Papson, *Nike Culture: The Sign of the Swoosh* (London: Sage, 2004).
Goodrum, Charles and Helen Dalrymple, *Advertising in America* (New York: Harry N. Abrams, 1990).
Gordon, George (Lord Byron), *Don Juan* (1823), in Frederick Page (ed.), *Byron Poetical Works* (Revised Edition) (Oxford: Oxford University Press, 1987).
Graukroger, Steven, 'Romanticism and decommodification: Marxism's conception of socialism', in *Economy and Society* (1986), 15, (3).
Greenblatt, Stephen, 'Racial memory and literary history', in *PMLA* (2001), 116, (1).
Gunn, Giles, 'Introduction: Globalizing literary studies', in *PMLA* (2001), 116, (1).
Hardt, Michael and Antonio Negri, *Empire* (Cambridge, Mass: Harvard University Press, 2000).
—, *Multitude: War and Democracy in the Age of Empire* (New York: Penguin, 2004).
Heffernan, Nick, *Capital, Class and Technology in Contemporary American Culture: Projecting Post-Fordism* (London: Pluto, 2000).
Held, David, *Global Covenant: The Social Democratic Alternative to the Washington Consensus* (Cambridge: Polity, 2004).
Hemingway, Ernest, 'Hills like white elephants' (1927), in *Men Without Women* (New York: Scribner's, 1928).

Bibliography

—,*The Moveable Feast* (1936) (London: Random House, 1994).
—,*Across the River and Into the Trees* (New York: Scribner's, 1950).
—,*The Garden of Eden* (New York: Scribner's, 1986).
Hertz, Noreena, *The Silent Takeover: Global Capitalism and the Death of Democracy* (London: Heinemann, 2001).
—,*Trainspotting*, in John Hodge, *Trainspotting and Shallow Grave* (London: Faber and Faber, 1996).
Hodge, John, *The Beach* (London: Faber and Faber, 2000) (Film script).
hooks, bell, *Outlaw Culture: Resisting Representations* (New York: Routledge 1994).
Houellebecq, Michel, *Atomised*, trans. Frank Wynne (London: Heinemann, 2000).
—,*Platform*, trans. Frank Wynne (London: Heinemann, 2002).
—,*Lanzarote*, trans. Frank Wynne (London: Heinemann, 2003).
Howes, David (ed.), *Cross-Cultural Consumption: Global Markets and Global Realities* (London: Routledge, 1996).
Huggan, Graham, *The Postcolonial Exotic: Marketing the Margins* (London: Routledge, 2001).
Human Rights Watch, *The Enron Corporation: Corporate Complicity in Human Rights Violations* (New York: Human Rights Watch, 1999).
Huntke, Steffen, *Conspiracy and Paranoia in Contemporary American Fiction: The Works of Don DeLillo and Joseph McElroy* (Frankfurt: Peter Lang, 1994).
Hurston, Zora Neale, 'Characteristics of negro expression', in Nancy Cunard (ed.), *Negro Anthology* (London: Wishart, 1934).
Iyer, Pico, *The Global Soul: Jet Lag, Shopping Malls and the Search for Home* (London: Bloomsbury, 2000).
Jaggi, Maya, 'Poetry in the projects', in *Guardian* (22 July 2000).
Jameson, Fredric, 'The politics of theory: ideological positions in the postmodernism debate', in *New German Critique* (1984), 33.
—,'Postmodernism and the Market', in Slavoj Zizek (ed.), *Mapping Ideology* (London: Verso, 1994).
—,'Notes on globalization as a philosophical issue', in Jameson, Fredric and Miyoshi, Misao (eds), *Cultures of Globalization* (London: Duke University Press, 1998).
Jarvis, Brian, *Postmodern Cartographies: The Geographical Imagination in Contemporary American Culture* (London: Pluto, 1998).
Jay, Paul, 'Beyond discipline? Globalization and the future of English', in *PMLA* (2001), 116, (1).
Jefferds, Susan, *The Remasculinization of America: Gender and the Vietnam War* (Bloomington: Indiana University Press, 1989).
Joyce, James, *Ulysses* (1922) (London: Bodley Head, 1993).
K'wan, *Road Dawgz* (Columbus, Ohio: Triple Crown, 2003).

Kayman, Martin, 'The state of English as a global language: Communicating culture', in *Textual Practice* (2004), 18, (1).

Kehde, Suzanne, 'Colonial discourse and female identity: Bharati Mukherjee's *Jasmine*', in Anne Brown and Marjanne Gooze (eds), *International Women's Writing: New Landscapes of Identity* (Westport, Conn: Greenwood, 1995).

Kelley, Robin, *Race Rebels: Culture, Politics and the Black Working Class* (New York: The Free Press 1994).

—, 'Playing for keeps: pleasure and profit on the postindustrial playground', in Wahneema Lubiano (ed.), *The House that Race Built* (New York: Vintage, 1998).

King, Anthony (ed.), *Culture, Globalization and the World System: Contemporary Conditions for the Representation of Identity* (Houndmills: Macmillan, 1991).

Klein, Naomi, *No Logo: Taking Aim at the Brand Bullies* (London: HarperCollins, 1999).

—, *Fences and Windows: Dispatches from the Front Lines of the Globalization Debate* (London: HarperCollins, 2002).

Knight, Peter, 'Everything is connected: *Underworld*'s secret history of paranoia', in *Modern Fiction Studies* (1999), 45, (3).

Koshy, Susan, 'The geography of female subjectivity: ethnicity, gender, and diaspora', in Lois Parkinson Zamora (ed.), *Contemporary American Women Writers: Gender, Class, Ethnicity* (Harlow, Essex: Addison Wesley Longman, 1998).

Kumar, Amitava (ed.), *World Bank Literature* (Minneapolis: University of Minnesota Press, 2003).

Lahiri, Jhumpa, *Interpreter of Maladies* (London: HarperCollins, 1999).

—, *The Namesake* (2003) (London: HarperCollins, 2004).

Leary, Timothy, *Chaos and Cyberculture* (California: Ronin, 1994).

LeClair, Tom, *In the Loop: Don DeLillo and the Systems Novel* (Urbana: University of Illinois Press, 1987).

Lencek, Lena and Gideon Bosker, *The Beach: The History of Paradise on Earth* (London: Secker and Warburg, 1998).

Locke, Alain (ed.), *The New Negro* (New York: Albert and Charles Boni, 1927).

Lyotard, Jean-Francois, *The Postmodern Condition: A Report on Knowledge*, trans. Geoff Bennington and Brian Massumi (Manchester: Manchester University Press, 1984).

McBride, Stephen and John Wiseman (eds), *Globalization and its Discontents* (London: Macmillan, 2000).

McFall, Liz, *Advertising: A Cultural Economy* (London: Sage, 2004).

McInerney, Jay, *The Story of My Life* (New York: Atlantic Monthly Press, 1988).

—, *Model Behaviour* (London: Bloomsbury, 1998).
Mansfield, Katherine, *The Collected Stories* (London: Penguin, 2001).
Mariani, Philomena (ed.), *Critical Fictions* (Seattle: Bay Press, 1991).
Marinetti, Filippo, 'The founding and manifesto of futurism' (1909), in Filippo Marinetti, *Selected Writings*, edited and translated by R.W. Flint (London: Secker and Warburg, 1972).
Marx, Karl, *Grundrisse, Foundation of the Critique of Political Economy (Rough Draft)* (1857), trans. Martin Nicolaus (London: Allen Lane, 1973).
Marx, Karl and Frederick Engels, *The German Ideology* (1857), trans. Clemens Dutt (1932) (London: Lawrence and Wishart, 1965).
Marx, Leo, *The Machine in the Garden* (New York: Oxford University Press, 1964).
Mattelart, Armand, *Advertising International: The Privatisation of Public Space*, trans. Michael Chanan (Routledge: London, 1991).
Mazza, Chris and Jeffrey DeStell (eds), *Chick-Lit: Postfeminist Fiction* (Normal, Illinois: FC2, 1995).
Meethan, Kevin, *Tourism in Global Society: Place, Culture, Consumption* (Houndmills: Palgrave, 2001).
Melville, Herman, *Moby-Dick, or, The Whale* (1851) (Oxford: Oxford World's Classics, 1998).
Mengham, Rob (ed.), *An Introduction to Contemporary Fiction* (Cambridge: Polity, 1999).
Micklethwait, John and Adrian Wooldridge, *A Future Perfect: The Challenge and Hidden Promise of Globalization* (London: William Heinemann, 2000).
Miles, Steven, *Consumerism as a Way of Life* (London: Sage, 1998).
Millard, Kenneth, *Contemporary American Fiction: An Introduction to American Fiction Since 1970* (Oxford: Oxford University Press, 2000).
Monbiot, George, *Captive State: The Corporate Takeover of Britain* (London: Macmillan, 2000).
Mongia, Padmina (ed.), *Contemporary Postcolonial Theory: A Reader* (London: Arnold, 1996).
Moses, Cathy, *Dissenting Fictions: Identity and Resistance in the Contemporary American Novel* (New York: Garland, 2000).
Mosse, George, *The Image of Man: The Creation of Modern Masculinity* (New York: Oxford University Press, 1996).
Mukherjee, Bharati, 'A four-hundred year-old woman', in Philomena Mariani (ed.), *Critical Fictions* (Seattle: Bay Press, 1991).
—, *Jasmine* (1989) (London: Virago, 1994).
—, 'Beyond multiculturalism: surviving the nineties', in *Journal of Modern Literature* (1996), 20, (1).
—, 'Oh, Isaac, Oh, Bernard, Oh Mohan', in Roger Rosenblatt (ed.), *Consuming Desires: Consumption, Culture and the Pursuit of Happiness* (Washington: Island Press, 1999).

Mullaney, Julie, *Arundhati Roy's* The God of Small Things (New York: Continuum, 2002).
Mullins, Paul, *Race and Affluence: An Archaeology of African-American Consumer Culture* (New York: Kluwer Academic, 1999).
Murphet, Julian, *Literature and Race in Los Angeles* (Cambridge: Cambridge University Press, 2001).
Neal, Mark, *Soul Babies: Black Popular Culture and the Post-Soul Aesthetic* (New York: Routledge, 2002).
Negroponte, Nicholas, *Being Digital* (London: Coronet, 1996).
Nelson, Emmanuel (ed.), *Bharati Mukherjee: Critical Perspectives* (New York: Garland, 1993).
Niblock, Sarch, ' "My Manolos, my self": Manolo Blahnik shoes and desire', in Kim Akass and Janet McCabe (eds), *Reading Sex and the City* (London: Taurus, 2004).
Nunn, Kem, *Tapping the Source* (1984) (London: No Exit, 1998).
—, *The Dogs of Winter* (1997) (London: No Exit, 1998).
—, *Tijuana Straits* (New York: Scribner's, 2004).
Nye, David, *American Technological Sublime* (Cambridge, Mass.: M.I.T. Press, 1994).
O'Brien, Susie and Imre Szeman, 'Introduction: the globalization of fiction/the fiction of globalization', in *South Atlantic Quarterly* (2001), 100, (3).
O'Hara, Daniel, *Empire Burlesque: The Fate of Critical Culture in Global America* (Durham, North Carolina: Duke University Press, 2003).
Oliver, Jeanne, *Crete* (Hawthorn, Victoria: Lonely Planet, 2000).
Oliver, W.H. and B.R. Williams (eds), *The Oxford History of New Zealand* (Revised Edition) (Oxford: Clarendon, 1987).
Olson, Charles, *Call me Ishmael: A Study of Melville* (1947) (London: Jonathan Cape, 1967).
Osteen, Mark, *The Economy of Ulysses: Making Both Ends Meet* (New York: Syracuse University Press, 1995).
—, *American Magic and Dread: Don DeLillo's Dialogue with Culture* (Philadelphia: University of Pennsylvania Press, 2000).
Palahniuk, Chuck, *Fight Club* (1996) (London: Vintage 1997).
—, *Invisible Monsters* (1999) (London: Vintage, 2000).
—, *Survivor* (1999) (London: Vintage, 2000).
—, *Choke* (2001) (London: Vintage, 2002).
—, *Lullaby* (New York: Random House, 2002).
—, *Diary* (2003) (London: Vintage, 2004).
—, *Non-Fiction* (London: Jonathan Cape, 2004).
Peyser, Thomas, *Utopia and Cosmopolis: Globalization in the Era of American Literary Realism* (Durham, North Carolina: Duke University Press, 1998).
Porter, David (ed.), *Internet Culture* (New York: Routledge, 1997).

Bibliography

Potter, Russell, *Spectacular Vernaculars: Hip-Hop and the Politics of Post-modernism* (Albany: State University of New York Press, 1995).

Prendergast, Tom, *Creating the Modern Man: American Magazines and Consumer Culture 1900–1950* (Columbia: University of Missouri Press, 2000).

Pynchon, Thomas, *The Crying of Lot 49* (1965) (London: Picador, 1979).

Quinn, Eithne, 'Who's the mack?: the politics of the pimp figure in gangsta rap', in *Journal of American Studies* (2001), 34, (1).

Rebein, Robert, *Hicks, Tribes and Dirty Realists: American Fiction after Postmodernism* (Lexington: University of Kentucky Press, 2000).

Rheingold, Howard, *The Virtual Community: Finding Connections in a Computerized World* (London: Minerva, 1995).

Rhode, Will, *Paperback Raita* (London: Pocket, 2002).

Ritzer, George, *The McDonaldization of Society: An Investigation into the Changing Character of Contemporary Social Life* (London: Thousand Oaks, 1993).

Robbins, Kevin and Frank Webster, 'Cybernetic capitalism: information technology and everyday life', in Vincent Mosco and Janet Waska (eds), *The Political Economy of Information* (Wisconsin: University of Wisconsin Press, 1988).

Roberson, Susan (ed.), *Women, America and Movement: Narratives of Relocation* (Columbia: University of Missouri, 1998).

Robertson, Roland, *Globalization: Social Theory and Global Culture* (London: Sage, 1992).

Rodrik, Dani, *Has Globalization Gone too Far?* (Washington DC: Institute for International Economics, 1997).

Rogin, Michael, *Subversive Genealogy: The Politics and Art of Herman Melville* (New York: Alfred Knopf, 1983).

Rosenblatt, Roger (ed.), *Consuming Desires: Consumption, Culture and the Pursuit of Happiness* (Washington: Island Press, 1999).

Ross, Andrew, *Strange Weather: Culture, Science and Technology in the Age of Limits* (London: Verso, 1991).

Roszak, Theodore, *The Making of a Counterculture: Reflections on the Technocratic Society and its Youthful Opposition* (1968) (2nd edition) (Berkeley: University of California Press, 1995).

Roy, Arundhati, *The God of Small Things* (1997) (London: HarperCollins, 1998).

—,*Power Politics* (Cambridge, Mass: South End Press, 2001).

—,*The Ordinary Person's Guide to Empire* (London: HarperCollins, 2004).

Rushdie, Salman, *Imaginary Homelands: Essays and Criticism 1981–1991* (London: Granta, 1991).

—,'Introduction', in Salman Rushdie and Elizabeth West (eds), *The Vintage Book of Indian Writing 1947–1997* (London: Vintage, 1997).

Said, Edward, 'Globalizing literary study', in *PMLA* (2001), 116, (1).
Savanandan, Ambalavaner, 'Globalism and the left', in *Race and Class: The Threat of Globalism* (1998), 40, (2/3), 5.
Savran, David, *Taking it Like a Man: White Masculinity, Masochism and Contemporary American Culture* (Princeton: Princeton University Press, 1998).
Sayer, Andrew, 'Postfordism in question', in *International Journal of Urban and Regional Research* (1989), 13, (4).
Schiller, Herbert, *Culture Inc.: The Corporate Takeover of Public Expression* (New York: Oxford University Press, 1989).
Schlosser, Eric, *Fast Food Nation: What the All American Meal is Doing to the World* (London: Penguin, 2002).
Shaw, William, *Westsiders* (London: Bloomsbury, 2000).
Simmons, Philip, *Deep Surfaces: Mass Culture and History in Postmodern American Fiction* (Athens: University of Georgia Press, 1997).
Sinclair, Upton, *The Jungle* (London: Heinemann, 1906).
Sklair, Leslie, *Globalization: Capitalism and its Alternatives* (Oxford: Oxford University Press, 2002).
Smith, Anthony, 'Towards a global culture?', in Mike Featherstone (ed.), *Global Culture: Nationalism, Globalization and Modernity*.
Smith, Neil, *Uneven Development: Nature, Capital and the Production of Space* (Oxford: Blackwell, 1984).
Soja, Edward, *Postmetropolis: Critical Studies of Cities and Regions* (Cambridge: Blackwell, 2000).
Standage, Tom, *The Victorian Internet* (London: Weidenfeld and Nicolson 1999).
Stein, Gertrude, *Tender Buttons* (1914), in Carl Van Vechten (ed.), *Selected Writings of Gertrude Stein* (New York: Vintage, 1972).
Stiglitz, Josef, *Globalization and its Discontents* (London: Allen Lane, 2002).
Stille, Alexander, 'Apocalypse soon', in *New York Times Book Review* (7 November 2002).
Stratton, Jon, 'Cyberspace and the globalization of culture', in David Porter (ed.), *Internet Culture* (New York: Routledge, 1997).
Stringer, Vickie, *Let that be the Reason* (Columbus, Ohio: Triple Crown, 2001).
Tanner, Tony, 'Afterthoughts on Don DeLillo's *Underworld*', in *Raritan* (1998), 17, (4).
Teeple, Gary, 'What is globalization?', in Stephen M'Bride and John Wiseman (eds), *Globalization and its Discontents* (London: MacMillan, 2000).
Thomas, Bryn, Tom Smallman and Pat Yale, *Britain* (3rd edition) (Melbourne: Lonely Planet, 1999).

Thomas, Jeannie, *Naked Barbies, Warrior Joes and Other Forms of Visible Gender* (Urbana: University of Illinois Press, 2003).
Thompson, Graham, *The Business of America: The Cultural Production of a Post-war Nation* (London: Pluto, 2004).
Thomson, Jeff, ' "What is called heaven": identity in Sandra Cisneros's *Woman Hollering Creek*', in *Studies in Short Fiction* (1994), 31, (3).
Thoreau, Henry David, *Walden* (1854) (London: Everyman, 1997).
Thornton, Sarah, *Club Cultures: Music, Media and Subcultural Capital* (Cambridge: Polity, 1995).
Tomlinson, John, *Cultural Imperialism: A Critical Introduction* (London: Continuum, 1991).
Toop, David, *Rap Attack: African Rap to Global Hip Hop* (Revised and expanded 3rd edition) (London: Serpent's Tail, 2000).
Trachtenberg, Alan, *The Incorporation of America: Culture and Society in the Gilded Age* (New York: Hill and Wang, 1982).
Turner, Nikki, *A Project Chick* (Columbus, Ohio: Triple Crown, 2004).
Twitchell, James, *Lead us into Temptation: The Triumph of American Materialism* (New York: Columbia University Press, 1999).
Varndoe, Kirk, '*Campbell's Soup Cans, 1962*', in Heiner Bastion (ed.), *Andy Warhol: Retrospective* (London: Tate, 2002).
Veblen, Thorstein, *The Theory of the Leisure Class: An Economic Study of Institutions* (1899) (London: Allen and Unwin, 1949).
Viner, Katharine, 'Hand-to-brand combat', in *Guardian* (12 September 2000).
Vollman, William, *Butterfly Stories* (London: Andre Deutsch, 1993).
Watkins, S. Craig, *Representing: Hip Hop Culture and the Production of Black Cinema* (Chicago: University of Chicago Press, 1998).
Weber, Max, *The Protestant Ethic and the Spirit of Capitalism* (1905) (New York: Scribner's, 1958).
Webster, Frank, *Theories of the Information Society* (London: Routledge, 1995).
Welsh, Irvine, *Trainspotting* (Edinburgh: Cannongate, 1993).
Wesley, Marilyn, *Violent Adventure: Contemporary Fiction by American Men* (Charlottesville: University of Virginia Press, 2003).
West, Cornel, *Race Matters* (New York: Beacon Press, 1993).
Williams, Raymond, *Problems in Materialism and Culture* (London: Verso, 1980).
Withey, Lynne, *Grand Tours and Cook's Tours: A History of Leisure Travel, 1750 to 1915* (London: Aurum, 1997).
Wolcott, James 'Blasts from the Past', in *The New Criterion* (1997), 16, (4).
Wolf, Martin, *Why Globalization Works* (New Haven: Yale University Press, 2004).
Wolfe, Tom, *The Bonfire of the Vanities* (1987) (London: Picador, 2002).

Wolff, Michael, *Burn Rate: How I Survived the Gold Rush Years on the Internet* (London: Weidenfeld and Nicolson, 1998).

Wordsworth, William, 'To the Editor of the *Morning Post*', in *Morning Post* (11 December 1844), reprinted in William Wordsworth, *Selected Prose*, edited by John Hayden (Harmondsworth: Penguin, 1988).

Wright, Richard, *Native Son* (1940) (New York: Harper Row, 1964).

Filmography

28 Days Later, Danny Boyle (dir.) (20th Century Fox/DNA/Film Council, 2002).
The Beach, Danny Boyle (dir.) (20th Century Fox/Figment, 2000).
Big Wednesday, John Milius (dir.) (Warner/A-Team, 1978).
Celebrity, Woody Allen (dir.) (Buenavista/Sweetland, 1998).
The Corporation, Mark Achbar, Jennifer Abbott and Joel Bakan (dirs), (Zeitgeist Films, 2004).
Dawn of the Dead, George Romero (dir.) (Target International/Laurel Group/Dawn Associates, 1978).
Fight Club, David Fincher (dir.) (20th Century Fox/Fox 2000/Regency, 1999).
Prêt-à-Porter, Robert Altman (dir.) (Buenavista/Miramax, 1994)
Super Size Me, Morgan Spurlock (dir.) (Hart Sh.arp Video LLC, 2004).
Trainspotting, Danny Boyle (dir.) (Polygram/Channel Four/Figment/Noel Gay, 1996).
Zoolander, Ben Stiller (dir.) (Paramount/Village Roadshow/VH1/NPV, 2001).

Discography

DJ-Shadow, 'Why Hip Hop Sucks in '96', *Endtroducing* (Mowax, 1996).
Wu-Tang Clan, 'C.R.E.A.M', *Enter the Wu-Tang 36 Chambers* (BMG/RCA/Loud, 1993).

Index

Abu-Lughod, Janet 85–6, 161
advertising 2–4, 15–16, 19, 22, 29–31, 32, 33–6, 37–8, 41–3, 51–4, 73–4
Ahmad, Aijaz 134, 146
Alessandrini, Anthony 142
Alexander, Richard 137
Allen Woody, *Celebrity* 31
Altman, Robert, *Prêt-à-Porter* 31
Appadurai, Arjun 4, 5, 6, 139, 163
Austen, Jane 35

Bakan, Joel, *The Corporation* 1–2
Baker, Stephen 9
Baker, T.N. 24
Ballard, J.G. 27
Balshaw, Maria 8
Banerjee, Debjani 141–2
Barbie 156–9
Bari, Deepika 149
Barnet, Richard and Cavanagh, John 79
Barr, Emily 124
Baudrillard, Jean 48
Beatty, Paul 6, 21–6, 61, 74
  Tuff 21–3, 25–6, 61
  White Boy Shuffle 21, 23–4
Belle, Jennifer 33
Berger, John 2
Bhabha, Homi 131–3
Bourdieu, Pierre 43–4
Boyd, William 63
Boyle, Danny 110–12, 13

The Beach 110
Trainspotting 111–13
brands 2, 4, 16–17, 19–20, 22–3, 27, 30–40, 41–5, 53–4, 73–4, 76–80, 82–4, 152–4, 156–8
Braques, George 37
Buell, Frederick 133, 146
Bushnell, Candace 26, 33–6, 57, 58, 59, 61, 74
  Sex and the City 33–6, 58–9
  Four Blondes 33
  Trading Up 33

Cain, James M. 95
Canclini, Nestor Garcia 4, 69, 86, 159–60
Carey, James 91, 98
Cashmore, Ellis 13
Chambers, Iain 134, 160–1
Chandler, Raymond 95
Chopin, Kate 37, 102, 104
Cisneros, Sandra 6, 156–62
  Woman Hollering Creek 156–62
Crystal, David 135
Csikszentmihalyi, Mihaly and Rochberg-Halton, Eugene 44

DJ Shadow, *Endtroducing* 14
Davis, Stuart 37
DeLillo, Don 6, 60–76, 89, 101
  Cosmopolis 60–1
  Libra 62, 64–5
  Ratner's Star 62

Index

The Names 62
Underworld 62–76
White Noise 62
Demuth, Charles 37
Diaz, Junot 7
DiCaprio, Leonardo 110
dirty realism 137
Dlaska, Andrea 143–4
Dos Passos, John 36–7, 38, 39, 44
Douglas Mary and Isherwood, Baron 44
Douglass, Frederick 16
Drake, Jennifer 141
Drieser, Theodore 35
Ducille Ann 156
Dyson, Michael 18

Edwards, Paul 20
Eggers, Dave 6, 124, 125–7
  You Shall Know Our Velocity 125–6
  'We can't fix anything . . . ' 125–7
Eliot. T.S. 71
Ellis, Bret Easton 6, 26, 27–33, 57, 58, 61, 74
  Glamorama 27–33, 53, 58, 61
  Less Than Zero 29, 30
  American Psycho 29, 31, 35
  The Informers 35
Ellison, Ralph 38
Enron 88–9
Erdrich, Louise 7
Ewen, Stuart, *Captains of Consciousness* 2–3

Faludi, Susan, *Stiffed* 46–7
Faulkner, William 37
Ferguson, Niall 85–6
Fielding, Helen 33
Fincher, David, *Fight Club* (film version) 51–5, 57
Fitzgerald, F. Scott 37
Ford, Richard 137
Franzen, Jonathan 7
Frazier, E. Franklin 17
Friedman, Jonathan 157–8

Friedman, Monroe, *A 'Brand' New Language* 39
Friedman, Thomas, *The Lexus and the Olive Tree* 68–70, 73

Garland, Alex 101, 104–27, 134, 162
  The Beach 101, 104–27
George, Nelson 13
Gibson, William 6, 90–101, 105, 162
  All Tomorrow's Parties 93–4, 97–9
  Count Zero 93
  Iduro 93–4, 96–7, 98
  Neuromancer 93, 94, 98
  Mona Lisa Overdrive 93
  Pattern Recognition 99–101, 103
  Virtual Light 93–4, 98, 104
Giddens, Anthony 4, 65, 93, 130
Gikandi, Simon 155
Gilroy, Paul 14
Goldman, Robert and Papson, Stephen 14
Godden, Richard, *Fictions of Capital* 40–1
Gordon, George (Lord Byron) 85
Greenblatt, Stephen 136
Grewel, Gurleen 141–2
Gunn, Giles 162

Hardt, Michael and Negri Antonio 4, 121–4, 132–3
Hebdige, Dick 44
Heffernan, Nick 9
Hemingway, Ernest 7, 36, 39–45, 61, 137
  'Hills like white elephants' 39, 41–5
Hertz, Noreena 79, 80, 82–3, 85
hip-hop 13–21, 24–6
Hodge, John 110–12, 113
  The Beach 110–11
  Trainspotting 111–12, 113
hooks, bell 13, 17
Hopper, Edward 37
Houellebecq, Michel 119–20, 124, 126
  Platform 119–20
  Atomised 120

Howes, David 157, 159
Huggan, Graham 134, 151–2
Hurston, Zora Neale 15–16, 18–19, 38
  'will to adorn' 15–16, 18–19

IKEA 52–3
Internet 64, 71–2, 90–101

Jameson, Fredric 3, 134–5
Janowitz, Tama 33
Jay, Paul 163
Jones, Edward 7
Joyce, James 36, 38, 39, 44

K'Wan 24–6
  Road Dawgz 25–6
Kayman, Martin 135–4
Kincaid, Jamaica 9
Klein, Naomi 2, 38–9, 68–70, 73, 77–89, 147, 148
Knight, Peter 68
Kumar, Amitava 136

Lahiri, Jhumpa 6, 128–40, 141, 149, 150, 151, 152, 155, 156, 161
  Interpreter of Maladies 128–40, 149, 150
Leary, Timothy 91
Lee, Spike 14
Lencek, Lena and Bosker Gideon, *The Beach* 104, 112–13
Locke, Alain, *The New Negro* 17
Lonely Planet 106–9, 114–15, 125
Lyotard, Jean-Francois 116

McDonaldization 120
McInerney, Jay 28, 33
Macauley, Thomas 135
Mansfield, Katherine 102, 104
Marx, Karl 61, 93
  Grundrisse 93
Marx, Leo 91
masculinity 45, 46–55
Meethan, Kevin 120
Melville, Herman 7, 75–89, 95
  Moby-Dick 75–89, 108

Micklethwait, John and Wooldridge, Adrian, *A Future Perfect* 70
Migga-Kiza, Joseph 95
Millhauser, Stephen 7
Milius, John, *Big Wednesday* 102
migration 4, 8, 127–7, 128–63
Modern Fiction Studies 9, 162
modernism 11
Moore, Michael 2
Monbiot, George 2, 79, 80
Mongia, Padmina 161–2
Morrison, Toni 7
Mowry, Jess 21
Mukherjee, Bharati 6, 140–6, 147–50, 151, 152, 155, 161, 162, 156
  Jasmine 141–6, 148, 149, 150
Mullaney, Julie 150
Mullins, Paul 16, 17
Murphet, Julian 8

Neal, Mark 23–4
Negri, Antonio, *see* Hardt, Michael and Negri Antonio
Negroponte, Nicholas 91
Nelson Emmanuel 141
Norton, Edward 51–2
Nunn, Kem 102–4, 105, 124, 126
  The Dogs of Winter 101, 102–4, 108
  Tijuana Straits 102
  Tapping the Source 102

Olsen, Charles 76, 77, 87
Osteen, Mark, *American Magic and Dread* 73–74

PMLA (Proceedings of the Modern Language Association of America) 9, 162
Palahniuk, Chuck 6, 26, 36, 45–59, 101, 105, 124
  Fight Club 45–59, 61, 104
  Invisible Monsters 56
  Choke 56
  Lullaby 56
  Diary 56
  Survivor 56–7

Index

See also Fincher, David
Pepys, Samuel 36
Picasso, Pablo 37, 39, 44
Pitt, Brad 51–2
Pope, Alexander 36
postcolonialism 9–10, 128–140, 155–6, 162–3,
postmodernism 9–10
Potter, Russell 26
Prada 30–1
Proulx, Annie 137
Pulitzer Prize 7, 128, 137,
punk 11
Pynchon, Thomas 62

realism 11, 27, 32
Rheingold, Howard 95
Robertson, Roland 5, 69, 163
Rodrick, Dani 3
romanticism 11, 113–15
Ross, Andrew 95
Roth, Philip 7
Roy, Anindyo 141
Roy, Arundhati 88, 146–56, 161, 162
    The God of Small Things 146, 150–6
    The Ordinary Person's Guide to Empire 147, 148
    Power Politics 146–148
Rushdie, Salman 9, 131–2, 137, 140, 146
Russo, Richard 7, 137

Said, Edward 162
Sapphire 21
Savanandan, Ambalavaner 2
Saunders, George 27
Sayer, Andrew 69–70
Schlosser, Eric, *Fast Food Nation* 1
Shakur, Tupac 13, 20
Shaw, William 17
Shell, Ray 21
Simmons, Philip 9
situationism 11
Sklair, Leslie 4, 156–7, 158
Souljah, Sistah 21
Smiley, Janes 137

Smith, Anthony 132
Smollett, Tobias 36
South Atlantic Quarterly 162
Spurlock, Morgan, *Super Size Me* 1
Stein, Gertrude 37
Stiglitz, Josef 2–3
Stille, Alexander 121
Stiller Ben 31
Stringer, Vickie 24–5
    Let that be the Reason 24
Sutcliffe, William 124
Sykes, Plum 33

Tan, Amy 7
Tanner, Tony 71
technology 4, 9, 64, 71–2, 87, 90–101, 163
Teeple, Gary 5
Thomson, Jeff 160
Thoreau, Henry David 24, 81–2
tourism *see* travel
Trachtenberg, Alan 91–2
travel 4, 8, 102–27, 128, 163
Triple Crown 24–6
Trueur, David 7
Turner, Nikki 24–5
Twitchell, James 81

Vollmann, William 118–19, 120, 124, 126
    Butterfly Stories 118–19

Walcott, Derek 71
West, Cornel 13, 24
Warhol, Andy 32
Webster, Frank 92, 98
Weisenberger, Lauren 33
Wharton, Edith 35
Williams, Hype 23
Williams, Raymond 43
Withey, Lynne 114
Welsh, Irvine, *Trainspotting* 111, 113
Wolfe, Tom 60
Wolff, Michael 95
Wordsworth, William 114–15
Wright, Richard 38, 39
Wu-Tang Clan, the 16–17